A YEAR OF DAILY OFFERINGS

JAMES KUBICKI, S.J.

A Year of Daily Offerings

~

Giving Your Life to God
One Day at a Time

IGNATIUS PRESS   SAN FRANCISCO

Cover photograph:
Cathedral of the Holy Cross and Santa Eulalia
Barcelona, Spain
dem10, istockphoto.com

Cover design by Riz Boncan Marsella

© 2024 by Ignatius Press, San Francisco
All rights reserved
ISBN 978-1-62164-703-4 (PB)
ISBN 978-1-64229-313-5 (eBook)
Library of Congress Control Number 2024935575
Printed in the United States of America ∞

To my brother Jesuits,
from whom, as a high school student,
I learned about
the Morning Offering

INTRODUCTION

What is the most valuable thing that you have? After going through all the possessions and people in your life, wouldn't you say that time is the most precious? We often speak of running out of time, but that really only happens when we die. Our present life is in time. We live and move in time.

Yet you often hear people talk about "killing time" or "wasting time". If time is the most precious thing we have, how could we consider "killing" it or "wasting" it?

Various books about achieving financial or professional success talk about the importance of time management. There is an entire market for books to help us "manage" our time. There are all sorts of calendars and daily planners to help us use our time in a way that helps us attain our goals. As the saying goes, "if you fail to plan, you plan to fail."

I can just see Jesus shaking his head at all the energy and foresight that most people use to attain some success that is fleeting.

Do you remember the parable he once told about a dishonest employee? You can find it in the Gospel of Luke 16:1–13. Parables are stories that are designed to shock. They're intended to force the listener or reader into deeper thought. And this one certainly meets that criterion.

An employee, the steward of a wealthy man, is about to be fired "for squandering his property". We don't know if he was simply inefficient or ineffective with his master's money, but his plan on finding out that he is about to be let go indicates a tendency toward dishonesty.

He decides to call in "his master's debtors one by one"

and have them change the records of what they owe the master. In that way he used his master's wealth to make friends for himself, friends who would remember him after he had lost his job and was in need.

What does Jesus say is the reaction of the master? You would think he would be outraged at the dishonesty of his employee. But instead, Jesus says, "the master commended the dishonest steward for his prudence."

Remember: a parable is meant to catch our attention, to shock us into deeper thought. Why did the master commend his employee? Because of his prudence, not because of his dishonesty. He showed that he was very clever in preparing for the future.

Then Jesus draws the lesson he is trying to make for all of us: "For the sons of this world are wiser in their own generation than the sons of light." In other words, people of the world know how to plan ahead. The children of the Kingdom of God seem less inclined to do so.

All earthly success is fleeting. It may lead to honors, to people making a statue of you and creating a memorial to you. But those things won't do you any good after you've run out of time, after you've died. So, shouldn't we put as much and greater emphasis on planning for the future beyond this life? Shouldn't we use our time to attain the ultimate goal of eternal life?

Most people who hear the parable of the dishonest employee are outraged and immediately perceive his dishonesty. Yet they are less likely to see the dishonesty of living their lives and using their time as though it belonged to them. We do not belong to ourselves. Our time is not our own to do with as we want. We are not gods but are creatures whom God has lovingly brought into existence. God has entrusted to us our lives with their talents and our time with its opportunities in order to return love for love. We and all we have belong to God not only because we are creatures whom God has created and continues to care for. We were "purchased" by God.

St. Paul puts it this way: "Do you not know that your body is a temple of the Holy Spirit within you, which you have from God? You are not your own; you were bought with a price. So glorify God in your body" (1 Cor 6:19–20).

What was the price paid for us by God? When mankind was enslaved to sin, God paid the ultimate price to liberate us. As the First Letter of Peter 1:17–19 says: "conduct yourselves with fear throughout the time of your exile. You know that you were ransomed from the futile ways inherited from your fathers, not with perishable things such as silver or gold, but with the precious blood of Christ, like that of a lamb without blemish or spot." The "precious blood of Christ", shed to redeem us, makes us precious. Every moment of our lives is precious. It is a gift given to us by God that we in turn offer back to the Giver, not grudgingly, but gratefully and lovingly.

This offering of ourselves is how each of the baptized exercises the priesthood that is theirs by their union in the Body of Christ, the Priest. In his encyclical *Mediator Dei*, Pope Pius XII wrote: "By the waters of baptism, as by common right, Christians are made members of the Mystical Body of Christ the Priest, and by the 'character' which is imprinted on their souls they are appointed to give worship to God. Thus they participate, according to their condition, in the priesthood of Christ" (no. 88).

The baptismal ceremony includes an anointing with sacred chrism, the same highly perfumed and blessed oil that is used to anoint and consecrate the walls of a new church, its altar, and the hands of a newly ordained priest. These are consecrated for a sacred purpose—worship. Similarly, the heads of the baptized or confirmed are anointed and consecrated for the sacred purpose of worship. But this worship is not only what we do once a week on Sunday. It is what we do with our entire life.

This was a clear teaching of the Second Vatican Council. *Lumen gentium* no. 34 states:

> The supreme and eternal Priest, Christ Jesus, . . . gives them [the laity] a sharing in His priestly function of offering spiritual worship for the glory of God and the salvation of men. . . . For all their works, prayers and apostolic endeavors, their ordinary married and family life, their daily occupations, their physical and mental relaxation, if carried out in the Spirit, and even the hardships of life, if patiently borne—all these become "spiritual sacrifices acceptable to God through Jesus Christ" [1 Peter 2:5]. . . . Thus, as those everywhere who adore in holy activity, the laity consecrate the world itself to God.

The council's document on the laity, *Apostolicam actuositatem* no. 4, further states:

> they do not separate union with Christ from their life but rather performing their work according to God's will they grow in that union. . . . Neither family concerns nor other secular affairs should be irrelevant to their spiritual life, in keeping with the words of the Apostle, "Whatever you do in word or work, do all in the name of the Lord Jesus Christ, giving thanks to God the Father through Him" (Col 3:17).

How can you become more conscious of your call as a member of the Body of Christ who shares in his priesthood and who offers yourself with Christ? This is where a daily offering prayer can help.

This book is designed to help you renew the daily offering one day at a time. It follows the seasons and saints of the year in a way that can help you make the daily offering and, over time, live it more consciously throughout your day. May the readings, prayers, and reflections of this book help us all live our priestly call to, in the words of St. Paul, "present your bodies as a living sacrifice, holy and acceptable to God, which is your spiritual worship" (Rom 12:1).

JANUARY

January 1: Solemnity of Mary, Mother of God, and the Annual World Day of Peace

We begin this new year by honoring the motherhood of Mary. When the Archangel Gabriel came to Mary, she had the choice whether to become the mother of the Prince of Peace or to reject God's will. Though confused, Mary surrendered herself completely to the will of God. It's been said that Mary first received into her heart what she then conceived in her womb—the Word of God. She was able to receive the Word because her heart was immaculate with no sinful obstacles to God's will. Mary's heart was one hundred percent devoted to God.

There are many resolutions that I could make today, but the most important one is to offer every day of the coming year to God, praying that his will be done in me just as it was done in Mary. I know that when God's will is done perfectly on earth as it is in heaven, there will be justice, harmony, and peace.

Jesus, as I begin this new year, I look to your Mother as the example I want to follow. This is my resolution: to live one day at a time, offering each day to you, asking that God's will be done in me and in my life. Your Blessed Mother's offering of herself allowed you, the Prince of Peace, to come into the world. As I follow her example, I believe that you will make me an instrument of your peace just as she was. Amen.

DAILY WORD: "Blessed are the peacemakers, for they shall be called sons of God" (Mt 5:9).

EVENING REVIEW: In what ways was I an instrument of peace today?

January 2: Sts. Basil and Gregory Nazianzen (4th Century)

Today's saints share a common feast because of the close friendship they shared from the time they were students. Together they pursued wisdom, and their pursuit led them to be baptized together in 358. In time, they both became bishops whose sound teaching led to their being named two of the four major Doctors of the Eastern Church.

St. Gregory said this about their friendship: "Our one single object and ambition was virtue, and a life of hope in the blessings that are to come. With this end in view, we ordered our lives and all our actions. Our great pursuit, the great name we wanted, was to be Christians, to be called Christians."

These saints demonstrate the importance of friendship. Friends either help one another to follow a good path, or they support each other in living foolishly. Each of us was created for heaven, and we are given each day to walk closer to our goal. We are also given to one another to help each other to attain heaven.

Jesus, you told your followers: I no longer call you servants, but "friends" (Jn 15:15). Friends share their interests and desires. May your desires be mine today. May I desire the salvation of the people whom I will meet today as much as you do. May I be a true friend to them as much as you are a true friend to me. May I be a Christian both in name and in my actions.

DAILY WORD: "A friend loves at all times" (Prov 17:17).

EVENING REVIEW: How did my friendship with Jesus help me to be a friend to others today?

January 3: The Most Holy Name of Jesus

Following Jewish Law, Jesus was circumcised eight days after his birth and given a name. In his case, it was the name that the Archangel Gabriel told Mary she was to call her son. Today we celebrate a feast in honor of the Name of Jesus.

A name represents the person who carries it. To "come in the name" of another is to represent that person. To honor the Name of Jesus is to honor him.

The Name of Jesus is all-powerful: "There is salvation in no one else, for there is no other name under heaven given among men by which we must be saved" (Acts 4:12). St. Paul said that this name is "the name which is above every name" and "that at the name of Jesus every knee should bow" (Phil 2:9–10). It's a holy name and ought never to be misused.

Many people are more comfortable calling Jesus "Christ" or "Lord," but those are titles. Friends are on a first-name basis. Since Jesus called his disciples "friends", we are free to address the Second Person of the Holy Trinity by his name.

Jesus, you told us to pray, asking God the Father for what we need and desire in your name (Jn 14:13). When we pray in your name, we know that we are praying as you yourself prayed. We have many needs and desires, but ultimately we pray your own prayer: "Abba, Father . . . not what I will, but what you will" (Mk 14:36). I offer myself to you now and ask that your will may be done in each moment of my day. Amen.

DAILY WORD: Blessed be the Name of Jesus!

EVENING REVIEW: How did I bring glory to the Name of Jesus today?

January 4: St. Elizabeth Ann Seton (1774–1821)

Born in New York City, Elizabeth Ann Seton was raised in the Episcopal Church. She married a wealthy businessman and had five children, but during a visit to Italy in 1803, her husband became ill and died. A Catholic family befriended her, and when she returned to the United States, she became a Catholic. Upon receiving the Eucharist for the first time, she wrote a friend: "At last, at last, God is mine and I am his! I have received him!"

Elizabeth moved to Baltimore, where she opened a school for girls in 1808. When several young women joined her in this work, they began the Sisters of Charity, the first American religious congregation for women. Pope St. Paul VI canonized her in 1975, the first native-born U.S. citizen to be given this honor.

In the Eucharist, Jesus gives me the greatest gift—himself. I in turn make a gift of myself to him with my daily offering. I renew it now with these words of St. Elizabeth Ann:

How consoling, how sweet, the presence of Jesus to the longing, harassed soul! It is instant peace and balm to every wound! What would be my refuge? Jesus is everywhere. . . . Yes, everywhere! But in His Sacrament of the Altar, as actually present and real as my soul within my body. In His sacrifice, daily offered, as really as once offered on the Cross. Merciful Savior! Can there be any comparison to this blessedness? Adored Lord, increase my faith, perfect it, crown it. Having drawn me to Thy fold, keep me in Thy sweet pastures and lead me to eternal life.

DAILY WORD: Jesus, as you gave yourself to me, so I give myself to you.

EVENING REVIEW: With what acts of charity did I offer myself to Jesus today?

January 5: St. John Neumann (1811–1860)

John Neumann was born in Bohemia and came to the United States as a seminarian. After his ordination, he was sent to Buffalo, where he served German-speaking immigrants. In time he joined the Redemptorist Order and became the bishop of Philadelphia. There he established a Catholic educational system and promoted Eucharistic devotion in which parishes offered forty straight hours of adoration to the Blessed Sacrament.

When he canonized Neumann in 1977, Pope St. Paul VI said: "To accomplish his task, love was necessary. And love meant giving; love meant effort; love meant sacrifice. . . . Love still means giving oneself for others, because Love has come down to humanity; and from humanity love goes back to its divine source! . . . The Eucharistic Sacrifice was the center of his life, and constituted for him what the Second Vatican Council would later call 'the source and summit of all evangelization'."

I join myself and my day now to the perfect offering of Jesus in the Eucharistic Sacrifice by praying these words of St. John Neumann:

How much I love you, O my Jesus. I wish to love you with my whole heart. Take entire possession of me. To you I consecrate all the powers of my soul and body, my whole being. Would that I could infuse into all hearts a burning love for you. What great glory would be given to you here on earth, if every heart were an altar on which every human will were laid in perfect conformity with your will to be consumed by the fire of your love.

DAILY WORD: Heart of Jesus, burning furnace of charity, make me one with you.

EVENING REVIEW: In what ways did I share the burning love of Jesus with others today?

January 6: St. André Bessette (1845–1937)

A humble Brother of the Congregation of the Holy Cross, St. André Bessette has been called "God's Doorkeeper" and the "Miracle Man of Montreal". He served the College of Notre Dame in Montreal as the porter and once joked, "My superiors showed me the door, and I stayed there forty years!" His humility and holiness led people from all over to seek his prayers and counsel.

He said: "I am ignorant. If there were anyone more ignorant, the good God would have chosen him in my place."

He encouraged those who asked for help to turn to St. Joseph. He often touched them with a medal of the saint or anointed them with oil from a lamp that he kept burning in front of a statue of St. Joseph. Doctors have attested to the miraculous nature of the subsequent healings, and it's estimated that between 1910 and 1937, 10,000 people were cured. St. André always gave credit to St. Joseph. The shrine that he built, the Oratory of St. Joseph, now sits on the highest point in Montreal. More than a million people came to pay their respects at his funeral.

Like his patron St. Joseph, André Bessette was a humble instrument in God's hands. He was a magnifying glass through which a ray of God's love shone to bring about great physical and spiritual healings.

St. Joseph, foster father of the Son of God, help me today to be like your devoted servant St. André. May all my thoughts, words, and actions magnify the love of God so that it may touch all the people I will meet or think about or pray for. Amen.

DAILY WORD: "My soul magnifies the Lord."

EVENING REVIEW: How did God's love touch others today through me?

January 7: St. Raymond of Peñafort (1175–1275)

Raymond, a professor of philosophy, Church law, and civil law, joined the Dominicans at the age of forty-seven. The pope asked him to organize all the Church's teachings and documents. This work gained Raymond the title "Father of Canon Law". He continued his teaching and writing until his death at one hundred years old, demonstrating that one is never too old to serve God.

Laws are often seen as restrictions on our freedom. But laws are part of nature. As physical beings, we follow certain laws—some by necessity, like gravity, and some by choice, like eating nutritious food and getting enough sleep. As spiritual beings, too, there are spiritual laws built right into our nature. Made in the image and likeness of God, we're made by and for love. That, Jesus taught, sums up the law.

I commit myself to following the law of love every moment of this day with this prayer adapted from the writings of St. Raymond:

I look on you, Jesus, the author and preserver of faith. As I drink the cup that you offer me today, I give thanks to you, the giver of all blessings. May you, the God of love and peace, set my heart at rest and speed me on my journey. May you shelter me in the hidden recesses of your love and bring me at last to that place where I will repose forever in the vision of peace, in the security of trust, and in the restful enjoyment of your riches.

DAILY WORD: "Blessed are those who keep [God's] testimonies, who seek him with their whole heart" (Ps 119:2).

EVENING REVIEW: How did I follow or not follow God's law of love today?

January 8

The Gospel tells the amazing story of the Magi who followed a star that led them from their homes to the distant small town of Bethlehem. We know them as the three kings or wise men. They came from the East, Gentile territory, to find the newborn king whose birth was shown to them in ancient writings and in the stars.

At one point, however, they don't seem very wise. Surely King Herod's reputation must have reached them. He was so jealous and possessive that he killed his own family members whom he feared wanted to replace him on the throne. Yet the Magi presented themselves to this murderous king and asked, "Where is he who has been born king of the Jews?" (Mt 2:2). Herod asked, when they found him that they should bring him news so that he might go and honor him as well. But the Magi were "warned in a dream not to return to Herod" and so returned to "their own country by another way" (Mt 2:12).

What they may have lacked in wisdom, they made up for in courage. They were brave to step out of their comfort zones, leave their homes, and seek someone to whom a star had given witness. It took courage to disobey Herod and slip out of Judea. We do not follow a star, but we do seek to follow God's will. And that takes courage! My daily offering reminds me to ask for the courage to follow God's will one day at a time.

Loving God, may I seek and follow your will every moment of this day.

DAILY WORD: Thy will be done, thy kingdom come!

EVENING REVIEW: Where did I need courage to follow God's will today?

The word "epiphany" means "showing through" or "manifestation". We are celebrating the manifestation of Jesus to the world. The Magi who came to worship Jesus represent all non-Jewish peoples. Jesus is the Savior of all people, Jewish and Gentile. Israel was chosen to reveal to the world the light of God's loving plan for mankind, but this did not happen until the Jewish child Jesus came as the light of the world (see Jn 8:12). With his appearance, the prophecy of Isaiah was fulfilled:

> Arise, shine; for your light has come,
>   and the glory of the LORD has risen upon you.
> For behold, darkness shall cover the earth,
>   and thick darkness the peoples;
> but the LORD will arise upon you,
>   and his glory will be seen upon you.
> And nations shall walk by your light,
>   and kings in the brightness of your rising.

(Is 60:1–3)

The followers of Jesus, who become one with him through Baptism, now give light to the world. In the Sermon on the Mount, Jesus told us: "You are the light of the world" (Mt 5:14). We now manifest God's glory to the world through our good deeds of love, for Jesus continued, "Let your light so shine before men, that they may see your good works and give glory to your Father who is in heaven" (5:16).

Lord Jesus, I believe that you are the light of the world. I also believe that, because I am a member of your Body, I too am the light of the world. I offer myself to you today so that I may be your light in the lives of all the people I will meet and for whom I am praying.

DAILY WORD: Lord, be my light so that I may be your light.

EVENING REVIEW: In what ways did I bring light into darkness today?

January 10

At the Epiphany, the three gifts the Magi brought were highly symbolic. The gifts witnessed to the mystery of the Christ Child before whom they bowed.

Gold is a gift for a king. In giving Jesus gold, the Magi recognized him as "the king of the Jews" (Mt 2:2) and as the King of kings over all people of all time.

Frankincense is placed on a hot coal and becomes smoke that, as it ascends, represents people's prayers to God. In offering Jesus frankincense, the Magi give witness to his true nature. He is not only human but divine. The Son of God is true God.

Myrrh is an aromatic spice that was used to anoint the bodies of those who have died. Offering this to the Child, the Magi recognize his mortality as a human sharing in the mortality of the race. They also witness to how the divine King will save the world—through his suffering and death.

Lord Jesus, I do not have gold to give you, but I offer you all I possess. I ask that I may use all things for your glory, and I pray that your Kingdom may reign over me and all those you have placed in my care. I do not have frankincense to give you, but I have my worship. I offer my body to you as a living sacrifice, holy and pleasing spiritual worship to you, my God (see Rom 12:1). I do not have myrrh to offer you, but I have my weakness, both physical and spiritual, and my sufferings. Join them to yourself and your perfect offering renewed at every Mass.

DAILY WORD: My King and my God, take all that I have and hold and possess.

EVENING REVIEW: How did I use my possessions in God's service today?

The Christmas Season ends with the celebration of the Baptism of our Lord. We don't want to be like spoiled children who tire quickly of their Christmas gifts and seek new thrills. Those who are truly grateful spend time with the presents they have received. And so we savor the gifts of the season.

What gifts have I received this year? What gifts did I give this year, and how were they received? Did I receive the gift of someone's time? Did I give that precious gift to others? What happy memories do I carry away with me? What regrets do I have?

I am grateful for the best Christmas present—the presence of Christ in my life. Jesus took flesh in the womb of the Virgin Mary and was born. He entered the world as we all do, a weak human in need of love. Pope Benedict XVI said: "He became a child. He made himself dependent and weak, in need of our love. Now—this God who has become a child says to us—you can no longer fear me, you can only love me" (Midnight Mass Homily, Christmas 2008).

Lord Jesus, I thank you for all the gifts of the Christmas Season. I thank you especially for the gift of yourself. You became flesh in order to draw near to us. You stay close to us in the Eucharist. May the gift of your birth help me, as part of your Body, to give my flesh to you today.

DAILY WORD: Lord, your presence is your greatest present.

EVENING REVIEW: How was Jesus present to others through me today?

Jesus joined the crowds who came to be baptized by John in the Jordan River. Sinless, he had no need to be baptized, but in entering the waters he identified himself with sinful, suffering mankind. He anticipated that at the end of his life he would take upon himself the sins of the world. St. Paul wrote: "For our sake he made him to be sin who knew no sin, so that in him we might become the righteousness of God" (2 Cor 5:21). Jesus made the water holy, the source of new life for those who would be baptized by water and the Spirit.

What happened to Jesus when he arose from the water also happened to us at our Baptisms. The Holy Spirit came upon each of us, and the Father declared, "You are my beloved son, you are my beloved daughter; with you I am well pleased" (see Lk 3:22; Mk 1:11; Mt 3:17). What a difference it would make if I really understood that I am a temple of the Holy Spirit and a beloved child of God the Father!

Father of Jesus and my Father, I believe that your Holy Spirit is as close to me as my breath. I believe that I am your beloved. Believing this frees me from having to prove myself. I need to put on no masks or facades today. I need to play no games to win other people's attention and affection because I know that I am loved by you as much as you loved Jesus your Son.

DAILY WORD: I am a child of God the Father, who loves me very much.

EVENING REVIEW: In what ways did I experience the loving care of my Father today?

January 13: St. Hilary of Poitiers (300–368)

St. Hilary was a convert to Christianity. His search for the truth led him to the Bible and, in particular, to the Gospel of John. He was made a bishop, and his writings earned him the title Doctor of the Church. St. Hilary reflected upon the line of St. Paul, "Do you not know that your body is a temple of the Holy Spirit within you, which you have from God? You are not your own" (1 Cor 6:19). He interpreted that verse by referring to Psalm 127—"Unless the Lord builds the house, those who build it labor in vain." St. Hilary wrote:

> Such a temple must be built by God; if it were constructed by human effort, it would not last; it is not held together by resting on merely worldly teachings, nor will it be protected by our own vain efforts or anxious concern. Its foundations must be rooted in the prophets and apostles. It must be held together by a cornerstone. An ever-increasing unity will make it grow into a perfect mankind, to the scale of Christ's body. Its beauty and charm are the adornment given to it by supernatural grace.

Holy Spirit, breathe your new life in me today. Offering myself to you, I ask that you may always dwell in me so that all I think and say and do will build up the Body of Christ which is the Church.

DAILY WORD: Unless the Lord builds, I labor in vain.

EVENING REVIEW: How did the Holy Spirit use me today to strengthen the Church?

At Baptism, a new Christian is not only washed or immersed in water but is anointed with sacred chrism, the highly perfumed oil that is used to consecrate new churches, their altars, and the hands of a newly ordained priest. This anointing is what makes me an "Anointed One" or "Christian". The anointing prayer speaks of Jesus, who was consecrated by the Holy Spirit to be a priest, prophet, and king. I share in the priestly identity of Jesus.

Before the time of Jesus, Jewish priests offered sacrifices of animals or grain. Placed on the altar and set afire, the smoke ascended to the heavens as a prayerful offering to God. Jesus replaced those sacrifices with his one perfect offering on the Cross. Sharing in the priesthood of Jesus, I am now called to offer the daily sacrifice of my life. As St. Paul wrote, "Present your bodies as a living sacrifice, holy and acceptable to God, which is your spiritual worship" (Rom 12:1).

Praying a daily offering and then living it throughout my day is how I exercise the priestly identity I have received through Baptism.

Lord Jesus, as a member of your Body, I share in your priestly identity and mission. You want me to join the moments of my day to your perfect offering. You saved the world through your sacrificial death and Resurrection. But not all have accepted the salvation you won for them. Take the offering of my day and unite it to your own perfect offering. In that way every moment will have eternal significance and play a role in the ongoing salvation of the world.

DAILY WORD: I offer this moment to you, O God, as a living sacrifice.

EVENING REVIEW: What was holy and pleasing in this day I offered God?

Who did the people of his time say that Jesus was? Most thought of him as a prophet and he was. The Holy Spirit anointed Jesus as a prophet and, at my Baptism, anointed me as a prophet, too. What does it mean to be a prophet?

The prophets of old were those who heard the word of God and then spoke that word to the people around them. They were not so much fortune-tellers as people who, with the eyes of faith, could discern the signs of the times. They were able to see that if certain paths were followed, they would lead to either disaster or well-being.

Sharing in the prophetic identity and mission of Jesus, I, too, am a prophet. My discerning eyes of faith develop as I reflect upon the Scriptures. There I meet the living Word of God who became flesh, who speaks to me and helps me to see as he sees, think as he thinks, and feel as he feels.

I also meet the Word of God in the events of my life. God speaks to me through the people and events of my daily life. God teaches me, affirms me, and challenges me. My evening review helps me to listen for God's voice in my daily life.

Lord Jesus, through Baptism your Holy Spirit anoints me to be a prophet. May I listen well to your word that comes to me in the Scriptures and in today's events. Help me to speak your word both in what I say and in what I do today.

DAILY WORD: "Speak, LORD, for your servant hears" (1 Sam 3:9).

EVENING REVIEW: How did I bring God's word to people today?

January 16

As a descendant of King David, Jesus possessed royal blood.
When the Holy Spirit came upon Jesus in the Jordan River,
he was anointed a king, but not like the political kings of
his time or ours. He was anointed a servant king who told
his disciples: "The kings of the Gentiles exercise lordship
over them. . . . But not so with you; rather, let the greatest
among you become as the youngest, and the leader as one
who serves. . . . I am among you as one who serves" (Lk
22:25–27).

At Baptism, I was anointed. Jesus shared with me his royal
dignity. Joined to the Body of Christ, I am part of "a chosen
race, a royal priesthood, a holy nation, God's own people"
(1 Pet 2:9). Like Jesus and unlike worldly kings and queens,
I do not seek wealth and power. I seek to share in the royal
power of Jesus, which is the power of a love that is revealed
in service and sacrifice. The earthly throne that Jesus had
was the Cross, for he said, "I, when I am lifted up from the
earth, will draw all men to myself" (Jn 12:32). If I share
that throne now, I have the promise that I will share a heavenly throne.

*Lord Jesus, Son of David, you said that you came not to be served
but to serve. You gave me a striking example of service when you bent
down and washed the dirty feet of your apostles at the Last Supper.
Be with me today so that I may not so much seek to be served as to
serve.*

DAILY WORD: I am a royal daughter (son).

EVENING REVIEW: In what ways did I live my Christlike royal
identity today?

January 17: St. Anthony (251–356)

St. Anthony left everything to live a life of solitude, prayer, and penance in the desert of Egypt. The Scriptures inspired him to do so. One day, on his way to church, he was thinking how the apostles left everything to follow Jesus and how the early Christians sold everything and gave the money to the apostles, who then distributed it among the poor. Just as he entered the church, he heard these words of Jesus being proclaimed: "If you would be perfect, go, sell what you possess and give to the poor, and you will have treasure in heaven; and come, follow me" (Mt 19:21). He thought it no coincidence, but rather that the Word of God was being spoken directly to him. He sold everything and went to follow Jesus as a hermit.

We take nothing material with us as we pass from this life to the next. But we do take with us all we have lovingly given away to others. We take with us the virtues we have fostered.

We renew our daily offering now, reflecting on these words of St. Anthony:

Let us not think, as we look at the world, that we have renounced anything of much consequence, for the whole earth is very small compared with heaven. Therefore let the desire of possession take hold of no one, for what gain is it to acquire these things that we cannot take with us? Why not rather get those things that we can take with us—prudence, justice, temperance, courage, understanding, love, kindness to the poor, faith in Christ, freedom from wrath, hospitality? If we possess these, we shall find that they will prepare for us a welcome there in the land of the meek-hearted.

DAILY WORD: I give, and I find treasure in heaven.

EVENING REVIEW: What did I give and what treasure did I find today?

29

January 18: Beginning of the Octave of Prayer for Christian Unity

On this day in 1908, in a small chapel on a remote hillside fifty miles from New York City, Fr. Paul Wattson and Sister Lurana White began the custom of offering an octave (eight days of prayer) for Christian unity. They were Episcopalians who had founded the Franciscan Friars and Sisters of the Atonement that, in a few years, became the first Anglican religious order to seek full communion with the Roman Catholic Church. The special Octave of Prayer for Christian Unity has continued ever since.

Jesus himself prayed for Christian unity on the night before he died. At the Last Supper, he prayed: "I pray for them . . . for those you have given me. . . . I pray not only for them, but also for those who will believe in me through their word, so that they may all be one, as you, Father, are in me and I in you, that they also may be in us, that the world may believe that you sent me" (see Jn 17). The unity of Christians is an essential witness to the truth of Christianity.

The traditional form of the Morning Offering includes the line "for the reunion of all Christians".

Lord Jesus, your Heart is wounded and broken by the divisions among your followers. I want to console you this day by committing myself to do all I can to overcome these divisions that give scandal to the world. May every prayer and action of mine today bring healing to the Church, your Body. May the Holy Spirit, who guided you, guide me and all Christians to the fullness of truth.

DAILY WORD: I offer this for the reunion of Christians.

EVENING REVIEW: How did I foster harmony today?

January 19

There are many reasons why people do not believe in God. The bishops at the Second Vatican Council identified one reason that may be surprising—you and me! They wrote: "Believers can have more than a little to do with the birth of atheism. To the extent that they neglect their own training in the faith, or teach erroneous doctrine, or are deficient in their religious, moral, or social life, they must be said to conceal rather than reveal the authentic face of God and religion" (Vatican II's *Gaudium et spes*, no. 19).

By not living an authentic Christian life, we contribute to the growth of atheism. The world looks at Christians and says, "How can we believe in Jesus when his followers act the way they do and are so divided?" Jesus anticipated this at the Last Supper when he prayed that his followers would be one just as he and the Father are one so that the world would believe (see Jn 17:21–23).

Let us exercise "spiritual ecumenism" now, joining Christians of various denominations around the world this week in offering ourselves for unity. Together we accept the words of St. Paul, who wrote:

I therefore, a prisoner for the Lord, beg you to walk in a manner worthy of the calling to which you have been called, with all lowliness and meekness, with patience, forbearing one another in love, eager to maintain the unity of the Spirit in the bond of peace. There is one body and one Spirit, just as you were called to the one hope that belongs to your call; one Lord, one faith, one baptism, one God and Father of us all, who is above all and through all and in all. (Eph 4:1–5)

DAILY WORD: May I reveal the authentic face of God.

EVENING REVIEW: Today, how well did I do, bearing with others through love?

January 20: Sts. Fabian and Sebastian (3rd Century)

St. Fabian and St. Sebastian, pope and soldier, respectively, were both martyrs of the early Church. They fulfilled Jesus' prediction: "If they persecuted me, they will persecute you" (Jn 15:18–20). They lived in a time when it was illegal to be a Christian, and there was plenty of evidence to convict them. If the same were true today, would there be enough evidence to convict me? Does my life witness to the truth and love of Jesus Christ?

Today, throughout the world, Christians—of all denominations—are dying for the faith. A month after being elected, Pope Francis said,

> Let us ask for the help of Mary Most Holy so that the Church throughout the world may proclaim the Resurrection of the Lord with candor and courage and give credible witness to it with signs of brotherly love. Brotherly love is the closest testimony we can give that Jesus is alive with us, that Jesus is risen. Let us pray in a special way for Christians who are suffering persecution; in our day there are so many Christians who are suffering persecution—so, so many, in a great many countries: let us pray for them, with love, from our heart. May they feel the living and comforting presence of the Risen Lord.

These modern martyrs represent an ecumenism of blood. Though separated as a result of Christianity's divisions, they are one in their love for the One for whom they gave their lives.

God, our One Father, I offer my day to you as a bloodless martyrdom, uniting myself to the Cross of Jesus which all Christians hold dear.

DAILY WORD: I offer this for my persecuted brothers and sisters.

January 21: St. Agnes (ca. 291–304)

According to tradition, Agnes was only fourteen when she was martyred. Her courage and purity have won her an honored place in the Communion of Saints. Her name means "Lamb", and every year on this day in Rome, two lambs are sheared. The wool is sent to a convent where nuns weave it into palliums, the stole-like vestment archbishops wear as a sign of their unity with the pope, the bishop of Rome.

Right before we receive the Body and Blood of Christ in Holy Communion, we hear the words: "Behold the Lamb of God, behold him who takes away the sins of the world. Blessed are those called to the supper of the Lamb." Jesus is the Lamb of God who unites himself to us so that we become "lambs of God" as well, offering ourselves with Jesus for the reconciliation and salvation of the world. This is the meaning of the daily offering.

As we continue offering our days this week for Christian unity, we pray that it might be a unity visible to non-Christians. The world listens more, as Pope St. Paul VI said, to our witness than to our words. The world must see our witness of Christian unity. In his first address to the cardinals who elected him pope, Benedict XVI said strongly: "Each one of us must come before him, the supreme Judge of every living person, and render an account to him of all we have done or have failed to do to further the great good of the full and visible unity of all his disciples."

Lamb of God and Good Shepherd, I offer myself to you. May all your flock be one.

DAILY WORD: Lord, make me an instrument of unity today.

EVENING REVIEW: What did I do or not do to further unity among Christians today?

January 22: National Day of Prayer and Penance for Sins against Life

In 1995, Pope St. John Paul II issued two encyclicals. On March 25, he issued *The Gospel of Life*; exactly two months later he issued *Ut Unum Sint*, about ecumenism. In the former, he wrote: "Service of the Gospel of life . . . increasingly appears as a valuable and fruitful area for positive cooperation with our brothers and sisters of other Churches and ecclesial communities." And in the latter, he wrote: "With increasing frequency Christians are working together to defend human dignity. . . . Before the world, united action in society on the part of Christians has the clear value of a joint witness to the name of the Lord."

Abortion was legalized in the U.S. on this day in 1973. Imagine if all Christians united to pray and work for an end to abortion. Such visible unity is what Jesus prayed for to his Father at the Last Supper, "that the world may know that you have sent me" (Jn 17:23).

We offer ourselves today for this double intention: an end to abortion and the unity of Christians. The following is from a prayer that Pope Benedict XVI offered at a Vigil for the Unborn on November 27, 2010.

Lord Jesus, source and lover of Life, we beg you. Reawaken in us respect for every unborn life, make us capable of seeing in the fruit of the maternal womb the miraculous work of the Creator, open our hearts to generously welcoming every child that comes into life. Accompany the choices of legislative assemblies with the light of your Spirit, so that peoples and nations may recognize and respect the sacred nature of life, of every human life. Amen.

DAILY WORD: Lord, I offer my life for life.

EVENING REVIEW: How did I foster greater respect for life today?

January 23: St. Marianne Cope (1838–1918)

On this day in 1838, Marianne Cope was born in Germany. When she was two, her parents immigrated to upstate New York. In time she became a Sister of St. Francis in Syracuse and helped found two hospitals. In 1883, she and six other Sisters went to Hawaii, where she served lepers, including St. Damien of Molokai.

Two days after her death, an article in the *Honolulu Advertiser* stated: "Without blare of trumpets, Sister Marianne entered upon her duties, and through thirty long, wearisome years living apart from the world and its comforts, she labored in the cause of a stricken people. She risked her own life in all that time, faced everything with unflinching courage, and smiled sweetly through it all."

Finding courage and strength in the Heart of Jesus, she wrote to encourage others: "Creep down into the heart of Jesus. He alone can comfort you in your supreme hour of sorrow." Filled with the love of the Sacred Heart that knows no boundaries, having been pierced for all people, she wrote: "The charity of the good knows no creed and is confined to no one place." And aware of the precious gift of time, she said: "Let us make best use of the fleeting moments. They will not return. Let us make the very best use of the precious moments and do all in our power for His dear sake and for His greater honor and glory."

Lord, I thank you for the precious moments of the day ahead of me. They will never return to me, and so I offer them to you. Keep them safe in your loving Heart.

DAILY WORD: I do this for love of you, Jesus.

EVENING REVIEW: What works and prayers of charity did I offer today?

January 24: St. Francis de Sales (1567–1622)

When he was eighteen, Francis was tempted to despair. He was obsessed with the thought that he had lost the love of God and was doomed to hate God forever in hell. He decided to make a pure act of love for God, thinking that if he was going to be separated from God forever, he wanted at least to love God as much as he could on earth. Then he prayed a Memorare to Our Lady, and all fear and despair left him. He was filled with a deep, abiding peace and spent the rest of his life sharing that peace with everyone he met.

Some people thought he was too easy on sinners because he emphasized God's love for them. He replied: "If there were anything more excellent than meekness, God would certainly have taught it to us; and yet there is nothing to which he so earnestly exhorts all as to be meek and humble of heart. Why would you hinder me from obeying the command of my Lord?"

To another critic he said: "Are these sinners not part of my flock? Has not our blessed Lord shed his blood for them? These wolves will be changed into lambs. If Saul had been cut off, we should never have had St. Paul."

I offer myself today for the conversion of sinners, including myself, and for the reunion of Christians, with this prayer of St. Francis de Sales:

My God, I give you this day. I offer you, now, all of the good that I shall do, and I promise to accept, for love of you, all of the difficulty that I shall meet. Help me to conduct myself during this day in a manner pleasing to you. Amen.

DAILY WORD: The measure of love is to love without measure.

EVENING REVIEW: In what ways did I love without measure today?

36

January 25: Feast of the Conversion of St. Paul

We end the Octave of Prayer for Christian Unity by remembering how St. Paul went from a Pharisee and persecutor of Christians to one of the greatest Christian missionaries of all time.

The change began when he met Jesus on the road to Damascus and heard these words "Saul, Saul, why are you persecuting me?"

The words of Jesus' question make clear that he and his followers, his Church, are one. Later Paul would elaborate on this unity (see 1 Cor 12). Christ is the Head, and the Church is his Body. We are made one with Christ through Baptism and the Eucharist.

After his profound and dramatic conversion, you might think Paul never struggled with sin. Romans 7 and 2 Corinthians 12:7–10 make it abundantly clear that Paul continued to be tempted and to give in to sin. When he prayed that the "thorn in the flesh . . . an angel of Satan" might leave him, the Lord told him: "My grace is sufficient for you, for my power is made perfect in weakness" (2 Cor 12:9).

Jesus saved the world through weakness—the weakness of a baby born in a stable and the weakness of a man nailed to a cross. But through weakness, the power of love triumphed. I offer myself with my weaknesses as I reflect on Paul's words (2 Cor 4:7, 16–17):

But we have this treasure in earthen vessels, to show that the transcendent power belongs to God and not to us. We are afflicted in every way, but not crushed. . . . For this slight momentary affliction is preparing for us an eternal weight of glory beyond all comparison, because we look not to the things that are seen but to the things that are unseen, for . . . the things that are unseen are eternal.

DAILY WORD: Lord, I offer you my weakness.

EVENING REVIEW: What struggles and weaknesses did I offer up today?

January 26: Sts. Timothy and Titus (1st Century)

Am I contagious? Yes, during flu season we want to be careful about spreading viruses, but we Christians are supposed to be contagious when it comes to the Gospel. That's how others can "catch" the Good News. Pope Benedict XVI said that any "gesture of charity and authentic devotion to Christ . . . is contagious: it instils love, joy, and light" (Homily March 29, 2010).

St. Paul was so filled with the love of Christ that he was contagious. Having remembered his conversion yesterday, today we celebrate two who caught the Gospel from him. To Timothy, Paul once wrote: "The saying is sure and worthy of full acceptance, that Christ Jesus came into the world to save sinners. And I am the foremost of sinners; but I received mercy for this reason, that in me, as the foremost, Jesus Christ might display his perfect patience for an example to those who were to believe in him for eternal life" (1 Tim 1:15–16). In this same letter, Paul wrote about the importance of intercessory prayer: "I urge that supplications, prayers, intercessions, and thanksgivings be made for all men, for kings and all who are in high positions, that we may lead a quiet and peaceable life, godly and respectful in every way. This is good, and it is acceptable in the sight of God our Savior, who desires all men to be saved and to come to knowledge of the truth" (2:1–4).

Lord God, I offer my day to you for this intention: that everyone may come to know the truth of your love revealed in Jesus, your Son, and accept the salvation he won for them on the Cross. Amen.

DAILY WORD: May others catch the Good News through me.

EVENING REVIEW: In what ways did I instill love, joy, and light in others today?

January 27: St. Angela Merici (1474–1540)

Angela was an angelic messenger to all, but especially to young girls. Orphaned when she was fifteen, she joined the secular, or third-order, Franciscans. In time she organized a group of single laywomen into the first religious order of women dedicated to education—the Ursulines. She was convinced that society would become more Christian through the good formation of its future wives and mothers.

I renew my daily offering with this prayer of St. Angela:

As our Savior says: "A good tree is not able to produce bad fruit." He says: a good tree, that is, a good heart as well as a soul inflamed with charity, can do nothing but good and holy works. For this reason St. Augustine said: "Love, and do what you will", namely, possess love and charity and then do what you will. It is as if he had said: Charity is not able to sin. My Savior, illumine the darkness of my heart, and grant me grace rather to die than to offend Your Divine Majesty any more. Guard, O Lord, my affections and my senses, that they may not stray, or lead me away from the light of Your face, the satisfaction of every afflicted heart. I ask You, Lord, to receive all my self-will that by the infection of sin is unable to distinguish good from evil. Receive, O Lord, all my thoughts, words, and deeds, interior and exterior, that I lay at the feet of Your Divine Majesty. Although I am utterly unworthy, I beseech You to accept all my being.

DAILY WORD: United to you, Lord Jesus, I can bear good fruit.

EVENING REVIEW: What thoughts, words, and deeds did I lay at God's feet today?

January 28: St. Thomas Aquinas (1225–1274)

Thomas has been called the greatest theologian of all time. Yet, as a youth his peers nicknamed him "Dumb Ox" because of his size and quiet demeanor. His teacher, St. Albert the Great, predicted that the sound of this "dumb ox" would be heard all over the world. Thus it has happened, as his *Summa Theologica* continues to hold pride of place in theological education.

Thomas was a man who combined study and prayer. The hymns he wrote for the celebration of the feast of Corpus Christi are still sung today. In a mystical encounter, he once heard the Lord tell him, "Thomas, you have written well of me. What reward would you have?" He responded, "Nothing but yourself, Lord." This is the reward that I, too, am given every time I receive the Holy Eucharist.

As Jesus offers himself to me in the Eucharist, so I return myself and my day to him. The following is a prayer of St. Thomas entitled "For All Good Things".

Loving God, who sees in us nothing that You have not given Yourself, make my body healthy and agile, my mind sharp and clear, my heart joyful and contented, my soul faithful and loving. And surround me with the company of people and angels who share my devotion to You. Above all, let me live in Your presence, for with You all fear is banished, and there is only harmony and peace. Let every day combine the beauty of spring, the brightness of summer, the abundance of autumn, and the repose of winter. And at the end of my life on earth, grant that I may come to see and to know You in the fullness of Your glory. Amen.

DAILY WORD: I give myself to you in all the things I do.

EVENING REVIEW: How did I live in the presence of God today?

The first month of the calendar year is coming to an end. Where does the time go? It seems like just yesterday I began this month, this year, and made resolutions for my physical and spiritual health. How am I doing? Have I been faithful to my resolutions, especially the one to make an offering of every day to God?

Whether or not I've followed through on these resolutions, what's important is for me to keep trying. My life is spent and my offering given one day at a time. Failure is no reason to quit.

What counts is perseverance. St. Paul writes: "Let us not grow weary in well-doing, for in due season we shall reap, if we do not lose heart" (Gal 6:9).

The Letter to the Hebrews also speaks of perseverance: "Since we are surrounded by so great a cloud of witnesses, let us also lay aside every weight, and sin which clings so closely, and run with perseverance the race that is set before us, looking to Jesus, the pioneer and perfecter of our faith" (Heb 12:1-2).

Keep in mind Aesop's fable about the race between the hare and the tortoise. One may start fast, but slow, steady perseverance wins the race.

Lord Jesus, as I approach the end of this first month of the new year, I renew my commitment to make an offering of every day to you. Alone, I am helpless. United to you in the Eucharist, I can persevere and win the race.

DAILY WORD: One moment at a time, I offer myself to you.

EVENING REVIEW: What has helped me to be mindful of the daily offering I have made?

In his "Spiritual Exercises", St. Ignatius Loyola has "Rules for the Discernment of Spirits", where he says that behind the various movements of our hearts are different spirits, good and bad. The Spirit of God never uses discouragement to move our hearts, for discouragement—which literally means to lose heart—leads one to give up or to despair.

What discourages me? What can cause me in small ways or large to give up? How do I react to my weaknesses and failures? If I find myself tempted to give up because I am not perfect, then I am clearly listening to the bad spirit.

St. Pius of Pietrelcina, better known as Padre Pio, has some helpful words that echo St. Ignatius:

> The Spirit of God is a spirit of peace. Even in the most serious faults he makes us feel a sorrow that is tranquil, humble, and confident, and this is precisely because of his mercy. The spirit of the devil, instead, excites, exasperates, and makes us feel, in that very sorrow, anger against ourselves, whereas we should on the contrary be charitable with ourselves first and foremost. Therefore if any thought agitates you, this agitation never comes from God, who gives you peace, being the Spirit of Peace, but from the devil.

Lord Jesus, you did not come into the world to condemn us but to save us. I am weak and often discouraged by my weakness. I lose heart. Help me to take heart, to take your Heart, which is strong. I believe that you give your Heart to me in the Eucharist, where you are truly and fully present. As you offer yourself to me, so I offer myself to you.

DAILY WORD: Holy Spirit, encourage me now.

EVENING REVIEW: How was my heart moved by discouragement or encouragement today?

January 31: St. John Bosco (1815–1888)

John Bosco liked to play jokes on people, and as a youth he learned how to juggle so that he could entertain the children of the urban slums of Italy. Once he got their attention, he would teach them about Jesus. He told them, "Enjoy yourself as much as you like, just keep away from sin." Inspired by the gentle approach of St. Francis de Sales, he founded the Salesians, one of the largest teaching orders of men and women in the world today.

Sharing the love of the Heart of Jesus, John had an overwhelming desire for the salvation of every person. He was grieved that people might never know the love of God, receive it, and be saved. Jesus died to save all people, but not everyone has accepted the salvation he won for them. Now we, as members of his Body, play a role in helping people receive that salvation. This is what it means to offer our day "for the salvation of souls". I do so now with these words of St. John Bosco:

My God, fortunate is he who has tasted how sweet it is to work for the salvation of souls! He is not afraid of cold or heat, hunger or thirst, offenses or insults, no, not even of death. O Lord, give me crosses and thorns, if only I can save souls. Give me souls, Lord, and take all the rest. O Lord, I wish to make a complete sacrifice of my life to You, to work for Your glory until I draw my last breath, bearing patiently all adversities and contradictions in my work. Help me to spend all my strength for the salvation of souls.

DAILY WORD: I offer all for the salvation of souls.

EVENING REVIEW: Was there anything especially difficult, and therefore especially powerful, in this day I offered God?

FEBRUARY

February 1

In the United States, with the exception of Thanksgiving, on what day do people eat the most food? Hint: it's the day of the most-watched television show of the year. Yes, it's Super Bowl Sunday. Many people prepare for weeks, putting together menus of finger-foods and drinks and lists of invitees. If Jesus were around today, would he be on my list?

A first reaction might be: "Oh no! Not Jesus! We won't have any fun if he comes." But Jesus enjoyed a good party. He was criticized for having meals with the public sinners of his time—tax collectors and prostitutes (see Lk 15:1‑2). He was called "a glutton and a drunkard" (see Lk 7:34). His first recorded miracle was to change water into wine when the party had run short (see Jn 2:1‑11). Of course, Jesus did not sin by over-indulging, but he did enjoy a good time with friends and strangers.

Today I am mindful in my daily offering of giving God not only my prayers, works, and sufferings, but also my joys. Jesus wants to share in those as well. Offering my joys to God helps me to have a grateful heart. The word "Eucharist" means "thanksgiving". I offer myself with Jesus in the Eucharist as an act of thanksgiving for my life and all its blessings.

Lord Jesus, you are the Word made flesh, Wisdom Incarnate. You played on the surface of the earth and "found delight" in human children (see Prov 10:31). You want to share in all my legitimate pleasures and joys. I give them to you now, for shared happiness makes the happiness greater for both you and for me.

DAILY WORD: "Rejoice in the Lord always" (Phil 4:4).

EVENING REVIEW: What joys and did I offer God today?

February 2: Presentation of Our Lord

Today's feast, forty days after Christmas, celebrates the Presentation, described in Luke 2:22–38. Following Jewish law, Mary and Joseph brought the baby Jesus to the Temple to present him to God. This rite remembers the night of the Passover, when the angel swept through Egypt killing the firstborn males of those whose doorposts had no lamb's blood on them. Thus, the firstborn Israelites were spared. After this, the Egyptians drove the Israelites from their land, opening the way for them to journey to the Promised Land. The law of Moses directed the people to remember this great event in their history by consecrating every firstborn male to God. Thus was Jesus consecrated.

I too am consecrated, not according to the law of Moses, but according to the law of the New Covenant. At Baptism, I was consecrated and offered to God. My daily offering reminds me of this.

Today is also known at Candlemas Day. New candles to be used in worship are blessed today. We remember the Light that appeared at Christmas and Epiphany and remember as well that our consecration makes us light for the world. St. Sophronius wrote these words for the feast:

Our candles show how bright our souls should be when we go to meet Christ. The light has come and has shone upon a world enveloped in shadows. The true light has come, the light that enlightens every person who is born into this world. Let all of us be enlightened and made radiant by this light. Let all of us be so filled with it that no one remains in the darkness.

46

DAILY WORD: Let your light shine through me, Lord.

EVENING REVIEW: In what ways did the light of Christ grow in me today?

February 3: St. Blaise (d. 316) and St. Ansgar (801–865)

Ansgar, a French monk, went to Scandinavia as a missionary in the ninth century. Blaise, a fourth-century bishop, was a martyr. Tradition has it that a woman came up to him one day pleading that he help her son who was choking on a fish bone that was lodged in his throat. Blaise stopped and prayed; immediately the boy was cured. From that came the tradition of blessing throats on the feast day of St. Blaise using the newly blessed candles from yesterday's Feast of the Presentation.

If we have a special day designated for blessing throats, why not one for blessing backs, knees, hips, hearts, and stomachs? But today's blessing prayer covers all those as well: "Through the intercession of St. Blaise, bishop and martyr, may God deliver you from ailments of the throat and from every other evil. In the name of the Father, and of the Son, and of the Holy Spirit. Amen."

God is concerned about the health of our entire bodies along with our souls. The two go together. Our spiritual health often affects our physical health and vice versa. When I offer myself to God, I pray that his ultimate good will be done in my life. That may not always mean healing from physical ailments. But our offered ailments, like all offered suffering, can become particularly powerful prayers for others. Thus, our spiritual health can flourish even in times of poor physical health. God gives us grace to maintain the spiritual health that leads us to eternal life.

Lord, join the sufferings of my day to your Cross for the salvation of the world.

DAILY WORD: Deliver me from evil.

EVENING REVIEW: What particular physical sufferings did I offer to God as a prayer for others today?

February 4

At the Last Supper, Jesus told his disciples: "I have earnestly desired to eat this Passover with you before I suffer" (Lk 22:15). Then he took bread and wine and said "This is my body. . . . This . . . is the new covenant in my blood." Jesus was eager to give himself totally to his disciples. By giving himself to his disciples as he celebrated this Passover with them, he was anticipating that on the next day he would offer himself on the Cross for the salvation of all.

We now celebrate this New Passover with every Mass. Jesus is once again eager to give himself to us in the great sacramental mystery that he instituted at the Last Supper. He gives himself totally to us—Body and Blood, soul and divinity. That includes his Heart, which in Scripture refers to the essence of the person.

Since Jesus has given himself totally to me, I eagerly desire to give myself totally to him. I return love for love by making an offering of this day, asking only that he will fill me with his love.

O loving Heart of Jesus, you are concealed in the Holy Eucharist, and there you still beat with love for me. I worship you with fervent affection, with all my will and all my love. When you allow me to receive you, you dwell within me. Make my heart beat with yours. Purify my heart of all that is proud and sensual, all that is hard and cruel. Fill my heart with you so that the events of the day may not disturb it, but in your love I may have peace. Amen.

DAILY WORD: Make my heart like yours, Jesus.

EVENING REVIEW: In what ways did my heart beat in union with the Heart of Jesus today?

February 5: St. Agatha (d. 250)

Agatha, a Sicilian woman who had consecrated herself to a life of virginity, was a third-century martyr. She was so popular that not long after her death, a church was built in her honor in Rome and her name was included in the Roman Canon, Eucharistic Prayer I, which we continue to use.

In a homily about Agatha, St. Methodius said: "Agatha, the name of our saint, means 'good'. She was truly good, for she lived as a child of God. Agatha teaches people by her example to hasten with her to the true Good, God alone."

At one time a man came up to Jesus and asked him: "Good Teacher, what must I do to inherit eternal life?" Jesus responded, "Why do you call me good? No one is good but God alone" (Mk 10:17–18). Jesus was not trying to deny the fact that he was the Son of God. Rather, he was teaching the man that all goodness comes from God and all praise goes to God. At another time Jesus declared: "I can do nothing on my own authority; . . . I seek not my own will but the will of him who sent me" (Jn 5:30).

When I make my daily offering, I am seeking to do the will of God. I am trying to be good with the goodness of God. If that goodness is recognized by others, then I, like Jesus, give all credit to God.

Good and gracious God, in Baptism you have claimed me as your own child. May the good things I do today reflect your goodness and give you glory. Amen.

DAILY WORD: May the good I do today give glory to God.

EVENING REVIEW: What good was I able to accomplish today with God's help?

February 6: St. Paul Miki and Companions (d. 1597)

Today the Church honors the early martyrs of Japan—a Jesuit seminarian named Paul Miki and two other Jesuits; six Franciscan missionaries from Spain, Mexico, and India; and seventeen Japanese lay people. All were tied to crosses and stabbed with spears.

An eyewitness gave the following account:

> When the crosses were set up, it was a wonderful thing to see the constancy of all of them. Our brother Paul Miki, seeing himself raised to the most honorable position that he had ever occupied, openly proclaimed that he was a Japanese and a member of the Society of Jesus. And that he was being put to death for having preached the Gospel. He gave thanks to God for such a precious favor. Another Christian shouted to him that he would soon be in paradise. "Like my Master", said Paul, "I shall die upon the cross. Like him, a lance will pierce my heart so that my blood and my love can flow out upon the land and sanctify it to his name."

I may never face persecution and a death like this, but I'm called to give thanks to God for the "precious favor" of being a Christian and for being called to preach the Gospel by the way I live my life. Today I may have crosses to bear. I will join them to the Cross of Jesus, and in that way our love—Jesus' and mine united—will flow out upon the world for the salvation of others.

Jesus, your Cross is the sign of your love. Accept me and my crosses this day. By following your example, may I follow you into the eternal joy of heaven.

DAILY WORD: Jesus, I take up my cross and follow you today.

EVENING REVIEW: What crosses did I carry and offer up today?

February 7

On this day in 1920, a twenty-three-year-old American seminarian from Virginia named Frank Parater died of rheumatic fever at the Pontifical North American College in Rome. His "Rule of Life" contains the following challenges:

> Don't be petty; be large-minded. Don't be a bluffer; no man can keep from having his bluff called. Don't boast; an egotist is the worst boast; cultivate humility. Be frank, but not critical. A word of praise does more good than a sermon on faultfinding. Be gentle—"a gentleman never inflicts pain." Love the poor. Remember all men are humans, and let your charity be unbounded: but be strict with yourself (not scrupulous)—remember that someday God will judge every action of your life as a merciful Judge.

Frank was devoted to the Sacred Heart of Jesus. "The Sacred Heart never fails those who love him", he said. When he arrived in Rome, Frank had a premonition of his death, which occurred three months later. After his death, his friends found this testament among his writings: "I have nothing to leave or give but my life, and this I have consecrated to the Sacred Heart of Jesus to be used as He wills."

Sacred Heart of Jesus, all I am and have is a gift from you. You gave your life to save me. I give my life and this day to you. Be close to me so that together we—you the Head and Heart and I a part of Your Body—may offer ourselves for the spread of the Gospel and the salvation of all.

DAILY WORD: Merciful Heart of Jesus, use me as you will.

EVENING REVIEW: How did Jesus and I work together today?

February 8: St. Josephine Bakhita (1868–1947)

In the first pages of his encyclical *Spe salvi*, Pope Benedict XVI holds up Josephine Bakhita as an example of hope:

> To come to know God—the true God—means to receive hope. We who have always lived with the Christian concept of God, and have grown accustomed to it, have almost ceased to notice that we possess the hope that ensues from a real encounter with this God. The example of a saint of our time can to some degree help us understand what it means to have a real encounter with this God for the first time. I am thinking of the African Josephine Bakhita. . . . She was born . . . in Darfur in Sudan. At the age of nine, she was kidnapped by slave-traders, beaten till she bled, and sold five times in the slave-markets of Sudan. Eventually she found herself working as a slave for the . . . wife of a general, and there she was flogged every day till she bled; as a result of this, she bore 144 scars throughout her life.

Josephine found both freedom and faith in Italy, where she was baptized and joined the Canossian Daughters of Charity. She saw in Jesus one who understood her sufferings, for he, too, was scourged. Pope Benedict continues: "Now she had 'hope'—no longer simply the modest hope of finding masters who would be less cruel, but the great hope. [She said:] 'I am definitively loved, and whatever happens to me—I am awaited by this Love. And so, my life is good.'"

Lord, no matter what happens to me today, I trust in you because I believe in your love for me.

DAILY WORD: I have hope because I am loved by God.

EVENING REVIEW: How did God's love give me hope today?

Yesterday was also the feast of St. Jerome Emiliani (1486–1537), who, after having served a time in the military, devoted himself to serving the poor, especially orphans.

St. Jerome wrote about faith in a letter to members of the religious congregation he founded:

> Our goal is God, the source of all good. As we say in our prayer, we are to place our trust in God and in no one else. In his kindness, our Lord wished to strengthen your faith, for without it, as the evangelist points out, Christ could not have performed many of his miracles. God wishes to test you like gold in the furnace. If then you remain constant in faith in the face of trial, the Lord will give you peace and rest for a time in this world, and forever in the next.

People are often surprised that Jesus, who is God and all-powerful, was at times limited. What could have limited his ability to heal people? The Gospel tells us: "[Jesus] did not do many mighty works there, because of their unbelief" (Mt 13:58).

Lord Jesus, you trusted in the Father's love for you. You believed that you could do all things in cooperation with the One who sent you. You call me to have faith that you are "by the power at work within us able to do far more abundantly than all that we ask or think" (Eph 3:20). Increase my faith so that you may accomplish your will in me and through me today. I give you my day so that together we might "work many mighty deeds". Amen.

DAILY WORD: Father, I trust in you.

EVENING REVIEW: How was my faith tested and purified today?

February 10: St. Scholastica (480–547)

St. Scholastica was the twin sister of St. Benedict, considered the founder of monasticism in the Western Church. She, too, lived a monastic life and would visit her brother once a year at a house just outside the walls of his monastery. According to St. Gregory the Great, on her last visit, Scholastica must have sensed she was nearing death. She asked her brother to spend the entire night talking about "the delights of the spiritual life". He refused, saying, "I simply cannot stay outside my cell." She bowed her head and prayed, and immediately a violent storm with lightning and rain erupted, and Benedict was forced to remain with her.

St. Gregory the Great commented: "It is not surprising that she was more effective than he; since, as John says, 'God is love', it was absolutely right that she could do more, as she loved more."

It was the power of love that transformed Jesus' death on the Cross into life. Love is the greatest power in the world because, as John wrote, Almighty God who created and redeemed and sustains the world is Love (1 Jn 4:8, 16). In Love's image and likeness, I too am made by love and for love.

Holy Trinity, One God—Father, Son, and Holy Spirit—I adore you today. You are a communion of Three Persons, yet one God. You are the Great Mystery, Love itself. May your ways be my ways today. I give myself to you so that your loving will may be accomplished in me and in all I do today. Amen.

DAILY WORD: May God's love guide all I do.

EVENING REVIEW: How did I see the power of God's love working through me today?

February 11: Our Lady of Lourdes

For thirteen weeks in 1942, a Catholic book ranked number one on the *New York Times* best-seller list. The following year, it was made into a movie that was nominated for twelve Academy Awards, including Best Picture. "The Song of Bernadette" tells the story of a young French girl to whom the Blessed Virgin Mary appeared eighteen times between February 11 and July 16, 1858. When asked her name, Mary said that she was the Immaculate Conception, thus confirming the doctrine that had been officially defined less than four years before. Mary also showed Bernadette a trickle of water that became a spring and grotto of healing water to which pilgrims have flocked ever since.

We honor Mary today under the title of the location of this miraculous spring, Our Lady of Lourdes. Visiting there on the 150th anniversary of the apparitions, Pope Benedict XVI said: "Mary entrusts her smile to you, so that you yourselves may become, in faithfulness to her son, springs of living water. Whatever you do, you do in the name of the Church, of which Mary is the purest image. May you carry her smile to everyone!"

Lord Jesus, your birth and childhood brought smiles to your Mother's face. Now Mother Mary smiles upon me because I am part of your Body. Joined to her in the Church, I now bring her smile to the world. As I offer myself to you, Risen Savior, I pray that I may give your Mother's smile to all the people I meet today. May I be a source of comfort, hope, and joy to all. Amen.

DAILY WORD: I offer this to you, Jesus, with a smile.

EVENING REVIEW: How did my smile help others today?

In a traditional form of the Morning Offering, we offer to God all the "prayers, works, joys, and sufferings" of the day. The "prayers" naturally include all the ways in which we pray on a given day—morning and night prayers, the Angelus, Scripture reading, the rosary, Eucharistic adoration, and, of course, Mass. But there are numerous opportunities throughout the day when we can offer spontaneous prayers to bring God's grace to the situations and people we encounter. Perhaps our best opportunities for prayer occur in the stressful and confusing moments we encounter.

The desert monastics of the early Church tried to pray continuously through an exercise called the Jesus Prayer. Synchronizing their breathing with the phrases, they repeated: "Lord Jesus Christ / Son of the Living God / have mercy on me / a sinner." That constant prayer brought the power of Jesus into everything they did. (Some people simplify the prayer to "Lord Jesus Christ / have mercy on me" or "on us" or "on them".) Mentally repeating those words can be especially effective during difficult moments when your mind races and your breathing becomes shallow. The Jesus Prayer is also useful for resisting temptation. As someone said, "When the devil comes knocking at the door of your mind, send Jesus to answer the door."

Lord Jesus, I know that I and the people around me will need your help at various times throughout this day. Help me to keep you in mind during those times. Remind me to turn to you so that I can make your presence more explicit in my life, so that I can rely on your power and not on myself.

DAILY WORD: Lord Jesus Christ, have mercy on me.

EVENING REVIEW: What spontaneous prayers did I offer today?

February 13

Sister Lucia, the oldest of the children to whom Mary appeared at Fatima, died on this day in 2005. She and her two younger cousins were watching over the family's flock of sheep when Mary suddenly appeared to them on May 13, 1917. Mary asked them to return on the same day of the month for the next five months. They did, and in the last month, on October 13, with thousands of witnesses present, great signs appeared in the sky, and Mary revealed herself as Our Lady of the Rosary.

Each time that Mary appeared, Lucia always began the conversation with her by asking a question: "What do you want of me?" We should notice that Lucia did not begin by asking Mary for favors for herself, but by asking Our Lady what she could do for her. This is a good lesson for our own prayer. Mary told Lucia to continue coming each month, pray the rosary, and make sacrifices for the conversion of sinners.

In her book *Calls from the Message of Fatima*, Sister Lucia wrote:

> Our love for God must be like that of husband and wife. When their love is genuine, the wife willingly sacrifices herself in order to see her husband happy, and the husband sacrifices himself for his wife so that she, too, may be happy. It is the familiar mutual exchange of love, which requires immolation, gift, and surrender. And the fruit of this exchange is peace, joy, and well-being. Our love, too, must also be self-sacrificing.

Lord Jesus, I accept your total, self-sacrificing love for me. I want to love you as you have loved me. Today, I want to return love for love by giving myself to you as a "living sacrifice" (Rom 12:1).

DAILY WORD: Lord, what do you want of me?

EVENING REVIEW: What prayers and sacrifices did I offer today?

February 14: Sts. Cyril and Methodius (9th Century)

On this day of valentines, candy, and flowers, the Church honors two brothers who brought Christianity to the Slavic peoples of Eastern Europe—Cyril and Methodius. Cyril died on this day in the year 869. At a time when many Church leaders thought that Hebrew, Greek, or Latin were the only proper languages for Scripture and the Mass, these brothers translated the Bible and liturgical prayers into the language of the people. Cyril invented an alphabet that is still used today by Slavic peoples. The pope approved and blessed their efforts, and the faith spread.

I, too, am called to be a translator. To the people I meet, my words and actions translate the message of Christianity so that they may better understand it and be moved to accept it. As God's Word became flesh through the Blessed Virgin Mary when she said "yes" to God's will, so the Word takes flesh through me today as I begin my day saying "yes" to God's will for my life.

Loving God, you revealed the greatest love the world has ever known when your Son, the Word—your perfect communication to us—became flesh in the womb of Mary. Jesus came so we could know and accept your love. He continues to reveal your love to the world through his Body, the Church. United to him today, I offer myself to you so that through me you may communicate your love to all those I meet.

DAILY WORD: The Word becomes flesh.

EVENING REVIEW: How did my actions translate the Gospel so that the people I met today could understand God's love for them?

February 15: St. Claude de la Colombière (1641–1682)

Yesterday was a heart-filled day for the world; today is a Heart-filled day for us. Today the Church honors the spiritual director of St. Margaret Mary Alacoque, to whom Jesus revealed his Sacred Heart all on fire with love for mankind. St. Claude was a French Jesuit who served as chaplain to the Visitation Sisters in Paray-le-Monial. He confirmed the authenticity of the apparitions that Margaret Mary was receiving.

St. Claude prayed this heartfelt offering prayer:

The Sacred Heart is still burning with love for men and women, always open to pour out on them all kinds of graces and blessings, always moved by our miseries, always urged by the desire of sharing Its treasures with us and of giving Itself to us, always disposed to receive us and to be to us a refuge, a home, and a paradise even in this life.

O most adorable and lovable Heart of my beloved Jesus, I offer You my heart with all the love of which it is capable. I give myself wholly to You. Sacred Heart of Jesus, teach me perfect forgetfulness of self, since that is the only way by which one can enter into You. Since all that I shall do in the future will be Yours, grant that I may never do anything unworthy of You. Lord, do in me Your will. It is for You to do everything, Divine Heart of Jesus Christ. You alone will have the glory of my sanctification, if I become a saint, and it is for that reason alone that I would desire to be perfect.

DAILY WORD: "Jesus, you are my true friend" (words of St. Claude).

EVENING REVIEW: In what ways did I lose myself in loving others today?

Doctors say that keeping active is good for our health. While there are many different forms of exercise, some with more benefits than others, in the end the ones that are best for you are the ones that you enjoy. Why? Because we repeat what we enjoy. We need that enjoyment to get into a lasting habit of regular exercise.

The same is true for spiritual exercise. There are many ways of praying. What helps one person encounter God may not be the same for another. We are each unique. Thus, one of the keys to fostering a regular prayer life, just like a regular routine of physical exercise, is to find ways of praying that you enjoy.

Perhaps it's praying in a natural setting where you can sense something of God's greatness and beauty. You may enjoy prayerfully reading the Bible or another spiritual book. You may like praying the rosary as you take a daily walk or travel on your daily commute. Eucharistic adoration may be a profound experience for you. You may enjoy singing along with uplifting songs while driving in the car or doing housework. God wants to meet with you in any number of ways. He loves spending time with you.

Holy and Blessed Trinity, I offer you today all of my moments of prayer. I know that when I share my feelings and thoughts with you, and when I listen to you speak in the depths of my heart, you keep me spiritually healthy. Give me the habit of spiritual exercise. Help me to have a faithful prayer life.

DAILY WORD: To you, O LORD, I lift up my soul (see Ps 25).

EVENING REVIEW: How did I pray today?

February 17: Seven Holy Founders of the Servite Order (13th Century)

The belief that money and possessions will make one happy isn't new. Through the ages God has raised up countercultural men and women who show the world that human beings are more than flesh and blood and the things they possess. Around the time of St. Francis of Assisi, God inspired seven businessmen in Florence to leave the city and dedicate themselves to a life like that of the early Christians, sharing everything in common and praying for the Church and the world. They called themselves the Servants of Mary.

Recently, on their 700th anniversary, the Servite prior general wrote to those who still follow this path, urging them to practice true Christian community:

> There are obstacles in the path of community life, and they have to be fought against. For example, that sort of "gossip" that creates prejudices, that extinguishes trust, that does not "speak well" about others. Before speaking or criticizing, we must ask ourselves about the basis, the usefulness and worth of our words. We must insist on what unites us, on the work of our group, on our aims, on mutual trust. It is in community that we live united, of one heart and mind, in prayer, in listening to the Word of God, in the breaking of the bread of the Eucharist.

Loving God, I offer myself and my day to you so that through me you may foster harmony in the communities in which I live and work today—my family, my workplace, the Church. May I say only those things that are good and are necessary for the edification of others (see Eph 4:29).

DAILY WORD: "How good and pleasant it is when brothers dwell in unity!" (See Ps 133.)

EVENING REVIEW: How did I help or hinder harmony today?

February 18

Sometimes a priest or deacon will dismiss the congregation with the words: "Go forth, the Mass is ended." It's true that the celebration of the Mass is ended, but the offering we make with Jesus at each Mass should continue in our daily lives.

In his Apostolic Exhortation *The Sacrament of Charity*, Pope Benedict XVI said that the Eucharist is a mystery to be believed, celebrated, and lived. Commenting on Romans 12:1, where Paul says each Christian is to be a "living sacrifice", the pope said: "In these words the new worship appears as a total self-offering made in communion with the whole Church." He added that "the worship of God in our lives . . . tends by its nature to permeate every aspect of our existence. Worship pleasing to God thus becomes a new way of living our whole life, each particular moment of which is lifted up, since it is lived as part of a relationship with Christ and as an offering to God."

My daily offering helps me to make every moment of my life an act of worship. It helps me to live the Mass in my daily life. A priest once had cards printed to highlight this reality: "The Mass never ends. It must be lived by each of us. Let us go to better love and serve the Lord."

Lord Jesus, just as you continually renew the offering of yourself in every celebration of the Mass, so I renew my self-offering with every moment of this day. I unite myself and my day to your perfect offering of yourself on the Cross and in the Mass. May I live the Mass today.

DAILY WORD: O God, I worship you with my life.

EVENING REVIEW: How did I live the Mass today?

February 19: St. Conrad of Piacenza (1290–1351)

St. Conrad was a happily married, well-to-do man who enjoyed hunting. One day he and his friends lit a fire to drive their prey into the open. The fire quickly got out of control, killing farm animals and destroying crops and houses. Conrad and his friends, afraid they would be caught and punished, slipped away. The authorities arrested an innocent man who had been gathering firewood, charged him with arson, and sentenced him to death. When Conrad saw the man being led away, he came forward and confessed his guilt. He was tried, convicted, and ordered to pay for the damage. After they had lost everything, Conrad and his wife saw in this circumstance a call from God to pursue different vocations. Conrad became a hermit, and his wife joined the Poor Clares. They spent the rest of their lives offering their prayers and lives to make reparation for the harm that had been done.

Conrad overcame his fear of punishment so that an innocent man would not suffer. He took responsibility for his actions, and he was indeed punished. Yet God brought good out of the disaster. As St. Paul wrote: "We know that in everything God works for good with those who love him" (Rom 8:28).

Lord Jesus, at different times I have struggled with fear. I have been afraid to suffer the consequences of my bad choices. I dedicate this day to you. May it play a small part in the work of repairing the damage that my sins have done to me and to others.

DAILY WORD: I offer this to balance out the wrong I have done.

EVENING REVIEW: In what ways has God used the things that did not turn out as I wanted to bring about something better?

February 20: Sts. Jacinta (1910–1920) and Francisco (1908–1919)

Our Lady of Fatima appeared to the children Jacinta Marto and her brother, Francisco, as well as to their older cousin, Lucia. Jacinta and Francisco are the youngest people who were not martyrs to be canonized. They are saints, not because Mary appeared to them, but because they lived their short lives with heroic virtue. Mary asked them to pray and to make sacrifices. She said: "Sacrifice yourself for sinners, and say many times, especially when you make some sacrifice: 'O Jesus, it is for love of You, for the conversion of sinners, and in reparation for sins committed against the Immaculate Heart of Mary.'" Francisco and Jacinta responded wholeheartedly to her request.

The Heart of Jesus has one desire—the salvation of every person. The Son of God became human and sacrificed himself, dying on a cross and then rising, for one reason—so that the human race would be freed from sin and death. Not everyone knows God's loving mercy, and many are at risk of ignoring or rejecting it. As Jesus offered himself on the Cross for the salvation of all people, so I, as a member of the Body of Christ, join in the ongoing work of salvation, interceding for people so that they may be open to the grace God wants to give them. I offer myself and my day for this intention. I want to respond wholeheartedly to this desire of God that continues to come to us through Mary's various apparitions.

Lord Jesus, I offer you all the prayers and sacrifices of this day in union with your own perfect offering of yourself on the Cross.

DAILY WORD: "Jesus, it is for love of you and for the conversion of sinners."

EVENING REVIEW: What sacrifices did I offer today for the conversion of those at risk?

February 21: St. Peter Damian (1007–1072)

Peter Damian, an orphan, was raised by his older brothers. One of them, seeing his potential, sent Peter away to study, and in time he became a professor, a priest, and a Camaldolese Benedictine monk.

Familiar with suffering, Peter wrote a letter of encouragement to one of his brothers, sharing with him the first verse from Sirach 2: "My son, if you come forward to serve the Lord, . . . prepare yourself for temptation." He reminded him that loving parents discipline their children, that a goldsmith hammers the gold to beat out the dross, and a potter puts the clay pot into a furnace to strengthen it. He went on:

> For God's chosen ones there is great comfort; the torment lasts but a short time. Then God bends down, cradles the fallen figure, and whispers words of consolation. Therefore do not let your weakness make you impatient. Instead, let the serenity of your spirit shine through your face. Let words of thanks break from your lips. In serenity look forward to the joy that follows sadness. Hope leads you to that joy and love enkindles your zeal.

Lord Jesus, St. Peter wrote that faith is "more precious than gold which though perishable is tested by fire" (1 Pet 1:7). I offer you the trials and sufferings of this day not only as a sacrifice joined to your own perfect sacrifice for the salvation of the world, but also as the way that my faith may grow. Trials are difficult, but I accept them and offer them to you for my ultimate good and the good of others.

DAILY WORD: May this help my faith grow.

EVENING REVIEW: In what ways did the trials of today help me grow?

February 22: Feast of the Chair of St. Peter

No, we are not honoring a piece of furniture today. We honor the divine authority that a chair represents. Every bishop has a special chair from which he presides in his home church or cathedral. This chair is called the cathedra, from the Latin and Greek for chair. The cathedra represents the bishop's authority that he exercises in service to his diocese.

The Chair of St. Peter represents his special authority to lead and govern the Church. This authority was given to St. Peter after he professed his belief that Jesus was "Christ, the Son of the living God". In response, Jesus told him, "Blessed are you, Simon Bar-Jona! For flesh and blood has not revealed this to you, but my Father who is in heaven. And I tell you, you are Peter, and upon this rock I will build my Church, and the gates of Hades shall not prevail against it. I will give you the keys of the kingdom of heaven" (Mt 16:16–19).

St. Jerome (d. 419) once wrote to the pope: "I decided to consult the Chair of Peter, where the faith is found exalted by the lips of an apostle. I now come to ask for nourishment for my soul there. I follow no leader save Christ, so I enter into communion with the Chair of Peter, for this I know is the rock upon which the Church is built."

Lord Jesus, I offer my day to you today in particular for the Successor to St. Peter who currently sits on his chair. May he be guided by the Holy Spirit and nourish the flock that you have entrusted to him (see Jn 21:15–17).

DAILY WORD: I offer this for our pope.

EVENING REVIEW: How did I help in feeding the flock today?

February 23: St. Polycarp (d. 155)

St. Polycarp was a second-generation Christian and disciple of St. John the Apostle who became bishop of Smyrna (in modern Turkey). When he refused to sacrifice to idols, he was sentenced to be burned to death on a pyre. Some friends tried to persuade him to go through the motions of sacrificing, but he replied, referring to Christ, "For eighty-six years I have been his servant, and he has done me no wrong. How can I blaspheme against my king and savior?"

Witnesses report that as the fire engulfed him, it bulged out like the sail of a ship in the wind and formed a vault around Polycarp. Inside, he glowed like bread being baked. Since the fire did not touch Polycarp, one of the soldiers thrust his sword into his body and killed him.

Joined to the Body of Christ, I too am called to be bread. I am like bread baked in an oven of various trials and sufferings. But in this way, I become bread for others, offering myself and my sufferings for them. I make the last recorded words of Polycarp my own as I renew my offering:

Lord, almighty God, Father of your beloved and blessed Son Jesus Christ, through whom we have come to the knowledge of yourself, I bless you for judging me worthy of this day, this hour, so that I may share the cup of Christ and so rise again to eternal life in soul and body, immortal through the power of the Holy Spirit. May I be received in your presence today as a rich and pleasing sacrifice. Amen.

DAILY WORD: Receive me, Lord, as a rich and pleasing sacrifice.

EVENING REVIEW: How was I bread that was given to nourish others today?

The Letter of James says: "Blessed is the man who endures trial, for when he has stood the test he will receive the crown of life which God has promised to those who love him" (1:12). Temptation is part of life. Jesus, fully sharing in our humanity, was tempted. Like Jesus, we too have an enemy who wants to prevent God's will from being accomplished in us. What is God's will? That I and every human being be saved from sin and death (see 1 Tim 2:4).

The Letter to the Hebrews says that Jesus was "in every respect . . . tempted as we are" (4:15) and "learned obedience through what he suffered" (5:8). All virtues are like muscles in that they require exercise to stay healthy and to develop. Temptation is an opportunity to grow spiritually.

What are my predominant temptations? Doubt? Anger and resentment? Impatience? Gossip? Lust? Worry and fear? Lying? Envy? Every temptation has an opposite virtue: faith, forgiveness, patience, charity, chastity, trust, honesty, gratitude. God is giving me the opportunity to develop such virtues as I face temptations.

Lord Jesus, I believe that you were tempted in every way that I am and did not sin but grew stronger in virtue. You have shown me the way to live in the fullness of grace. Help me to stay close to you today so that I may grow stronger. I offer the temptations of this day to you, praying that they may help me grow in the virtues you want me to have.

DAILY WORD: I can overcome every temptation with God's help.

EVENING REVIEW: What were my temptations today? How did I grow or fail to grow through them?

In his Sermon on the Mount (Mt 5:13–16), Jesus told his disciples (and us): "You are the salt of the earth." What does he mean?

Salt is very humble. If used well, it does not draw attention to itself but enhances the flavors of the food with which it is mixed. It is also a preservative that keeps food from spoiling. So, as salt, I am to bring out the goodness of others and to preserve it from being spoiled by sin.

Jesus also said: "I am the light of the world; he who follows me will not walk in darkness, but will have the light of life" (Jn 8:12). This may sound proud, but it isn't. Light is also very humble. We do not look at the light but allow it to enlighten our surroundings so that we can see. As light, Jesus showed others through his words and deeds the way to the Father.

Joined to Christ, I too am called to help others see and find God. As Jesus said: "your light must shine before others, that they may see your good deeds and glorify your heavenly Father."

As salt and light have a purpose beyond themselves, so do I. My life's purpose is to give glory to God.

Lord Jesus, you call me to be salt and light for the world. May my every thought, word, and deed today answer that call. Only with your help can I be what you have called me to be. I offer myself to you so that my life's purpose may be fulfilled and others will glorify our heavenly Father with me.

DAILY WORD: I am salt and light.

EVENING REVIEW: How did I bring out the goodness in others or enlighten them to see God's glory today?

The Letter of James sees the tongue as one of the most important parts of the body (3:1–12). Though it is small, it is powerful. Just as a small spark can start a fire that burns millions of acres, so the tongue is a spark that has power to set the world on fire either with God's love or with hatred. St. James continues: "With it we bless the Lord and Father, and with it we curse men, who are made in the likeness of God. From the same mouth come blessing and cursing" (Jas 3:9–10).

The letter goes on to say that "this ought not to be so." Just as a spring cannot bring forth both pure and polluted water, so it is with the tongue. If the words it speaks come from a pure heart, then it will set the world on fire with good. But if the heart is polluted with sin, the tongue will gush forth words of evil.

Gossip is one way that the tongue delivers evil. Talking negatively about others does not change them and, instead, poisons others. Thus, St. Paul told the Ephesians to say only those things that are good, that build up the Body of Christ, and that "impart grace to those who hear" (4:29). He also said: "let your speech always be gracious, seasoned with salt" (Col 4:6).

How can I make sure that I will do this? I must have the love of Christ in my heart.

Lord Jesus, unite my heart to yours so that all I say today may come from a pure heart.

DAILY WORD: May all I say give you glory, Lord.

EVENING REVIEW: Did my words today build up or tear down?

February 27: St. Gabriel of Our Lady of Sorrows (1838–1862)

Francis Possenti was the eleventh child of thirteen, fathered by a distinguished lawyer. Francis was intelligent, handsome, and popular. He was considered the best dresser and dancer in his Italian town. He studied hard and socialized with his many friends. Just before college graduation, he became so ill that he made a promise to the Blessed Virgin Mary that if he recovered, he would enter a religious congregation. He did recover and quickly forgot his promise.

Then one Sunday, as he glanced at a banner of Mary Help of Christians that was being carried in procession, he felt Mary's eyes on him and heard in his heart the words "Keep your promise!" He soon joined the Passionist Order and was given the name by which we know him today, Brother Gabriel of Our Lady of Sorrows. Gabriel soon contracted tuberculosis and died at 24.

Often our feelings determine our actions. We tend to make promises to God when we feel desperate, and we ignore God when we feel good. C. S. Lewis said: "God whispers to us in our pleasures, speaks in our conscience, but shouts in our pains: it is his megaphone to rouse a deaf world." We often judge our spiritual lives by how we are feeling. But the key is not how we feel but what we do.

God, my Abba, my Father, I surrender myself into your hands today. No matter how I feel, I ask that your will be done in me so that my life may be a sign of my love for you—love that shows itself more in action than in feeling.

DAILY WORD: Doing, not feeling.

EVENING REVIEW: How did I let or not let my feelings control me today?

February 28

This time of year has been called "March-uary". It's the time of year when winter seems to go on forever and spring will never come. We want to leave the deadness of winter and experience the new life of spring.

St. James admonishes us to live in the present: "you have no idea what your life will be like tomorrow. You are a puff of smoke that appears briefly and then disappears. Instead, you should say, 'If the Lord wills, we shall live and we shall do this or that'" (Jas 4:14–15).

Jesus offered a similar perspective when he told a parable about a rich man who planned to build bigger barns to hold all his wealth. "God said to him, 'Fool! This night your soul is required of you; and the things you have prepared, whose will they be?' So is he who lays up treasure for himself, and is not rich toward God" (Lk 12:16–21).

My daily offering helps me to live in the present, to live each day as a gift from God. All I really have is this day in which to become "rich in what matters to God". What matters to God? Ultimately love—my love for God and for God's other children, my neighbor. My day is filled with moments that are all opportunities to love.

Father, this day is your loving gift to me. Each moment of it is precious to me and to you. May each moment demonstrate my grateful love to you as I seek to do your will at all times.

DAILY WORD: Does this matter to God?

EVENING REVIEW: How did I grow rich in what matters to God today?

February 29

It's been said that in the Bible there are 366 instances of the words "Be not afraid" or "Do not fear." That's one for every day of the year including leap year! Fear and worry can be a big part of life. It was fear that led our ancestral parents Adam and Eve to doubt God's love and to seek control.

Jesus spoke against worry. "I tell you, do not be anxious about your life. . . . And which of you by being anxious can add one cubit to his span of life? . . . Therefore do not be anxious about tomorrow, for tomorrow will be anxious for itself." When we worry, we cram tomorrow's potential troubles into today, making it hard to function in the moment. As Jesus said: "Let the day's own trouble be sufficient for the day" (Mt 6:24–34). Live one day at a time!

Worrying doesn't even prepare us to face future problems; rather, worry can become the tool of self-fulfilling prophecy. As worry is a temptation against trust, it is also an opportunity to grow in that virtue. Worry is a call to practice the slogan: "Let go and let God."

Lord Jesus, when I worry, I am letting fear take control of my life. But your Word says, "There is no fear in love, but perfect love casts out fear. For fear has to do with punishment, and he who fears is not perfected in love" (1 Jn 4:18). Jesus, my life is in your hands, not my own. Without fear or worry, then, I receive this day as a gift from you and return it to you, asking only that your will be done.

DAILY WORD: Let go and let God.

EVENING REVIEW: Did I worry today? How did I deal with it?

MARCH

March 1

The word Lent comes from the Anglo-Saxon word *lencten*,
meaning spring. In the spring, people prepare the soil and
plant seeds. In Lent, Christians do something similar, but
in a spiritual way. Through fasting we clear the soil of our
hearts, asking God to purify them and rid them of the weeds
of sin. We prepare our hearts to receive the seeds of God's
Word, both Scripture and the words God speaks to our hearts
during prayer. We spend more time in prayer as we prepare
for Easter, Christianity's greatest feast.

The word "lent" is also the past tense of the verb "to
loan". During Lent, we have the opportunity to realize that
our lives are not our own. They are on loan to us from
God. St. Paul writes: "Do you not know that your body
is a temple of the Holy Spirit within you, which you have
from God? You are not your own; you were bought with
a price. So glorify God in your body" (1 Cor 6:19–20).

In many of his parables, Jesus spoke of this reality. We
are stewards of God's talents, all the things that are given
to us for a time and for which we will ultimately render an
accounting.

*Master, you have blessed me in so many ways. You suffered and died
for me. In doing so, you freed me from sin and death and purchased
me for God, our loving Father. My life is not my own to do with
as I wish. I belong to you. I believe this, and I show my belief by
offering this day and my entire life to you. Amen.*

DAILY WORD: I am not my own. I belong to God.

EVENING REVIEW: In what ways did I glorify God today?

We begin Lent by receiving ashes on our foreheads, a reminder that we are dust and to dust we shall one day return. This is not a morbid thought but a bracing dose of reality. We often behave as if our lives will never end. We put off doing things that we know we ought to do, thinking that there will be plenty of time later. But the truth is that one day will be our last, of which Jesus said, "you know neither the day nor the hour" (Mt 25:13).

Lent begins with this line from the second reading at Mass: "Behold, now is the acceptable time; behold, now is the day of salvation" (2 Cor 6:2). We are called to live in the now, the present.

Today is the day of salvation because the past is gone and the future may not come. We only really have the present day, in fact, the present moment. Here is where I accept the salvation Christ won for me. Now is when I accept the loving will of the Father. It is God's will that I know Jesus and be saved from sin and death.

Jesus, you revealed in the clearest possible way that God is love and that God wills that I be saved. You died to accomplish this. It is up to me now to accept the salvation you won for me. I do accept it and offer you every moment of this day so that I may be closer to you. May I be ready to meet you when my life on earth ends.

DAILY WORD: "Now is the day of salvation."

EVENING REVIEW: What things that I have put off doing did I do today?

March 3: St. Katharine Drexel (1858–1955)

Born into a very wealthy Philadelphia family, Katharine Drexel and her sister inherited millions when her father and stepmother died. At her canonization in 2000, Pope St. John Paul II said:

> From her parents she learned that her family's possessions were not for them alone but were meant to be shared with the less fortunate. . . . She began to devote her fortune to missionary and educational work among the poorest members of society. Later, she understood that more was needed. With great courage and confidence in God's grace, she chose to give not just her fortune but her whole life totally to the Lord.

In 1891, St. Katharine founded a religious congregation for women devoted to the Blessed Sacrament and dedicated to serving the Native and African-American people of the United States. St. John Paul also said: "May her example help young people . . . appreciate that no greater treasure can be found in this world than in following Christ with an undivided heart."

The following is adapted from a prayer that St. Katharine wrote:

I adore you, my Eucharistic God. I praise you for a love beyond my comprehension. You have given me the gift of yourself, the gift of infinite love. I glorify you in union with our Mother Mary, and I ask you to help me to imitate this love of yours. Please, give me the grace to follow the will of the Father in every detail just as you did. I want to be all yours as you are all mine. Amen.

DAILY WORD: I want to be all yours as you are all mine.

EVENING REVIEW: How did I use my possessions to serve God today?

March 4: St. Casimir (1458–1484)

Casimir Jagiellon, a royal prince of the Polish-Lithuanian Commonwealth, was sent by his father to lead an army against Hungary. Because the dispute was quickly settled, Casimir turned back and became known as "the Peacemaker". Unfortunately, his father was not so peaceful and was unhappy with his son for not following through with his unjust plans. He confined his son to a damp prison where he probably contracted the lung disease that killed him. Less than forty years after his death he was canonized.

A contemporary of his wrote:

> By the power of the Holy Spirit, Casimir burned with a sincere and unpretentious love for almighty God that was almost unbelievable in its strength. So rich was his love and so abundantly did it fill his heart that it flowed out from his inner spirit toward his fellow men. As a result, nothing was more pleasant, nothing more desirable for him, than to share his belongings, and even to dedicate and give his entire self to Christ's poor, to strangers, to the sick, to those in captivity, and to all who suffer.

Lord Jesus, fill my heart with the love that filled your Heart and the heart of St. Casimir. The Gospel says that your Heart was moved with pity for the crowds of wounded people that you saw (see Mt 9:36; 14:14; 15:32). St. Casimir's heart was also moved when he saw anyone in need. Keep my eyes and heart open to see you in every person I meet today, especially those who are suffering in any way. I offer myself to you so that your love may flow through me to touch them.

DAILY WORD: May your love fill my heart and flow out to all.

EVENING REVIEW: How was my heart moved with pity today?

A man who was lost stopped to ask a local how many miles it was to the town to which he was headed. The local replied, "Well, if you keep going in this direction, I'd say it's about 25,000 miles, but if you turn around and take a right at the next crossroads, it's only about three miles." Sometimes, in order to get to where you want to go, you have to turn completely around.

The word "conversion" comes from the Latin word for turn. It means to get back on track and headed in the right direction. Sometimes that takes time. A large ocean vessel like the Queen Mary, going full speed, took over a mile just to stop. The weight of our years and accumulated habits often make it difficult to change overnight. We need an annual period of conversion simply to begin the process of changing into the person we were made to be.

During Lent, I ask myself if I am headed in the right direction. Are there things that are weighing me down on my journey to the heaven that Jesus opened up for me with his suffering, death, and Resurrection?

Loving God, your Son Jesus said, "In my Father's house are many rooms . . . I go to prepare a place for you" (Jn 14:2). I offer myself to you. Take my hand and help me to follow you today so that I may not wander from the path that leads me to that dwelling place your Son has prepared for me. Amen.

DAILY WORD: Lord, help me turn to you and stay on track.

EVENING REVIEW: Did I get off track today? Are there any bad habits I fell into today that keep me from making progress on my journey to heaven?

March 6

The Eastern Byzantine Catholic and Orthodox Churches have a prayer that is recited daily during Lent. It was written by St. Ephrem of Syria. It speaks of four things to root out of one's life: discouragement, which never comes from God but is always the voice of the devil; sloth or laziness, which prevent us from doing what needs to be done; ambition, which is a form of pride that makes us want to get and stay ahead of others; and idle chatter, which is a distraction both to ourselves and to others.

Then St. Ephrem's prayer goes on to ask for four things: purity of mind and heart, which helps us oppose the culture of death that views people as objects to be used or thrown away; lowliness, which is the opposite of self-inflating pride; patience, which seeks God's time and not our own; and brotherly love, which is charity in action.

The prayer then asks for awareness of one's own sins and the grace not to judge others. It ends with part of the Jesus Prayer, asking for God's mercy.

Praying in this way during Lent can help us offer ourselves to God for purification and growth in the virtues, especially charity.

Master of my life, dispel from me the sins of discouragement, laziness, ambition, and idle chatter. Rather grant to me, your servant, the virtues of purity, lowliness, patience, and love for others. Lord, make me keenly aware of my own faults, and let me not judge my brothers or sisters. O God, blessed now and forever, be merciful to me, a sinner, and have pity on me. Amen.

DAILY WORD: You are Master of my life.

EVENING REVIEW: Regarding St. Ephrem's Prayer, how did I give in to the faults and grow in the virtues mentioned in it?

March 7: Sts. Perpetua and Felicity (d. 203)

Perpetua was a young mother, and Felicity was her pregnant servant and friend. They were imprisoned in Carthage in North Africa, and, since it was illegal to execute a pregnant woman, the officials waited until Felicity gave birth, all the while hoping to persuade the women to renounce their Christian faith. Perpetua's own father tried to persuade her to abandon her beliefs. In answer, Perpetua pointed to a water pot and asked him if it could be called by any other name than what it was? When he said no, she told him, "Just so, I cannot call myself by any other name than what I am—a Christian." Both women remained steadfast in their faith, even as they were mauled by wild animals and then killed by the sword.

Perpetua means perpetual or everlasting. Felicity means happiness or bliss. The two were happy to persevere in the faith even while undergoing threats, torture, and death. They came to enjoy everlasting happiness by giving up their lives rather than their faith. Through our daily offering, we surrender our lives and try to be faithful to our Christian name. Doing this, one day at a time, we trust that we will follow the martyrs into the everlasting happiness of heaven.

Lord Jesus, the martyrs Perpetua and Felicity loved you so much that they gave up life itself rather than you. Make me more aware of your love so that I may love you as they did. May everything I think, say, and do today be consistent with who I am. May I be a Christian perpetually and blissfully. Amen.

DAILY WORD: "Your merciful love is better than life" (Ps 63:3).

EVENING REVIEW: How was I tested today in my perseverance in the faith and in loving God by loving my neighbor?

March 8: St. John of God (1495–1550)

For his first forty years, many of which were spent as a mercenary soldier in various armies, John lived a wild and sinful life. After leaving the military, he experienced a conversion that led him to do penance, praying especially for the many people he had killed. In time he opened a house to care for the poor and the sick. After his death, the group that had formed to help him became known as the Brothers Hospitallers of St. John of God. Since God is love, as the Evangelist wrote (1 Jn 4:8, 16), it is not surprising that the charity that John exhibited would lead people to call him by the name by which we know him today, John of God.

He once wrote:

> If we look forward to receiving God's mercy, we can never fail to do good so long as we have strength. For if we share with the poor, out of love for God, whatever he has given to us, we shall receive, according to his promise, a hundredfold in eternal happiness. Who would not entrust his possessions to this best of merchants who handles our affairs so well? With outstretched arms he begs us to turn toward him, to weep for our sins, and to become the servants of love, first for ourselves, then for our neighbors. Just as water extinguishes a fire, so love wipes away sin.

O God, I am sorry for my sins. I offer you this day to repair the damage they have done. I entrust myself—all I am and have—to you. May I love even as I have been loved.

DAILY WORD: "Love covers a multitude of sins" (1 Pet 4:8).

EVENING REVIEW: In what ways did I love and do penance today?

March 9: St. Frances of Rome (1384–1440)

When she was eleven, Frances told her parents that she wanted to become a nun. They rejected her request and instead, two years later, arranged a marriage for her with a man named Lorenzo. They married and had three children. The couple prayed together and opened their house to the poor of Rome. It has been said that for the last twenty-three years of her life, Frances' guardian angel was visible to her.

An early biographer wrote of her:

> God had not chosen her to be holy merely for her own advantage. Rather, the gifts he conferred upon her were to be for the spiritual and physical advantage of her neighbor. For this reason, he made her so lovable that anyone with whom she spoke would immediately feel captivated by love for her and ready to help her in everything she wanted. Divine power was present and working in her words, so that in a few sentences she could bring consolation to the afflicted and the anxious, calm the restless, pacify the angry, reconcile enemies, and extinguish long-standing hatreds and animosities. For this reason, people flocked to Frances from all directions, as to a safe refuge.

Lord Jesus, you are the Word-Made-Flesh. You continue to speak your words to the world through each member of your Body, the Church. I give myself to you so that I, like our Mother Mary, may be totally open to the Holy Spirit. In that way you, the Word of God, will take flesh through me today. Speak through me as you spoke through St. Frances of Rome, that I may give to each person I meet your word of comfort or challenge, your word of love. Amen.

DAILY WORD: Put your words in my mouth (see Is 51:16).

EVENING REVIEW: How was divine power present in my words today?

There are three traditional Lenten practices that are interrelated—prayer, fasting, and almsgiving.

Prayer puts us in touch with God. Through prayer we try to see ourselves and the world as God sees us. As we pray with the Scriptures or the events of our day, we try to enter more deeply into the Heart of Jesus and share his concerns and desires.

What do we see when we look at the world through God's eyes and with the Heart of Jesus? A world that is hungry. There is the physical hunger of so many who do not have the resources simply to live. There is the spiritual hunger that everyone has—the hunger that only God can fill. St. Augustine wrote: "You have made us for yourself, O Lord, and our hearts are restless until they rest in you."

Our fasting reminds us of the material hunger of the millions of poor and suffering people. It also reminds us of our own spiritual hunger for God. Fasting can help us simplify our lives, leading us to share more of our possessions with others.

Prayer and fasting together lead to almsgiving. We are led to decrease our consumption and to share what we have with those who have far less than we have.

Lord God, help me to be faithful today to the traditional Lenten practices that have helped people to be more Christian. I offer you my prayer so that my mind and heart may be transformed. I offer you my meals and entertainment so that I may make more room for you. I offer you my possessions and time so that those with less may have more.

DAILY WORD: I do this for love of you.

EVENING REVIEW: How did I fast, pray, and give alms today?

Lent is a time of fasting. Fasting is simply a way that we pray with our bodies. When we feel hungry and empty during the day, we remember our need for God. And we can fast from more than food. We can fast from television, the internet, and social media. Why? We do this fasting to make more room for God in our lives, giving the time instead to prayer and works of charity, like visiting the sick or writing letters to prisoners.

St. Peter Chrysologus wrote:

> Let us offer our souls in sacrifice by means of fasting. There is nothing more pleasing that we can offer to God. Offer your soul to God, make him an oblation of your fasting, so that your soul may be a pure offering, a holy sacrifice, a living victim, remaining your own and at the same time made over to God. Whoever fails to give this to God will not be excused, for if you are to give him yourself, you are never without the means of giving.

Lord Jesus, by fasting during this time of year, I want to imitate you in your own forty-day fast in the desert. As you confronted temptation, you quoted the "Book of Deuteronomy" and said: "Man does not live by bread alone, but . . . man lives by everything that proceeds out of the mouth of the LORD." I want to empty myself so that I may be filled with you, O Word of God. I offer myself so that you may fill me with yourself and make me a pure channel for your mercy. Amen.

DAILY WORD: I offer this up to you.

EVENING REVIEW: In what ways did I fast today? How did this open me to God's love?

Along with fasting, one of the three traditional Lenten practices is prayer. Of course, we should pray every day, but during Lent, we try to give more time to prayer. Fasting from certain activities can give us that time.

St. John Chrysostom said the following about prayer:

> Prayer and converse with God is a supreme good: it is a partnership and union with God. As the eyes of the body are enlightened when they see light, so our spirit, when it is intent on God, is illumined by his infinite light. I do not mean the prayer of outward observance but prayer from the heart, not confined to fixed times or periods but continuous throughout the day and night.

The morning offering helps us to live our day as a continuous prayer. St. John continues: "Our spirit should be quick to reach out toward God, not only when it is engaged in meditation; at other times also, when it is carrying out its duties, caring for the needy, performing works of charity, giving generously in the service of others, our spirit should long for God and call him to mind, so that these works may be seasoned with the salt of God's love and so make a palatable offering to the Lord of the universe."

Holy Spirit, as I give myself to you today, I ask you to be as close and as constant a presence to me as my very breath. Fill me with your light so that it may shine through me at all times. Guide me and all my actions so that they will be seasoned with the salt of your divine love.

DAILY WORD: Breathe in me, Holy Spirit.

EVENING REVIEW: How was I conscious of God's presence throughout my day?

Fasting, by which we reduce our consumption, and prayer, by which we open ourselves to God's guidance, lead to almsgiving, an act of mercy.

Pope St. Leo the Great said the following in one of his Lenten homilies:

> There is no more profitable practice as a companion to holy and spiritual fasting than that of almsgiving. This embraces under the single name of mercy many excellent works of devotion, so that the good intentions of all the faithful may be of equal value, even where their means are not. The works of mercy are innumerable. Their very variety brings this advantage to those who are true Christians, that in the matter of almsgiving not only the rich and affluent but also those of average means and the poor are able to play their part. Those who are unequal in their capacity to give can be equal in the love within their hearts.

In another homily, St. Leo said: "No act of devotion on the part of the faithful gives God more pleasure than that which is lavished on his poor. Where he finds charity with its loving concern, there he recognizes the reflection of his own fatherly care."

Father of the poor, you sent your Son Jesus, who, for our sake, "though he was rich, yet for your sake he became poor, so that by his poverty [we] might become rich" (2 Cor 8:9). I offer myself to you, asking that I may be more like your Son. You are less concerned with the magnitude of my works of mercy than with the spirit of generosity and love with which they are done. May I do all for love of you.

DAILY WORD: As God has given, so do I give.

EVENING REVIEW: How did my works of mercy give pleasure to God today?

"Lip service" is insincerity. It is a form of hypocrisy in which one says one thing but acts in a way contrary to one's words. Jesus condemned lip service when he said: "Not every one who says to me, 'Lord, Lord,' shall enter the kingdom of heaven, but he who does the will of my Father who is in heaven. On that day many will say to me, 'Lord, Lord, did we not prophesy in your name, and cast out demons in your name, and do mighty works in your name?' And then will I declare to them, 'I never knew you; depart from me, you evildoers'" (Mt 7:21–23).

It's not enough to pray. We cannot make a daily offering with our lips and then serve ourselves all day. Our prayer, our offering must be lived at every moment. Our prayer, if it is sincere, must lead to action, to deeds of service, lest it be merely lip service. St. Paul wrote: "present your bodies as a living sacrifice, holy and acceptable to God" (Rom 12:1). One problem with a "living sacrifice", unlike the sacrifices of the Israelites—dead animals and grain—is that it can crawl off the altar! A "living sacrifice" must be offered at every moment.

Loving God, you sent your Son Jesus as the one sacrifice that replaced all others. He reconciled all things to you with the perfect offering of himself. Joined to his Body, I offer myself with him to you. Help me live this offering at all times today.

DAILY WORD: Whatever I do, in word or deed, I do in the name of Jesus (see Col 3:17).

EVENING REVIEW: Was I able to live my daily offering at every moment today? How?

In ancient times, today was known as the Ides of March. A festival in honor of the Roman god of war, Mars (from which we get the name March), was held on it. It was on this day in the year 44 B.C. that Julius Caesar was assassinated. In his play about this event, William Shakespeare wrote the famous line spoken by a character known as "Soothsayer": "Beware the Ides of March."

To this warning, Caesar responded, "He is a dreamer. Let us leave him; pass." Caesar rejected both the prophet and the warning that came to pass.

Jesus came as a prophet to warn people. He loved mankind too much to let it go on its merry way along a path of destruction. The first words of Jesus in the Gospel of Mark are: "The time is fulfilled, and the kingdom of God is at hand; repent, and believe in the gospel" (1:15).

Jesus was also rejected as a dreamer and false prophet. At the end of his life, he was mocked, blindfolded, struck, and told to play the prophet and declare who struck him (see Lk 22:63–65). Then he was crucified.

Lord Jesus, you are the prophet sent by the Father to warn mankind that it is on a path of self-destruction. I accept your warning, repent of my sins, and believe in the gospel. I want to show you that I am serious about this by making an offering of myself, praying that the loving will of the Father may be done in my life today.

DAILY WORD: "The Kingdom of God is at hand."

EVENING REVIEW: How did I show my repentance and belief today?

Jesus said to the apostles on the evening after he rose from the dead, "Peace be with you. As the Father has sent me, even so I send you" (Jn 20:21). What did the Father send Jesus to do? To reconcile people to himself and to one another. We are now sent by Jesus to continue this work of reconciliation.

Works of penance are one way that we do this. While God forgives sins through the Sacrament of Reconciliation, the effects of those sins remain and need to be healed. As the *Catechism of the Catholic Church* states: "Many sins wrong our neighbor. One must do what is possible in order to repair the harm. . . . Absolution takes away sin, but it does not remedy all the disorders sin has caused" (no. 1459).

Prayer, fasting, works of charity, and sacrifices offered to God are powerful spiritual ways that we allow God's healing power to flow through us and into our broken world. This is known as reparation—repairing the damage of sin, both our own and that of the world. Speaking of these spiritual means that overcome evil and its effects, St. Paul wrote: "For though we live in the world we are not carrying on a worldly war, for the weapons of our warfare are not worldly but have divine power to destroy strongholds" (2 Cor 10:3).

Father, as Jesus accepted his call to repair the damage of sin, so I offer myself to you today that the work of reparation may continue. One with Jesus, may sin decrease and grace increase through me.

DAILY WORD: As the Father sent Jesus, so does he send me.

EVENING REVIEW: What spiritual weapons did I use today to battle sin and repair the damage that sin has caused?

March 17: St. Patrick (385–461)

St. Patrick was a British teenager who was kidnapped by Irish pirates and taken to Ireland. Made a slave, he was forced to tend herds of sheep and swine. During those long, solitary hours, he prayed. As he put it, "Love of God and faith grew, and the spirit was moved, so that in one day I would say as many as a hundred prayers, and at night nearly as many." After six years, he escaped. His prayer had removed any resentment toward those who had enslaved him, and in a dream he saw a native of Ireland come to him with countless letters begging him to return. He studied theology, was ordained, and returned to evangelize Ireland.

This is a wonderful story of how God writes straight with crooked lines, or, as St. Paul put it, how "in everything God works for good with those who love him" (Rom 8:28). The following is part of a prayer that St. Patrick is said to have written as he prepared to meet a pagan king who could have easily decided to kill him.

I arise today through the strength of Christ's birth and his Baptism, through the strength of his crucifixion and his burial, through the strength of his Resurrection and his Ascension. I arise today through God's strength to pilot me; God's might to uphold me, God's wisdom to guide me, God's hand to guard me, God's way to lie before me, God's shield to protect me. Christ with me, Christ before me, Christ behind me, Christ in me, Christ on my right, Christ on my left. I arise today through a mighty strength, the invocation of the Trinity.

DAILY WORD: Christ with me and in me.

EVENING REVIEW: How did all things work for my good today?

March 18: St. Cyril of Jerusalem (315–386)

As a young priest, St. Cyril was placed in charge of preparing catechumens for Baptism. During Lent around 348, in the Church of the Holy Sepulchre in Jerusalem, he offered a summary of the faith—known as the "Jerusalem Catechesis". Shortly thereafter, he was named bishop of Jerusalem and fought against various heresies, especially Arianism, which denied the divinity of Jesus. His motto was "The Christian is a bearer of Christ."

St. Paul wrote: "Do you not know that you are God's temple and that God's Spirit dwells in you?" (1 Cor 3:16). Here is what St. Cyril wrote about the Spirit:

> The Spirit comes gently. He is not felt as a burden, for he is light, very light. The Spirit comes with the tenderness of a true friend and protector to save, to heal, to teach, to counsel, to strengthen, to console. The Spirit comes to enlighten the mind first of the one who receives him and, then, through him, the minds of others as well. As light strikes the eyes of a man who comes out of darkness into the sunshine and enables him to see clearly things he could not discern before, so light floods the soul of the one counted worthy of receiving the Holy Spirit and enables him to see things beyond the range of human vision.

Come Holy Spirit, as I offer myself, I ask you to enlighten me so that I may clearly see God's hand in my life today. Fill me with your light so that I may be a light for all whom I meet.

DAILY WORD: I bring Christ to all.

EVENING REVIEW: In what ways was I a light for others today?

March 19: St. Joseph, Spouse of the Blessed Virgin Mary

In 1870, Pope Blessed Pius IX proclaimed St. Joseph the patron of the universal Church. As the guardian of Jesus, he continues to protect the Body of Christ, the Church. St. Teresa of Ávila once wrote: "I have never known anyone to be truly devoted to St. Joseph who did not noticeably advance in virtue, for he gives very real help to souls who commend themselves to him."

O glorious St. Joseph, you were chosen by God to be the foster father of Jesus, the most pure spouse of Mary ever Virgin, and the head of the Holy Family. You have been chosen as the heavenly patron and protector of the Church. Therefore, it is with great confidence that I implore your powerful assistance for the whole Church on earth. Protect in a special manner, with true fatherly love, the pope, our bishops, and all who labor for souls amid the trials and tribulations of this life. Grant that all peoples of the world may come to know and follow Christ.

Dear St. Joseph, accept the offering of myself, which I now make to you. I dedicate myself to your service, that you may ever be my father, my protector, and my guide in the way of salvation. Obtain for me great purity of heart and a fervent love for the spiritual life. May all my actions, after your example, be directed to the greater glory of God, in union with the hearts of Jesus and Mary and your own paternal heart. Pray for me that I may share in the peace and joy of your holy death.

DAILY WORD: St. Joseph, pray for me.

EVENING REVIEW: How did I imitate St. Joseph today by supporting and protecting the Body of Christ?

Who is the most beautiful person in the world? Most people think of the answer in terms of physical beauty, which is, as the saying goes, only "skin deep". There is a much deeper beauty that one can see in photos of the wrinkled face of St. Teresa of Kolkata. It is the beauty of love, of holiness.

Every human person is made in the image and likeness of God, and every baptized person has been transformed into a child of God. As St. John wrote, "See what love the Father has given us, that we should be called children of God; and so we are" (1 Jn 3:1). This is not some sort of name game, but reality. Through the grace of Baptism, we have really become children of God.

Moreover, we are God's work of art. We are God's "workmanship" (Eph 2:10). As such, each of us is more valuable than the most "priceless" painting. But we have an enemy who wants to ruin God's artistry. Satan is the great disfigurer and destroyer who shows his hatred for God by attacking us.

Lent is a time to see our real beauty and the threats to it.

God my Creator, I believe that you have made me in your image and that you are forming me into your likeness. You do that through the events of my daily life. I offer myself to you, asking that I may be pliable, rather than hard and resistant, in your loving hands. Make me more and more like your own Son Jesus, your perfect reflection.

DAILY WORD: I am God's work of art.

EVENING REVIEW: How did God mold and form me today? In what ways was the devil trying to disfigure me?

March 21

In the northern hemisphere, it's the first full day of spring, the vernal equinox, when there are equal hours of light and darkness. The earth turns in a cycle that brings the greatest amount of daylight in June and the least amount in December. There is nothing we can do to hasten or hinder this movement toward greater light or darkness.

Our lives, too, consist of light and darkness, but we have a choice. We can choose to live in greater light or less. Jesus talked about this contrast, saying: "The light has come into the world, and men loved darkness rather than light, because their deeds were evil. For every one who does evil hates the light, and does not come to the light, lest his deeds should be exposed. But he who does what is true comes to the light, that it may be clearly seen that his deeds have been wrought in God" (Jn 3:19–21).

Am I living in the light or in darkness? Do I have secrets that I would be ashamed for others to know? Spring is a time for housecleaning, and Lent is a time for spiritual housecleaning. We open our windows to let in the fresh air and light of the Holy Spirit. We get rid of whatever increases the darkness or prevents growth and life.

Lord Jesus, Light of the world, I offer myself to you today. Help me to live in the light of truth—the truth of God's love and the truth that I am not God but a beloved creature who depends upon the Creator for my very existence. Bless my Lent so that your light may increase in me and in the world.

DAILY WORD: Choose light!

EVENING REVIEW: How much light and darkness were present in my choices today?

Jesus said: "Truly, truly, I say to you, unless a grain of wheat falls into the earth and dies, it remains alone; but if it dies, it bears much fruit. He who loves his life loses it, and he who hates his life in this world will keep it for eternal life" (Jn 12:24–25). Aren't we supposed to love ourselves? Doesn't God love us, and shouldn't we therefore love ourselves? Are we really supposed to hate our life in this world?

These words of Jesus are challenging. Another way of looking at them is to ask: If Jesus came to me today and invited me to join him in heaven, what would I say? Is there anything holding me back from wholeheartedly accepting his invitation? Is there anything more important to me than heaven?

It could be something very good—like a long and healthy life or loved ones or a project that will help many people, like a cure for cancer. But I have to be honest with myself and with God. Do I want God or something else? Lent is a time to ask these questions and, like Jesus, to die to ourselves, letting go of everything except the will of God, who wants to give me eternal life in heaven.

Loving God, as I offer myself to you each day and pray that your will be done in my life, I die to myself and my own desires no matter how good they may seem. For all things on earth are passing, but you remain forever. May I always be ready to come to you.

DAILY WORD: This too shall pass.

EVENING REVIEW: Am I ready?

March 23: St. Turibius of Mogrovejo (1538–1606)

Turibius was born in Spain, became a professor of law, and was appointed a judge by King Philip II. When the archbishop of Lima, Peru, died, his name came up as a replacement though he wasn't even ordained. He objected but soon saw God's will in this. He was ordained and spent the next twenty-six years in Latin America, where he paid special attention to the native Inca people. His courage is revealed in one of his favorite sayings: "Christ said, 'I am the truth.' He did not say, 'I am the custom.'"

With the following prayer of St. John Henry Newman, I recognize that God has a plan in which I am to play an important role:

God has created me to do Him some definite service; He has committed some work to me which He has not committed to another. I have my mission—I never may know it in this life, but I shall be told it in the next. . . . I am a link in a chain, a bond of connexion between persons. He has not created me for naught. I shall do good, I shall do His work; I shall be an angel of peace, a preacher of truth in my own place, while not intending it, if I do but keep His commandments. . . . Therefore I will trust Him. Whatever, wherever I am, I can never be thrown away. If I am in sickness, my sickness may serve Him; in perplexity, my perplexity may serve Him; if I am in sorrow, my sorrow may serve Him. . . . He does nothing in vain. . . . He knows what He is about. He may take away my friends, He may throw me among strangers, He may make me feel desolate, make my spirits sink, hide the future from me—still He knows what He is about.

DAILY WORD: I have my mission.

EVENING REVIEW: How did I fulfill my mission today?

March 24

Prior to changes in the Church's liturgical calendar, today was celebrated as a feast in honor of the Archangel Gabriel, who played such an important role in tomorrow's feast of the Annunciation.

Gabriel greeted the Blessed Virgin Mary with these words: "Hail, full of grace, the Lord is with you!" When Mary heard this greeting, "she was greatly troubled" (see Lk 1:26–38). Gabriel told her not to be afraid and that she would bear a son, "the Son of the Most High". This was made possible through the Holy Spirit and "the power of the Most High", which would "overshadow" her. Mary accepted the will of God that came to her through Gabriel, saying, "Let it be to me according to your word."

Pope St. John XXIII reflected: "One of the most glorious angelic spirits, Gabriel, announces the divine birth; heaven and earth meet in an ecstasy of love; the Son of God descends from on high and in the womb of a pure Virgin becomes the Son of Man."

Lord God, you sent Gabriel to your chosen servant Mary to reveal to her your will that she become the mother of your Son. She received your Word into her heart and conceived your Word in her womb. I offer myself to you as Mary did. May your will be done in my life today. Make me, like Gabriel, a messenger of your salvation to all the people I will meet or pray for today.

DAILY WORD: May it be done to me according to God's will.

EVENING REVIEW: How did God's Word come to me today?

March 25: The Annunciation of the Lord

Nine months before Christmas, we celebrate the conception of Jesus. When Mary said "yes" to God, a new human life, which was also divine, was conceived within her. Cell by cell that life grew and developed. Within three weeks, his first physical organ appeared as his heart began to beat right under the heart of his Mother.

In his 2003 encyclical about the Church and the Eucharist, Pope St. John Paul II called Mary "The Woman of the Eucharist". He wrote:

> In a certain sense Mary lived her Eucharistic faith even before the institution of the Eucharist, by the very fact that she offered her virginal womb for the Incarnation of God's Word. The Eucharist, while commemorating the passion and resurrection, is also in continuity with the incarnation. At the Annunciation Mary conceived the Son of God in the physical reality of his body and blood, thus anticipating within herself what to some degree happens sacramentally in every believer who receives, under the signs of bread and wine, the Lord's body and blood. As a result, there is a profound analogy between the *Fiat* which Mary said in reply to the angel, and the *Amen* which every believer says when receiving the body of the Lord.

Lord Jesus, as Mary said "Fiat—let it be done to me", so I say "Amen" when I receive your Body and Blood in the Eucharist. My "Amen" declares my desire to be one with you and to be transformed by you. As I offer myself to you, I say "Amen" to all that you want of me today.

DAILY WORD: Amen, may your will be done in me.

EVENING REVIEW: How did I live my "Eucharistic Amen" today?

Lent can seem very negative. We begin with ashes and the reminder of death. We continue by giving up good things like meat on Friday and sweets. Our daily Mass readings move us toward Jesus' confrontation with his enemies and eventually his suffering and death. We look inwardly at our sins and don't like what we see. We get anxious to be done with Lent and to celebrate the joyful season of Easter.

Yet there is an element of joy in Lent as well. St. Bernard once said: "Sorrow for sin is indeed necessary, but it should not involve endless preoccupation. You should dwell also on the glad remembrance of the loving kindness of God." In other words, while it's good to take a serious look at ourselves, we should not become obsessed with making ourselves better. For just as we can water seeds and weed around them, we cannot make them grow. Only God gives life and growth to them and to us.

The joy of Lent is captured in Preface I for this season. It calls Lent God's "gracious gift" and says that the "faithful await the sacred paschal feasts with the joy of minds made pure." Our conversion from sin and our growth bring joy because we know we are being "led to the fullness of grace that you bestow on your sons and daughters."

Father, thank you for this joyful season of Lent. Thank you for the graces and growth of this time. I offer myself to you so that you will make me more and more like your Son. Make my mind pure and help me to focus my attention on you and my neighbor.

DAILY WORD: I have joy because I am your child.

EVENING REVIEW: What joys did I offer God today?

The word "disciple" comes from the Latin verb "to learn". A disciple is one who is instructed in the way of the master. Through the Gospel, Jesus instructs us—disciples of the 21st century—and this involves not only receiving the lessons he teaches but also applying them. And that requires discipline.

Writing about discipline, St. Paul liked to use sports images: "Every athlete exercises self-control in all things. They do it to receive a perishable wreath, but we an imperishable. Well, I do not run aimlessly; I do not box as one beating the air; but I pommel my body and subdue it" (1 Cor 9:25–27). Life's journey or race involves hard work and training. Our tendency is to want things fast and easy. We don't like to delay gratification. Lent is a time for us to engage in training that makes it easier for us to choose those things that will help us attain an imperishable and heavenly crown.

To the Philippians, St. Paul also wrote: "But one thing I do, forgetting what lies behind but straining forward to what lies ahead, I press on toward the goal for the prize of the upward call of God in Christ Jesus" (3:13–14).

Lord Jesus, you call me to follow you, to be your disciple. To do that I must not only listen to your teaching but put it into practice. I must die daily to my own self-interests and focus entirely on my ultimate goal of heaven. I place myself in your hands today so that you may guide me to my goal.

DAILY WORD: I strain forward.

EVENING REVIEW: How did I train my body today to attain my goal?

March 28

What gave Jesus the greatest pleasure? What did he most enjoy doing? Putting ourselves in Jesus' place, we can imagine the smile that came to his face when he saw the joy that he brought to the blind and the lame whom he healed. And how he shared the joy of the leper, who had been alienated from society and watched his skin and extremities waste away, and whom Jesus touched and healed.

But something else gave Jesus even greater pleasure. Though wonderful, the physical cures were temporary. The eyes of the blind would close in death and the limbs of the lame would again become rigid and lifeless. The skin of the leper would one day turn to dust.

What gave Jesus the greatest pleasure was to bring spiritual healing, to touch the immortal part of a person. Jesus loved to forgive sins. It was for this reason that he came to earth, suffered, died on a cross, and rose from the dead. In Luke 15, Jesus told three parables designed to show those who complained about the attention he gave to sinners that heaven's greatest joy is mercy. Now, when we admit our sins and seek forgiveness and healing, we give Jesus the greatest joy.

Lord Jesus, thank you for continuing to forgive sins through the Sacrament of Reconciliation. I offer myself to you. Be merciful to me a sinner.

DAILY WORD: "There will be more joy in heaven over one sinner who repents" (Lk 15:7).

EVENING REVIEW: In what ways do I need both forgiveness and the healing of the effects of my sins?

March 29

Jesus wants us not only to receive his mercy—to be forgiven and healed—but to give mercy. In fact, "for with the
judgment you pronounce you will be judged, and the measure you give will be the measure you get" (Mt 7:2). When
Jesus taught his apostles to pray, he told them that the only
limit to God's mercy is the limit we put on our own mercy:
"Forgive us our trespasses as we forgive those who trespass
against us." After teaching this prayer, Jesus said: "if you
do not forgive men their trespasses, neither will your Father
forgive your trespasses" (Mt 6:15).

Forgiving those who have hurt us is good for us. Holding on to past hurts, replaying them in our minds and feeling their pain, hurts us. Resentment is like drinking poison
and hoping the other person dies. Resentment doesn't hurt
them, but us. Forgiveness heals.

We don't forgive and forget, unless we have amnesia or
dementia. It's natural to remember painful hurts. Every time
a negative or painful memory comes up, we choose to forgive by praying for the person or situation that caused it.
Jesus wants us to be free. He died forgiving those who killed
him, and he gives us the grace to forgive as well.

*Lord Jesus, I give myself to you with all my hurts and resentments.
Purify my memory and heal any hardness in my heart. Take my
heart and make it more like your own. May I be an instrument of
reconciliation and peace in your merciful and nail-scarred hands today and every day of my life.*

DAILY WORD: I forgive as I've been forgiven.

EVENING REVIEW: Whom do I need to forgive today?

March 30: St. John Climacus (569-649)

John was sixteen when he went to St. Catherine's monastery on Mt. Sinai. He eventually became abbot and wrote a book that is read in many monasteries every Lent. It's called "The Ladder of Paradise", and each of the thirty chapters presents helpful advice for making our way to our heavenly goal.

This book inspired an icon depicting a ladder that various Christians are climbing. Along the way, some are dragged off the ladder by demons who tempt them to fall into sin. Others reject the temptations and make their way up the ladder that reaches into heaven. There, at the top, is Jesus with his arms outstretched, greeting those who persevered in making the climb.

To persevere means to persist and to strive in spite of all difficulties. The opposite is to give up. It comes from the Latin *per*—through or thoroughly—and *severus* or strict. To keep climbing when we are tired or distracted and want just to give up requires a thoroughly strict effort. We tend to want an easier, softer way. Like water, of which the human body is mostly composed, we tend to take the path of least resistance, to settle for the lower spot, and stagnate, not moving or changing unless we are forced to do so.

Lent has been a time for us to commit ourselves to persevere.

Lord Jesus, you were exhausted, and you fell several times as you carried your Cross. Give me the strength today to follow you and carry my cross. Help me persevere.

DAILY WORD: I will not give up.

EVENING REVIEW: How did I persevere when I encountered difficulties today?

March 31

There's an old saying about March: it comes in like a lion and goes out like a lamb, or, if it comes in like a lamb, it goes out like a lion. In chapter 5 of the Book of Revelation, Jesus is both a lion and a lamb.

An elder says, "Weep not; behold, the Lion of the tribe of Judah, the Root of David, has conquered" (v. 5). Then, immediately after this, the author states, "Between the throne and the four living creatures . . . I saw a Lamb standing, as though it had been slain" (v. 6). Countless angels and living creatures and elders cry out in a loud voice: "Worthy is the Lamb who was slain, to receive power and wealth and wisdom and might and honor and glory and blessing!" (vv. 11–12).

Jesus is both a lion, the king of beasts, and the Lamb of God who takes away the sins of the world. Because he was slain, like a lamb, he is honored as a king.

As members of the Body of Christ, we are called to be lambs who offer ourselves as a sacrifice, joining the "living sacrifice" (Rom 12:1) of our lives to the perfect sacrifice of the Lamb of God. In that way we carry on the work of reconciliation. If we follow the Lamb in this way, we will share in the glory of the Lion.

Lord Jesus, Lion of Judah and Lamb of God, you offered yourself in sacrifice for my sins, and you now reign as King of heaven and earth. I choose to live the Mass today by offering myself in union with you for others' salvation.

DAILY WORD: I am your lamb today.

EVENING REVIEW: How did I offer myself as a "living sacrifice" today?

APRIL

April 1

It is April Fools' Day, a tradition that goes back to the English poet Chaucer around the year 1400. In Christianity, especially in the Eastern and Russian Orthodox Churches, there is a tradition of Holy Fools for Christ—people who chose to live in a way that would look foolish. They did this either to hide their holiness or to challenge the world to consider what is really important. For example, these Holy Fools would go around homeless and very poor in order to show the world that what really matters is not earthly but heavenly treasure.

The world often thinks of Christian believers as fools. According to St. Paul: "The word of the cross is folly to those who are perishing, but to us who are being saved it is the power of God. . . . For the foolishness of God is wiser than men, and the weakness of God is stronger than men" (1 Cor 1:18, 25).

Jesus had the last laugh. On the Cross he fooled the world, the devil, and death itself. Through his death he conquered death and brought eternal life. The world cannot save me from death. Only Jesus Christ can. I hold fast to the Cross by which he saved me.

Lord Jesus, I believe that by your death you saved me from eternal death. I believe that your Resurrection gives me the promise of eternal life. I choose today to be a fool with and for you rather than to be wise in the ways of the world, ways that only lead to destruction and death.

DAILY WORD: Christ crucified is the wisdom and power of God.

What crosses and weaknesses did I offer God today?

April 2: St. Francis of Paola (1436–1507)

Francis entered the order of his namesake when he was only thirteen, but felt called to greater solitude. After two years, he became a hermit. In time others joined him, and he founded the Order of Hermits of St. Francis of Assisi, which later came to be called the Order of Minims, or Little Ones.

In a world that encourages us to "super-size" everything, Francis gives witness that God's way is not the way of power and prestige, pride and possessions. St. Francis gave this advice in a farewell address to his community:

> Death is certain; life is short and vanishes like smoke. Fix your minds, then, on the Passion of our Lord Jesus Christ. Inflamed with love for us, he came down from heaven to redeem us. . . . He himself gave us an example of perfect patience and love. We, then, are to be patient in adversity. . . . Take pains to refrain from sharp words. If they escape your lips, do not be ashamed to let your lips produce the remedy, since they have caused the wounds. Pardon one another so that later on you will not remember the injury. The recollection of an injury is itself wrong. It adds to our anger, nurtures our sin, and hates what is good. It is a rusty arrow and poison for the soul. . . . You must change your life, therefore, so that God in his mercy will pardon you.

Lord Jesus, I fix my mind now on your Passion and death. You have given me an example to follow. As you offered yourself to free the world from sin, so I offer myself.

DAILY WORD: Through your suffering, O Lord, give me patience.

EVENING REVIEW: How did my thoughts and words cause
wounds or heal them?

April 3

In a sermon on the Song of Songs, St. Bernard of Clairvaux
wrote:

> Where can the weak find a place of firm security and peace,
> except in the wounds of the Savior? Indeed, the more se-
> cure is my place there the more he can do to help me. The
> world rages, the flesh is heavy, and the devil lays his snares,
> but I do not fall, for my feet are planted on firm rock. . . .
> What sin is there so deadly that it cannot be pardoned by
> the death of Christ? . . .
> They pierced his hands and feet and opened his side with
> a spear. Through the opening of these wounds I may drink
> "honey from the rock and oil from the hardest stone": that
> is, I may "taste and see that the Lord is sweet.". . .
> Through these sacred wounds we can see the secret of
> his heart, the great mystery of love. . . . Where have your
> love, your mercy, your compassion shone out more lumi-
> nously than in your wounds, sweet, gentle Lord of mercy?
> More mercy than this no one has than that he lay down his
> life for those who are doomed to death.

Lord Jesus, your passionate love for me led to your Passion. The
opening in your side reveals your Heart filled with love. I return
love for love now with this offering:

> *For love of me you came to earth;*
> *You gave your life for me.*
> *So every day you give me now,*
> *I give back happily.*
> *Take all my laughter, all my tears,*
> *Each thought, each word, each deed,*

And let them be my all-day prayer
To help all those in need.

DAILY WORD: I find my peace in your wounds.

EVENING REVIEW: How did I return love for love?

April 4: St. Isidore of Seville (556–636)

For one thousand years after his death, Isidore was the man most often quoted by scholars. His encyclopedic knowledge earned him the title "Schoolmaster of the Middle Ages" and led to his being proposed today as the patron saint of the internet. But he wasn't always a great scholar.

His brother Leander, twenty years older, was placed in charge of his education. He was so strict and demanding that Isidore ran away. As he sat in the woods, he noticed how drops of water falling on a nearby stone had worn a hole in it. He realized that if he persevered little by little in his studies he would satisfy his brother. He didn't have to learn everything all at once, but could study one day at a time and through perseverance could become the scholar his family wanted him to be.

Sometimes we get discouraged by our lack of growth or how slow it seems. We get discouraged at how far we must go to attain our goal of holiness. But if we focus on the present, on the activities and events of each day that God gives in order to help us grow, then little by little we will move closer to our ultimate goal—holiness and heaven.

Lord God, I know how weak I am. Like St. Isidore, I am often tempted to give up and to run away from my responsibilities. I believe that with each day you are giving me opportunities to grow in holiness. As I accept and give this day back to you, help me to focus on the present and not worry about how far I have to go.

DAILY WORD: One day at a time.

EVENING REVIEW: How did the hours of this day help me grow in holiness?

April 5: St. Vincent Ferrer (1350–1419)

Vincent was a Dominican who lived during one of the darkest periods in Church history—the Great Western Schism, when there were three different cardinals claiming to be pope. The nations of Western Europe and even various saints were divided over whom to support. Through courageous and challenging preaching, St. Vincent helped to overcome the divisions and bring about unity. Jean Gerson, a theologian at the time, wrote Vincent: "But for you, this union could never have been achieved."

St. Vincent once wrote this advice about preaching that is applicable to all speech:

> Your words should sound as though they were coming, not from a proud or angry soul, but from a charitable and loving heart. Your tone of voice should be that of a father who suffers with his sinful children, as though they were seriously ill or were lying in a huge pit; and he struggles to free them, raise them up, and cherish them like a mother, as one who is happy over their progress and the hope they have of heaven's glory. Finally, if you truly want to help the soul of your neighbor, you should approach God first with all your heart. Ask him simply to fill you with charity, the greatest of all virtues; with it you can accomplish what you desire.

Lord Jesus, at the Last Supper you prayed for the unity of your followers because through their union and peace the world would come to believe in you. I offer myself to you so that I may be an instrument of peace today in my family, among my friends, at work, and in my community.

DAILY WORD: May my words build up and not tear down.

April 6

The suffering, death, and Resurrection of Jesus prove that God loves us. Though mankind—individually and as a whole—had rejected and continues to reject God's love, it has not been abandoned. The Father sent the Son to redeem the world, and the Holy Spirit continues this work, opening hearts to accept the salvation Christ won for them. St. Paul wrote:

> We have peace with God through our Lord Jesus Christ. Through him we have obtained access to this grace in which we stand, and we rejoice in our hope of sharing the glory of God. . . . Hope does not disappoint us, because God's love has been poured into our hearts through the Holy Spirit who has been given to us. While we were yet helpless, at the right time Christ died for the ungodly. Why, one will hardly die for a righteous man—though perhaps for a good man one will dare even to die. But God shows his love for us in that while we were yet sinners Christ died for us. (Rom 5:1–8)

The love of God, the Holy Spirit in our hearts, moves us to share in the ongoing work of salvation. Not everyone knows and has accepted the love of God. Our prayers and interactions with people help them to know and accept Jesus. The *Catechism of the Catholic Church*, quoting the Council of Quiercy in 853, states: "There is not, never has been, and never will be a single human being for whom Christ did not suffer" (no. 605).

Jesus, I offer myself for the salvation of all so that your death won't be in vain.

DAILY WORD: Christ suffered and died for me and for you.

EVENING REVIEW: How did I help others know the love of God?

April 7: St. John Baptist de la Salle (1651–1719)

St. John was a French priest who dedicated himself to the education of the poor. He founded the Christian Brothers to expand and continue this work, and today they serve over 900,000 students in 80 countries. In 1950 Pope Pius XII named him the patron saint of teachers.

He once wrote: "The apostle Paul states that God has placed apostles, prophets, and doctors in the Church. If you meditate on this, you will be convinced that you, too, have been given your special place. Be driven by the love of God, then, because Jesus Christ died for all, that those who live may live not for themselves but for him who died and rose for them."

He also gave this advice:

Give up all bitterness toward your neighbor, no matter what. Each day look for every possible opportunity to do a kindness for those you do not like. After examining yourself on this matter every morning, decide what you are going to do, and do it faithfully with kindness and humility. Speak to and answer everyone with very great gentleness and deference. Keep in mind the way the Lord spoke and replied to others even when he was most harshly treated. Never comment on the faults or the behavior of your neighbors. Decide never to speak of the failings of others.

Lord Jesus, all your words and actions revealed the love of the Father, even when anger moved you to right the wrongs you saw. May all I do and say today reveal God's love.

DAILY WORD: I speak and act with kindness as Jesus did.

EVENING REVIEW: What kindness did I do for those I do not like? If I did not do anything, I do so now by offering a prayer for them.

April 8: St. Julia Billiart (1751–1816)

When she was just seven, Julia explained the catechism to other children, a sign of things to come, but only after some difficulty. When she was twenty-three, someone fired a shot at her father beside whom she was seated. The shot missed, but the trauma resulted in Julia becoming paralyzed. She continued her work of teaching the faith to children from her bed. At one point, during the Reign of Terror that followed upon the French Revolution, she escaped, hidden in a hay cart. Throughout all this, she repeated "How good is the good God!" When peace and religious liberty returned to France, other women joined Julia in her work, and the Sisters of Notre Dame de Namur was founded. On the feast of the Sacred Heart in 1804, a priest told her to step out in faith, and on the spot she arose, completely cured.

She once wrote: "However severe God's guidance may seem to us at times, it's always the guidance of a Father who is infinitely good, wise, and kind. He leads us to our goal by different paths. We must act as little children do in the dark—clasp the hand of father or mother and go where we are led."

Lord God, I believe, as St. Paul wrote, that you can make everything work together for my good (see Rom 8:28). I accept this day and all that is in it, and I return it to you. Use the events of my day to bring about my ultimate good and the good of others. May only your holy and loving will be done.

DAILY WORD: How good is the good God!

April 9

During Lent, people around the world make their final preparations for Baptism or reception into the Church, and the baptized prepare themselves for the renewal of their promises, rejecting the devil and proclaiming their belief in the creed. The power of Jesus' death and Resurrection is made present in the sacraments of Baptism and the Eucharist, symbolized in the water and blood that flowed from the Heart of Jesus pierced on the Cross.

St. Paul writes: "But you were washed, you were sanctified, you were justified in the name of the Lord Jesus Christ and in the Spirit of our God. . . . For you were bought with a price" (1 Cor 6:11, 20). What was the price? The blood of the Lamb of God shed on the Cross. As a result, we do not belong to ourselves.

Paul continues: "The body is not meant for immorality, but for the Lord, and the Lord for the body. And God raised the Lord and will also raise us up by his power. . . . Do you not know that your body is a temple of the Holy Spirit within you, which you have from God? You are not your own. . . . So glorify God in your body" (1 Cor 6:13–14, 19–20).

Lord Jesus, I believe that you died and rose to free me from sin and death. You paid the price for my salvation with your body. I offer you my body. I offer you all of the legitimate and good pleasures of this day. I offer you all the pains and discomforts of this day. I am yours, and yours alone I want to be. All glory be to you!

DAILY WORD: I belong to the Lord.

EVENING REVIEW: How did I glorify God in my body?

April 10

The baptized have been washed in the blood of the Lamb. This precious blood cleanses us from sin and gives a new life that begins here on earth and reaches its fullness in heaven. As a result, we live in a way that reveals this new life to the world.

St. Peter wrote:

> Conduct yourselves with fear throughout the time of your exile. You know that you were ransomed from the futile ways inherited from your fathers, not with perishable things such as silver or gold, but with the precious blood of Christ, like that of a lamb without blemish or spot. He was destined before the foundation of the world but was made manifest at the end of the times for your sake. Through him you have confidence in God, who raised him from the dead and gave him glory, so that your faith and hope are in God. Having purified your souls by your obedience to the truth for a sincere love of the brethren, love one another earnestly from the heart. (1 Pet 1:17–22)

Lord, to free me from sin and death you gave something much more precious than silver or gold, diamonds or rubies. You shed your Precious Blood for me. You offered all out of love for me. I must be very important to you. Now your Blood, in which I was washed at Baptism, makes me even more precious to you. How can I thank you enough? I will show my gratitude by conducting myself with reverence today—reverencing myself as precious to you and reverencing others for whom you also shed your Blood. May I love you by loving others intensely from a pure heart.

DAILY WORD: We are precious to the Lord.

EVENING REVIEW: What helped me to be conscious of the fact that I and everyone I met today are precious to God?

April 11: St. Stanislaus (1030–1079)

Today's saint was a Polish bishop who rebuked King Boleslaus II for immorality, injustice, and cruelty. When his challenge was ignored, he excommunicated the king. Enraged, the king went to the small chapel where Stanislaus was celebrating Mass, drew his sword, and killed him.

Within a year of his election as pope, St. John Paul II went to Poland to celebrate the 900th anniversary of Stanislaus' martyrdom. He spoke about the sacrament of Confirmation and said:

> This is the sacrament which brings to birth within us a sharp sense of responsibility for the Church, for the Gospel, for the cause of Christ in the souls of human beings, and for the salvation of the world. . . . All of life which opens up in view of this sacrament assumes the aspect of a great and fundamental test: a test of faith and of character. Saint Stanislaus has become, in the spiritual history of the Polish people, the patron of this great and fundamental test of faith and of character. In this sense we honor him also as the patron of the Christian moral order. In the final analysis the moral order is built up by means of human beings. This order consists of a large number of tests, each one a test of faith and of character. From every victorious test the moral order is built up. From every failed test moral disorder grows.

Dear God, I offer myself to you so that the moral order, which alone can bring justice and peace to the world, may be built up through me today. Give me the grace to be faithful and courageous.

DAILY WORD: I am responsible for the cause of Christ.

EVENING REVIEW: How was my faith and character tested today? How did I build up the moral order through my choices?

117

April 12

On this day in 1987, Father John Eagan, a Jesuit who had spent almost all of his life teaching and counseling high school boys, died at the age of sixty-one. A month earlier he had been diagnosed with inoperable liver cancer. In a letter to family and friends, he wrote about the peace he felt in spite of the prognosis:

> Most mornings of my life I like to get up early, go down to the Blessed Sacrament, and put myself in his presence. Once at home with the Lord, I always start my day with St. Ignatius' little prayer: "Take, Lord, and receive all I am and have. You've given it all to me; I give it all back to you. Do with me as you want. Just give me your love and your grace and that's enough." This morning start to each day has, over the years, become the foundation of my life. So now, when the Lord moves in and clearly asks me to travel this way with him, I find that "Yes" to him coming from deep places. And a sense of calm: all's well; I'm in his hands. He'll give me his love and his strength to walk the way till the end.

Fr. Eagan received each day as a gift and offered it back to God with the "Suscipe" prayer of St. Ignatius, founder of the Jesuits. In the end, this habit prepared him for the offering he was called to make of his health and his life.

God of life, today is your gift to me. I make a gift of it back to you. It's all I really have to give, and it's all you really want from me.

DAILY WORD: Take and receive all I am and have.

EVENING REVIEW: How did I practice surrender?

April 13: St. Martin I (d. 655)

Martin was elected pope in 649 and quickly called a council to deal with a heresy that denied that Jesus had a human will. The Emperor Constans II did not want any discussion of the issue. He had Martin arrested and brought to Constantinople, where he was condemned to death. Patriarch Paul of Constantinople intervened. Martin's life was spared, but he was sent into exile in Crimea.

Of his experience he wrote: "I have not been allowed to wash, even in cold water, for 47 days. I am wasted away and frozen through, and have had no respite from dysentery. The food that is given me makes me feel sick. I hope that God, who knows all things, will bring my persecutors to repentance after he will have taken me out of this world. As to this wretched body, God will have care of it. He is at hand. Why should I trouble myself?"

He died as a result of the mistreatment and is honored as the last pope to die as a martyr.

St. Peter wrote: "For one is approved if, mindful of God, he endures pain while suffering unjustly. . . . For to this you have been called, because Christ also suffered for you, leaving you an example, that you should follow in his steps" (1 Pet 2:19, 21).

Lord Jesus, I want to follow perfectly in your footsteps. That doesn't mean I have to look for pain and suffering. But when it comes my way, I will offer it to you as the martyrs did and unite it to your saving Cross. By following you in suffering, may I follow you in glory.

DAILY WORD: I bear this for you.

EVENING REVIEW: What sufferings did I offer God?

April 14

When the apostles saw the Risen Jesus, they couldn't believe their eyes. They thought they were seeing a ghost. Jesus proved that he was risen by showing them his wounds and having them touch him. He said,

"Why are you troubled, and why do questionings rise in your hearts? See my hands and my feet, that it is I myself; handle me, and see . . ." (Lk 24:38–39). He dispelled Thomas' doubt a week later in the same way, telling him, "Put your finger here, and see my hands; and put out your hand and place it in my side; do not be faithless, but believing" (Jn 20:27).

Why wasn't the risen body of Jesus healed of its wounds? They remain as an everlasting sign of his love. Seeing and touching those wounds with my mind and heart convinces me that Jesus died and rose for love of me.

A similar dynamic goes on in recovery and support groups where people share their stories. They show their wounds so that others may believe that recovery is possible, that God's power is able to overcome all pains and sorrows, addictions and sickness. It's a power that can even overcome death.

St. Peter, no doubt having Isaiah 53:5 in mind, wrote: "By his wounds you have been healed" (1 Pet 2:24).

Risen Lord, you showed your wounds to the apostles to overcome their doubts, to show them that you are more powerful than suffering and death. The sight of your wounds increased their faith. I offer you my physical, emotional, and spiritual wounds. Use them to bring healing and to increase others' faith in your powerful love.

DAILY WORD: Take my suffering and wounds.

EVENING REVIEW: How did my own woundedness help others today?

April 15

Today is a day of reckoning for all who pay taxes. I may
think that my salary and money are my own, but as a member
of a community that has needs—for education and roads
and sanitation—I am responsible for meeting those needs.
In an even deeper way, I am not my own. St. Paul writes:
"None of us lives to himself, and none of us dies to himself.
If we live, we live to the Lord, and if we die, we die to the
Lord; so then, whether we live or whether we die, we are
the Lord's. For to this end Christ died and lived again, that
he might be Lord both of the dead and of the living" (Rom
14:7–9).

I am a creature dependent on God for my existence. I did
not will myself to be born, nor do I have a right to will
myself to die. I belong to God, my Creator and Father. I
belong to Jesus, who gave his life so that I might have eternal
life.

St. Paul continues: "Why do you pass judgment on your
brother? Or you, why do you despise your brother? For we
shall all stand before the judgment seat of God; for it is
written, 'As I live, says the Lord, every knee shall bow to
me, and every tongue shall give praise to God.' So each of
us shall give account of himself to God" (Rom 14:10–12).

*God, my Creator and Father, you give and sustain my existence. I
believe I shall die the way I have lived. I offer this day to you. Help
me to live it well.*

DAILY WORD: I belong to you, God.

EVENING REVIEW: What account of myself do I give to God
for this day?

April 16: St. Bernadette (1844–1879)

Bernadette Soubirous was an undersized, asthmatic, and uneducated fourteen-year-old girl who had not yet received her First Holy Communion when the Blessed Virgin Mary appeared to her at Lourdes, France, on February 11, 1858. She appeared seventeen more times and asked Bernadette to pray, do penance for sinners, and have a church built in that place. During one of the apparitions, Mary indicated a flow of water that became a spring to which people have gone for healing ever since.

When asked who she was, Mary responded, "I am the Immaculate Conception." She told Bernadette: "I promise you happiness not in this world but in the other." Her promise came true. Bernadette suffered misunderstanding and rejection from family and friends as well as from the religious community she joined to escape from the harassment of the curious. She once referred to herself as "the broom placed behind the door once it had been used."

Bernadette is a saint, not because Mary appeared to her, but because of her heroic virtue. She wrote in her private journal: "I must die to myself continually and accept trials without complaining. I work, I suffer, and I love with no other witness than his heart. Anyone who is not prepared to suffer all for the Beloved and to do his will in all things is not worthy of the sweet name of Friend, for here below, love without suffering does not exist."

Mary, Mother of Jesus and my Mother, I offer myself to God through you. Make up for what is lacking in this day that I offer. Guide me to find total happiness in the next life.

DAILY WORD: "Jesus, my God, I love you above all things" (words of St. Bernadette).

EVENING REVIEW: How was I God's tool?

April 17

As spring is nature's season of hope, so Easter is the Church's season of hope. Hope is an active virtue. It's more than wishful thinking. I can say, "I hope it doesn't rain today", but there is nothing I can do about the day's weather. However, saying "I hope I pass the exam" is a hope about which I can do something. I can study!

My hope in the resurrection is not an idle hope like wishing for good weather but an active hope. It requires something on my part—work. Salvation is a gift from God for which I hope, but St. Paul told the Philippians to "work out your own salvation with fear and trembling" (2:12). My hope in the resurrection and eternal life in heaven requires work on my part.

I am here on earth to learn to breathe the atmosphere of heaven. It's a rare atmosphere of mercy, love, and peace. Jesus once told a parable (Lk 16:19–30) about a rich man and a poor man named Lazarus, who shared the same hope of life after death in "the bosom of Abraham". The rich man failed to attain his hope because he never learned to treat Lazarus with respect and compassion. From the netherworld he continued to treat Lazarus like a slave whom he could send on errands. True hope means doing everything to attain what I hope for.

Loving God, you made me for heaven. You sent Jesus to blaze a trail there through his life, death, and Resurrection. With each breath may I live in a way by which I can attain your hope for me.

DAILY WORD: "All the way to heaven is heaven" (St. Catherine of Siena).

EVENING REVIEW: How did I breathe or not breathe heaven's atmosphere today?

What will heaven be like? It's good to imagine because doing so helps me keep my goal in mind, and that helps me live each moment pointed in the right direction.

St. Thomas Aquinas said that the "first point about eternal life is that man is united with God. For God is the reward and end of all our labors."

Secondly, according to Thomas, heaven "consists in the complete satisfaction of desire, for there the blessed will be given more than they wanted or hoped for. Only God satisfies, he infinitely exceeds all other pleasures." I am made for union with God, and there will always be an emptiness and longing until I attain this goal.

Finally, St. Thomas writes that "eternal life consists of the joyous community of all the blessed, a community of supreme delight, since everyone will share all that is good with all the blessed." Or, as St. Augustine wrote, "we shall have no enemies in heaven; we shall never lose a friend." The word "goodbye" is not part of the vocabulary of heaven.

Each day is given to me as an opportunity to grow in union with God and to learn to love my neighbors because God wants us all to be part of the Communion of Saints.

Lord Jesus, you lived your earthly life in total conformity to the will of God, loving the Father above all and loving all his children to the point of even sacrificing your life for them. Help me to live this day with that same total love. I will do so with the confidence that the way you showed will lead to happiness in heaven.

DAILY WORD: Heaven is my goal.

EVENING REVIEW: How did thoughts of heaven help me stay on track today?

April 19

Religion has been criticized for offering people "a pie in the sky when they die". Until then, critics say, the poor are told to accept their brutal life. Karl Marx called religion "the opium of the people", a drug to take away the pain of life. However, the thought of heaven isn't so much a tranquilizer as a challenge.

In a Jubilee Year homily about the Ascension, Pope St. John Paul II said that Christ's Resurrection and glorification show all people "that our true and final homeland is not down here, but 'in heaven', namely, in God." But arriving there means following the path that will bring us there. That's the challenge.

St. John Paul went on to say that the thought of heaven "should not withdraw us from engagement in the world, as the lives of the saints demonstrate, but must reinforce it even more. In fact, only by fulfilling our mission on earth will we finally be able to be in the glory of God."

Christianity, with its hope of heaven, is far from an anesthetic; rather, it stimulates us to live faithfully the new life that was given to us in Baptism.

O Jesus, as I begin this day, I set my sights "on things that are above" (Col 3:2). Through Baptism I have died and risen with you. Even now I am living a new life. Help me to do this faithfully so that when my earthly journey is done and you return to raise the bodies of all, I may be ready for you to change this mortal body and make it like your own glorified body (Phil 3:21).

DAILY WORD: One good step at a time leads to heaven.

EVENING REVIEW: How did I fulfill my mission on earth today?

April 20

St. Adalbert was a missionary bishop whose feast is celebrated on the same day as St. George (April 23). Adalbert was born in Bohemia and became bishop of Prague before going as a missionary to the Hungarians and the fierce Prussians. He was martyred by them on April 23, 997.

One thousand years later, St. John Paul II went to his tomb in Poland after the fall of the Berlin Wall. He spoke about the challenge of evangelization in an increasingly secularized world:

> The witness of Saint Adalbert is ever present in the Church and constantly bearing fruit. We need to take up with fresh vigor his work of evangelization. Let us help those who have forgotten Christ and his teaching to discover him anew. This will happen when ranks of faithful witnesses to the Gospel begin once more to traverse our continent; when works of architecture, literature and art show in a convincing way to the people of our time the One who is "the same yesterday and today and for ever"; when in the Church's celebration of the liturgy people see how beautiful it is to give glory to God; when they discern in our lives a witness of Christian mercy, heroic love and holiness.

Merciful God, I offer you my day. Make me your faithful witness today. May people see in me your mercy and love so that they may discover a true Christian who reflects your Son.

DAILY WORD: May they see you in me.

EVENING REVIEW: In what ways, through my words and actions, did I give witness to God's mercy, love, and holiness?

April 21: St. Anselm (1033–1109)

St. Anselm was born in Italy, became a Benedictine monk in France, and was made the archbishop of Canterbury in England. An important theologian of his time, his reflections came from his deep love of God. He once wrote: "I seek not to understand in order that I may believe; rather, I believe in order that I may understand." And again: "I am desperate for Your love, Lord. My heart is aflame with fervent passion. When I remember the good things You have done, my heart burns with desire to embrace You. I thirst for You; I hunger for You; I sigh for you."

From such deep love naturally flows the offering of oneself to the Beloved. In the words of the contemporary Christian song "Hungry": "Hungry I come to you for I know you satisfy. I am empty, but I know Your love does not run dry. I'm falling on my knees, offering all of me. Jesus, you're all this heart is living for."

Convinced of God's love for me, I offer myself with this prayer of St. Anselm:

Lord God, almighty Father, good Jesus, have mercy on me a sinner. Grant that I may serve you and love you as much as you desire and that I may live according to your will. Do not abandon me, Lord, to human weakness or to ignorance, nor to my merits, nor to anything else than your will. Lord, in your goodness, do with me and with all my thoughts and deeds as it pleases you, so that only your will may always be done by me, in me, and for me.

DAILY WORD: You are all this heart is living for.

EVENING REVIEW: How did I renew my love for God and the offering of myself throughout the day?

God loved mankind before our creation and prepared for us a good place in which to live and grow. According to the Book of Genesis, after each moment of creation, God looked at all that was made and found it "good". But after man was created, God found creation "very good". Man is the climax of God's creative efforts. As the *Catechism of the Catholic Church* puts it, "God created everything for man, but man in turn was created to serve and love God and to offer all creation back to him" (no. 358).

It is a sin to misuse and abuse creation. We were placed on earth to work with God in caring for creation. The earth is our home, which we should not trash. Doing so has grave consequences for ourselves and for future generations. Ultimately it shows a lack of gratitude to God for the gifts that surround us.

Moreover, our destiny and that of creation are inextricably connected. Writing to the Romans, St. Paul says that "creation waits with eager longing for the revealing of the sons of God; for creation was subjected to futility, not of its own will but by the will of him who subjected it in hope; because the creation itself will be set free from its bondage to decay and obtain the glorious liberty of the children of God" (8:20–21). In the resurrection, God will not only transform our mortal bodies but the earth from which we came.

Loving Creator, help me to work with you in caring for the earth today. May my choices protect and not harm the environment.

DAILY WORD: All creation, give praise to God!

EVENING REVIEW: In what ways did I protect or hurt creation today?

April 23: St. George (d. 303)

Holy cards of St. George—patron saint of police, the military, and boy scouts—often depict him as a knight on horseback thrusting a lance into a dragon. He was indeed a soldier, but he lived long before knights, and dragons are mythical creatures. George, however, confronted a "dragon" of his time—the Roman emperor—about his persecution of Christians and ended up being tortured with clubs, red-hot irons, and poison before he was finally beheaded.

St. Peter Damian wrote this about him:

> As for St. George, he was consumed with the fire of the Holy Spirit. Armed with the invincible standard of the cross, he did battle. Let us not only admire the courage of this fighter in heaven's army but follow his example. Let us be inspired to strive for the reward of heavenly glory, keeping in mind his example, so that we will not be swayed from our path, though the world seduce us with its smiles or try to terrify us with naked threats of its trials and tribulations.

What are the dragons—the temptations and evils—that I battle? Do I have the courage and perseverance to fight them? Do I ask for the grace to do so as I begin each day?

Lord Jesus, you fought the devil as you resisted temptations in the desert. You cast out demons, freeing people from their oppression. Through your death on the Cross you overcame sin and death. Give me the strength I need today to battle the temptations that will come my way and to do my part in overcoming the evils in our world.

DAILY WORD: With the Cross as my strength, I do battle today.

EVENING REVIEW: What were the temptations that I overcame today? What were the battles I lost?

April 24: St. Fidelis of Sigmaringen (1577–1622)

The motto of the U. S. Marine Corps is "Semper Fi", short for "Semper Fidelis", which is Latin for "Always Faithful". The ideal of faithfulness inspired today's saint, whose baptismal name was Mark but who became "Fidelis" when he joined the Capuchin Franciscans in 1612. On that day, he reflected on a passage from the Book of Revelation: "Be faithful unto death, and I will give you the crown of life" (2:10).

Fidelis was indeed faithful unto death, going to Switzerland as a missionary and dying as a martyr during a sad time in history when Christians were at war with one another.

I may not be asked to be faithful in such a dramatic way, but every day my faithfulness is tested in small and ordinary ways. Am I faithful to daily prayer, to reading Scripture? Am I faithful to the moral code that comes to me through God's commandments? Am I faithful to Church teaching? Am I faithful to my commitments and relationships not only in deeds but in my thoughts?

To be always faithful, every day and for the long haul, isn't easy. This is why many people resist making commitments. Is it possible to be always faithful with all the changes that contemporary life brings? Not on my own, but with God, that which is impossible becomes possible.

Faithful God, you did not go back on your covenant with man. You were faithful unto death. You promised not to take back your love or refuse your mercy to anyone who asks. I offer myself to you today and ask for the grace to be faithful to this offering throughout this day and always.

DAILY WORD: Always faithful.

EVENING REVIEW: How was my faithfulness to God and my various commitments challenged today?

April 25: St. Mark

An early tradition identifies the evangelist Mark with John Mark, the cousin of Barnabas, one of St. Paul's co-workers. The three of them went together on Paul's first missionary journey (Acts 12:25), but after a while Mark returned to Jerusalem (Acts 13:13) and Paul decided Mark was undependable. When Barnabas wanted to include Mark on another missionary trip, Paul refused. Barnabas disagreed with the decision, and the two stopped working together (Acts 15:37–39).

Paul and Mark were eventually reconciled. In Rome, Paul told Timothy "Get Mark and bring him with you, for he is very useful in serving me" (2 Tim 4:11). It was in Rome that Mark met Peter, from whom he received the material for his Gospel.

Sometimes we think that in "the good ol' days" of the early Church everyone got along. Not true. There were differences of opinion and personality conflicts just as there are today.

It's easy to love and to work with people we like and with whom we agree. But Jesus didn't say "like one another." He said "love one another." We tend to think of love as a feeling and that we have to like everyone. No. True love means willing the good of another even when you don't like them. Jesus said, "love your enemies and pray for those who persecute you, so that you may be sons of your Father who is in heaven, for he makes his sun rise on the evil and on the good" (Mt 5:44–45).

Lord Jesus, during this day that I offer you, help me to love those whom I do not like.

DAILY WORD: Jesus, I love as you have loved.

EVENING REVIEW: How did I pray and do good things for those whom I dislike or even hate?

April 26

On the feast of St. Mark in 1467, in the Italian town of Genazzano, a strange and, according to tradition, miraculous event occurred. The townspeople were noisily celebrating the feast when suddenly a cloud descended upon their neglected and unfinished church, which, since the fifth century, was called Our Lady of Good Counsel. When the cloud lifted, an image of Mary and the Child Jesus was left behind. It was on a thin piece of plaster no thicker than an eggshell. Even more remarkable, the image seemed to float without any support on a small ledge. Though much of this church was eventually destroyed during World War II, the image remained unharmed and unmoved, still appearing to be suspended.

Veneration of Mary under the title Our Lady of Good Counsel became popular and led to its inclusion in the Litany to the Blessed Virgin Mary.

It makes sense to go to Mary for good counsel. Mary is the Mother of Wisdom incarnate, Jesus, who called himself "the way, and the truth, and the life" (Jn 14:6). Mary points us to Jesus and, as she did at the wedding feast in Cana, tells us, "Do whatever he tells you" (Jn 2:5).

As we renew the offering of ourselves, we turn to Mary with a prayer that was written in 1796:

O Mary of Good Counsel, inflame the hearts of all who are devoted to you, so that all of them have shelter in you, O great Mother of God. O most worthy Lady, let everyone choose you as teacher and wise counselor of their souls, since you are, as St. Augustine says, the counsel of the apostles and counsel of all peoples. Amen.

DAILY WORD: Mary, be my guide.

EVENING REVIEW: In what ways did I seek heavenly counsel today?

April 27

Tomorrow is the anniversary of St. Gianna Molla's death in 1962 at the age of 39. She was a medical doctor, wife, and mother of four. Her first three pregnancies were extremely difficult, her first going twenty-five days beyond the due date with labor lasting thirty-six hours. Two months into her fourth pregnancy, she was diagnosed with a large benign tumor of the uterus. She was given three options: (1) the safest: to have a hysterectomy, which would result in the death of the child; (2) to have the tumor removed and the child aborted; (3) the riskiest: to have the tumor removed and to continue the pregnancy. She chose the third and told her husband Pietro: "If you have to decide between me and the child, do not hesitate; I demand it, the child, save it."

The operation was successful, and seven months later she gave birth by Caesarean section to a healthy girl named Gianna Emanuela. But the mother's health quickly declined, and in seven days she died of an abdominal infection. Within ten years, the cause for her beatification was opened, and she was canonized in 2004, the first female physician and "working mom" to be declared a saint.

St. Gianna dramatically sacrificed herself, but her entire life was dedicated to making the love of God present. She once said, "Our body is a cenacle, a monstrance: through its crystal the world should see God." I pray that God may shine through me today with the following words of St. Gianna:

Lord, keep Your grace in my heart. Live in me so that Your grace may be mine. Make it that I may bear every day some flowers and new fruit.

DAILY WORD: Live in me, Jesus.

EVENING REVIEW: What "flowers and new fruit" did I bear today?

April 28: St. Louis de Montfort (1673–1716)

Louis was a priest who traversed France around the year 1700 giving talks, parish missions, and retreats. St. John Paul II encountered authentic Marian spirituality though his writings, especially "True Devotion to Mary", in which he found the phrase that became his episcopal and papal motto—"Totus Tuus" or "All Yours".
St. Louis explains:

All our perfection consists in being conformed, united, and consecrated to Jesus Christ; and therefore the most perfect of all devotions is, without any doubt, that which most perfectly conforms, unites, and consecrates us to Jesus Christ. Now, Mary being the most conformed of all creatures to Jesus Christ, it follows that, of all devotions, that which most consecrates and conforms the soul to Our Lord is devotion to His holy Mother, and that the more a soul is consecrated to Mary, the more it is consecrated to Jesus. Hence it comes to pass that the most perfect consecration to Jesus Christ is nothing else but a perfect and entire consecration of ourselves to the Blessed Virgin, and this is the devotion that I teach; or, in other words, a perfect renewal of the vows and promises of holy Baptism.

Both Jesus and Mary were perfectly united in their surrender to the will of God. When I offer myself and my day to God, I do so in imitation of them and with their help. I renew my offering with this prayer of St. Louis de Montfort:

Hail Mary, Daughter of God the Father; Hail Mary, Mother of God the Son; Hail Mary, Spouse of the Holy Spirit. Hail Mary, Temple of the Most Holy Trinity. I am all yours and all that I have is yours, O Virgin blessed above all things.

DAILY WORD: All for you, Jesus, through Mary.

EVENING REVIEW: What in my day was especially pleasing to Mary?

April 29: St. Catherine of Siena (1347–1380)

Catherine is one of the most unusual and important women in history. She was the youngest of twenty-five children. Drawn to a life of prayer, she received her first vision of Jesus when she was only six. She joined the lay Dominicans, devoted herself to prayer and works of charity, and prevailed upon the pope to leave Avignon in France and return to Rome. A terrible schism soon developed. She offered her life for the Church's healing and died when she was thirty-three. In 1970, Pope St. Paul VI named her and St. Teresa of Ávila the first female Doctors of the Church.

St. Paul said the greatest gift was charity (1 Cor 13). I offer my day to God who is love, asking that it may be filled with charity as I pray with St. Catherine:

O charity, you are that sweet and holy bond that joins the soul to its Creator. You overcome discord, unite the separated, and enrich those who are poor in virtue, because you give life to all virtues. You give peace and put an end to war. You enlarge the heart that it may welcome friends and enemies and all creatures, because it is clothed with the affection of Jesus and follows him. O Christ, sweet Jesus, whoever possesses charity is founded on you, the living stone. In you I read the rule and the teaching that I must hold to, for you are the way, the truth, and the life. So, by reading in you, who are the book of life, I shall be able to walk the straight path and attend only to the love of God and the salvation of my neighbor.

DAILY WORD: Today I love as you have loved me.

EVENING REVIEW: How was I charitable or uncharitable today?

April 30: St. Pius V (1504–1572)

Pope Pius V upset many of the cardinals who elected him. They were expecting him to throw a sumptuous banquet for them as was the custom, but he didn't and instead gave the money to the poor. Under his influence, the Church and the city of Rome experienced a spiritual renewal.

Pius was elected pope in 1566, three years after the Council of Trent. He implemented the decrees of the council, insisting that bishops and priests reside in their diocesan and parish boundaries. He revised the Church's prayer book, the Breviary, and the Roman Rite of the Liturgy. He called upon the entire Christian world to pray the rosary for the success of a Christian navy that was vastly outnumbered as it battled Turkish forces that had a stranglehold on the Mediterranean Sea, preventing both shipping and pilgrimages to the Holy Land. In gratitude for victory at the Battle of Lepanto, he instituted the Feast of the Most Holy Rosary.

In the Collect Prayer at Mass today, we ask God that, through the intercession of St. Pius V, "we may participate in your mysteries with lively faith and fruitful charity." The Second Vatican Council called for "active participation" in the Liturgy. This means more than externals like posture and voice. We must pray the Mass with "lively faith and fruitful charity" and then go forth to live the offering we have made with Christ to the Father.

Lord God, may I offer you worship not only when I prayerfully participate in the celebration of Mass but as I live the Mass in the daily offering of myself.

DAILY WORD: I offer myself to you in union with the offering of Jesus at Mass.

EVENING REVIEW: How did my thoughts, words, and deeds give worship to God?

MAY

May 1: St. Joseph the Worker

In socialist countries, today is celebrated as "The Day of the International Solidarity of Workers", but since 1955 the Church has celebrated it as a feast in honor of St. Joseph the Worker.

Made in the image and likeness of God, we are made to work with the Creator for the good of creation. Work is not a punishment but a way in which we fulfill the first commandment found in Scripture: "God blessed them, saying: 'Be fruitful and multiply, and fill the earth and subdue it.' . . . The LORD God took the man and put him in the garden of Eden to till it and keep it" (Gen 1:28; 2:15).

Through their work, people contribute to the good of creation, to developing the world into a garden in which all people can live at peace with their needs met. Jesus showed us the value of work done for God's glory when he followed Joseph's trade and worked with his hands as a carpenter. With every task he performed, he was saving the world because he lived each moment in perfect harmony with the will of the Father. Let us ask St. Joseph to help us do the same today.

God, our Father, creator and ruler of the universe, in every age you call men and women to develop and use their gifts for the good of others. With St. Joseph as our example and guide, help us to do the work you have asked and come to the rewards you have promised. Inspired by the example of St. Joseph, may our lives manifest your love and may we rejoice forever in your peace. Grant this through Christ our Lord. Amen.

DAILY WORD: I work for your glory, Lord.

137

EVENING REVIEW: What work did I consciously offer God today?

May 2: St. Athanasius (295–373)

Today we honor a great bishop and doctor of the Eastern Church, who, because of his steadfast defense of Church teaching against heresy, was exiled five times from his see of Alexandria, Egypt, and spent a total of seventeen years in exile. He wrote a biography of St. Anthony of the Desert (see January 17). The following excerpt challenges us to live one day at a time:

> Let's continue to be strenuous in pursuing virtue. Let's not grow tired of seeking it, for our Lord has become a guide for us and for every person who has a desire for the virtues. And so that it might not be tedious for us, St. Paul became our example when he said, "I die daily." Now, if we were to think each day that we had to die that day, we would never sin at all. This is the explanation of Paul's saying. If in the morning we imagined that we would never last till evening, and if at evening we thought that we would never see morning, we would never sin. If we were to keep the imminence of our death in mind, we would never be overcome by sin: lust which is fleeting would not reign over us; we would never harbor anger against another human being; we would not love the possessions which pass away; we would forgive every person who offended us. Therefore, let's be zealous in carrying out the work we have committed ourselves to, and let's travel to the end of the road on which have begun our journey.

Lord Jesus, all I really have is this day. Yesterday is gone. Tomorrow may not come. Help me live this day well.

DAILY WORD: This too shall pass.

EVENING REVIEW: How did the thought of death keep me faithful today?

May 3: Sts. Philip and James the Lesser

According to tradition, St. James, who is called the "Lesser" to distinguish him from the other apostle known as the "Greater", or elder, is the author of the New Testament letter that bears his name. Pope Benedict XVI said that this letter "shows us a very concrete and practical Christianity. Faith must be fulfilled in life, above all, in love of neighbor and especially in dedication to the poor." We must be "doers of the word" (Jas 1:22) whose faith is alive and a matter of not just thoughts, feelings, and words, but of action. For "faith apart from works is dead" (2:26).

St. Philip appears often in John's Gospel. He introduced his friend Nathanael (Bartholomew) to Jesus (1:45). He asked how the crowd could be fed before Jesus multiplied five loaves and two fish to feed them all (6:9–11). Yet even after experiencing this, he struggled. At the Last Supper, he told Jesus, "Lord, show us the Father, and we shall be satisfied" (14:8). To this Jesus exhibited frustration, saying, "Have I been with you so long, and yet you do not know me, Philip? He who has seen me has seen the Father; how can you say, 'Show us the Father'? Do you not believe that I am in the Father and the Father is in me?" (14:9–10). Jesus then went on to explain that his works reveal who he is and give glory to God.

Lord Jesus, I believe that you are in the Father and that through Baptism I am now in you. May all I do reveal that my faith is alive.

DAILY WORD: "Faith without works is dead."

EVENING REVIEW: How did my day reveal my deepest identity as a Christian and give glory to God?

May 4: St. José María Rubio (1864–1929)

Fr. Rubio, a diocesan priest who became a Jesuit, was known as the "Apostle of Madrid" and "Father of the Poor". He opened tuition-free schools for the poor and helped the unemployed find work. He fed them spiritually through sermons and retreats. The Eucharist was the center of his life and his love for the poor. He wanted to give them the total love that led Jesus to offer his body and blood on the Cross and in the Eucharist. In the Blessed Sacrament, he found the Sacred Heart of Jesus. He wrote: "In this Sacred Host lies hid the whole of God's omnipotence, all his wisdom, the perfect goodness of Jesus Christ, since therein rests his living heart as it is also in heaven."

According to St. John Paul II, who beatified him in 1985 and canonized him in 2003, Fr. Rubio's motto was "Do what God wants and want what God does!" That's what Jesus did. He always did what the Father wanted him to do. We want to do the same as Jesus did, not grudgingly and halfheartedly, but wholeheartedly sharing the desires of God. To want what God wants means to have my desires purified so that the only thing I desire is what God desires. In the end, it means to love, as Jesus did. It means to die to my own desires and even to lay down my life for others.

Father, I want no other desire than your desires. I want only to do your will as perfectly as your Son did. Through my union with his Eucharistic Heart, give me the courage and strength to do this today.

DAILY WORD: "I want what God wants."

EVENING REVIEW: In what ways did I want and do what God wants?

May 5

May is dedicated to the Blessed Virgin Mary. The Jesuit poet
Gerard Manley Hopkins reflected on this in his poem "The
May Magnificat". He wondered if May is Mary's month because it's brighter and sunnier. After the April showers, there
are the May flowers. Spring is in full bloom, and everywhere
we look, we see things growing. Mary sees it all. Mother
Nature reminds her of her own motherhood.

> All things rising, all things sizing
> Mary sees, sympathizing
> With that world of good
> Nature's motherhood.
> Their magnifying of each its kind
> With delight calls to mind
> How she did in her stored
> Magnify the Lord.

Each blade of grass, spring flower, cumulus cloud, or
robin's egg reflects the beauty of the Creator. Nature is
engaged in a symphony of praise. Even more wonderful is
the human contribution. Nature magnifies or gives praise
to God simply because of what it is. But human beings,
with free will, can choose not to join the symphony. We
can sin. However, when we choose to give glory to God,
the beauty of creation is magnified, made even more beautiful because the greatest note—love—has been added to the
song of praise.

*God of Nature, I praise and thank you for the beauty of creation
and for your most perfect work—Mary—whom you made without
sin in order to be the mother of your Son. May I, like Mary, say
"yes" to all you want of me today. I offer this day to you with love,
asking that it may join the chorus of praise that rises to you from all
over the earth.*

DAILY WORD: Praise and glory to you!

May 6

The English Jesuit poet Gerard Manley Hopkins wrote a poem entitled "The Blessed Virgin Compared to the Air We Breathe". Reflecting on a clear blue sky, he considers how without the atmosphere protecting the earth, the sun would leave it a waste. In the same way, sinful mankind could not endure the blazing glory of the All-holy Creator and so God chose a woman through whom he could enter the world in a way that would not destroy it.

> Through her we may see him
> Made sweeter, not made dim,
> And her hand leaves his light
> Sifted to suit our sight.

I am called to do the same now. In the words of the poet, I, like Mary, have this one work to do—"Let all God's glory through." I, like Mary, am to allow the Son to shine through me in such a way that the world may know and receive him.

A Carmelite, St. Elizabeth of the Trinity, echoed these thoughts in a prayer to Mary. May her words help me live my daily offering every minute today.

O Virgin most faithful, you remain night and day in profound silence, in ineffable peace, in a divine prayer that never ceases, your soul ever inundated with heavenly light. Your heart is like a crystal that reflects the divine One, the Guest who dwells in you, the Beauty that knows no setting. I adore the mystery of this God who is made flesh in you, O Virgin Mary.

DAILY WORD: Son of God, shine through me.

EVENING REVIEW: How did Christ shine through me today? Did I obscure the light in any way?

May 7

Most of the Ten Commandments prohibit immoral actions. Only two are positive directives. The third is "Remember to keep holy the sabbath day"; in other words, remember to honor your heavenly Father in a special way every week. The fourth is directed toward our earthly parents: "Honor your father and your mother."

Surely Jesus, who is the all-holy Son of God and without sin, followed all the commandments, including this one, by honoring his parents, his earthly mother and foster father. And, if we as Christians are to imitate Jesus, shouldn't we follow the example of Jesus and honor his Mother?

Jesus honored Mary, and, following his example, we also honor her. This means doing whatever she asks us to do. According to the Gospel of John, the first miraculous sign that Jesus gave to the world was in response to Mary's compassion (2:1–11). Jesus, his disciples, and Mary were guests at a wedding feast in Cana. Mary observed that the wine had run out, and she, concerned for the bride and groom, brought this fact to Jesus' attention. Jesus told her that his hour had not yet come, but Mary, knowing the compassion that the Son she had raised had for others, told the servers, "Do whatever he tells you." She knew he would respond to the need.

Honoring Mary as Jesus did means following her directions to do whatever Jesus tells me to do.

Father, help me follow your Son by honoring and obeying Mary and doing whatever your Son wants me to do today.

DAILY WORD: "Do whatever he tells us."

EVENING REVIEW: How did I honor Mary today by doing what Jesus wanted me to do?

May 8

During this month we set aside a day on which we honor our mothers, but the entire month is dedicated to the Mother of God and our Mother. We would be very cold, ungrateful, and unloving if we ignored or forgot about our mothers on Mother's Day. She's the one who gave us life, and she, or another who took her place, nurtured and cared for that life. Thus, we honor our mothers with a special day.

Mary is our spiritual mother. She gave each of us the new life of grace when, through her, the Savior, the Author of Life, came into the world. Without Mary, the Son of God could not have taken flesh, developed, been born, lived and suffered and died and then rose—all to save us. Thus, we owe Mary big time and should always be grateful to her.

Since Mary is the mother of Jesus, she is also our mother because we are one with him in his Body. Because we are the Body of Christ, Mary is our mother. Jesus confirmed this when, with his dying words on the Cross, he said "Behold, your mother!" (Jn 19:27). The Church has always interpreted these words, spoken to "the disciple whom Jesus loved", as words spoken to all the beloved followers of Christ throughout history.

Mother Mary, you gave birth to Jesus, my Savior. In doing so, you have also given birth to me because he has freed me from sin and given me a new life. Help me today to live as your child. May everything I do bring a smile to your face as you see the pleasure it brings to your Son.

DAILY WORD: I do this to please you, Mother.

EVENING REVIEW: What made my Mother happy or unhappy today?

Honoring the Blessed Virgin Mary is not something new. It's not something that the Church concocted years after she lived or even during her early days after Pentecost. According to the Bible (Lk 1:39–45), Mary was honored even before Jesus was born. At the Visitation, her kinswoman Elizabeth honored her with this greeting: "Most blessed are you among women. . . . Blessed is she who believed that there would be a fulfilment of what was spoken to her from the Lord." Hearing words like these was certainly quite an honor!

But this wasn't the first time that Mary received honor. Shortly before this, a creature from heaven itself, the Archangel Gabriel, honored Mary with this greeting: "Hail, full of grace, the Lord is with you! . . . Do not be afraid, Mary, for you have found favor with God" (1:28, 30). Honoring Mary comes right out of the Bible, where we see both heaven and earth praising her.

Mary is not God, but she is the Mother of God. We adore God and honor Mary as his perfect creation, the Mother of God's Son. Our honor and praise ultimately flow through Mary to the source of her blessedness, to God. In praising the daughter, we praise the Father. We echo Gabriel and Elizabeth every time we pray the Hail Mary.

Hail Mary, full of grace, the Lord is with thee. Blessed art thou among women and blessed is the fruit of thy womb Jesus. Holy Mary, Mother of God, pray for us sinners now and at the hour of our death. Pray for me now and unite yourself to this offering of my day so that it may be blessed and full of grace. Amen.

DAILY WORD: Hail Mary!

EVENING REVIEW: In what ways was Mary present to me today helping to make my offering more worthy of God?

May 10: St. Damien of Molokai (1840–1889)

Damien de Veuster was a Belgian missionary and member of the Congregation of the Sacred Hearts of Jesus and Mary. He arrived in Honolulu on March 19, 1864, and was ordained two days later in the church that still stands today, the oldest active cathedral in the United States. On this day in 1873, he volunteered for the great work of charity for which he is known.

People who had been diagnosed with Hansen's Disease, or leprosy, had been removed from all the Hawaiian Islands and confined to part of the island of Molokai. When he canonized Damien in 2009, Pope Benedict XVI said: "Not without fear and repugnance, he chose to go to the Island of Molokai to serve the lepers who lived there, abandoned by all. Thus he was exposed to the disease from which they suffered. . . . The servant of the Word consequently became a suffering servant, a leper with the lepers, for the last four years of his life."

St. John Paul II called Damien a "Servant of Humanity" and at his beatification said: "Where did Damien's charity and happiness in often difficult situations come from? He drew his strength from the contemplation of the Eucharist, the mystery of love in which Christ truly communicates with the one who receives him and whom he invites to total dedication."

Lord Jesus, your compassion for suffering mankind led you to share our suffering and death. St. Damien courageously followed your example, becoming one with the people he served. I offer my life to you now for the people for whom you suffered and died.

DAILY WORD: Heart of Jesus in the Eucharist, give me strength.

EVENING REVIEW: In what ways did I offer my sufferings to God today and in this way become one, as Jesus and Damien did, with suffering mankind?

May 11

On this day in 1610, the emperor of China did something very unusual. A foreigner, a Westerner from Italy, had just died. Normally foreigners were buried in the Portuguese colony of Macau. But the emperor had him buried in the capital city and inscribed on his tomb these words: "One who had attained renown for justice and written illustrious books." The tomb still exists and the man continues to be honored by the Chinese.

His name was Matteo Ricci, and he went to China as a Jesuit missionary in 1582. He soon discovered that the only way he could preach the Gospel was to first become thoroughly acquainted with Chinese culture and civilization and to share the knowledge of the West. He translated Euclid's "Elements of Geometry", introduced clocks, and created a map that shocked everyone because it depicted the true size of China in relation to the rest of the world.

Pope Benedict XVI called Ricci someone who was "gifted with profound faith and extraordinary cultural and academic genius". In the first pages of his personal journal, Ricci wrote: "Who can doubt that this whole expedition of which we are now writing is divinely directed, since it is entirely devoted to bringing the light of the gospel to souls." He also wrote: "This life is for us but a journey; we are not here forever, nor does our final goal lie here below."

Lord God, you desire all people to know you. I offer myself to you for this purpose. May I be a translation of your Word today so that all whom I meet may come to know and accept your love and desire for them.

DAILY WORD: I am your translation.

EVENING REVIEW: How did my words and actions help people know you or hinder them?

May 12: St. Pancras and Sts. Nereus and Achilleus (d. 304)

Sts. Nereus and Achilleus were brothers who served in the Roman army. According to Pope St. Damasus I, who wrote many epithets for the martyrs, they became Christians and threw away "their shields, their armor, and their blood-stained javelins. Confessing the faith of Christ, they rejoice to bear testimony to its triumph." The witness they gave was with their own lives, showing that, for a Christian, there is no fear of death.

St. Pancras was orphaned at an early age. An uncle took him in and eventually the two went to Rome, where they became Christians. In the last major persecution of the early Church, Pancras, only fourteen years old, was beheaded, showing that one is never too young to give witness to the faith.

Speaking to young people in 2010, Pope Benedict XVI said:

> I ask you to learn about the lives of the saints. You will see how God was their guide and how they made their way through each day in faith, in hope and in love. Christ is calling each of you to work with him and to take up your responsibilities in order to build the civilization of love. If you follow his Word, it will light up your path and lead you to high goals that will give joy and full meaning to your lives.

Lord Jesus, the word "martyr" means "witness". I respond to your call today, the high goal of giving witness to your Resurrection. I offer my life to you, asking that you will give me the courage to take up the responsibilities of the day in order to help build the civilization of love by which you desire to reign in every heart.

DAILY WORD: My life is a witness to you.

EVENING REVIEW: What kind of witness did I give today?

May 13: Our Lady of Fatima

On this day in 1917, the Blessed Virgin Mary appeared to three shepherd children—Lucia, Francisco, and Jacinta—in Fatima, Portugal. She appeared to them once a month until October, when she revealed herself as Our Lady of the Rosary, repeated her request that the rosary be prayed every day, and showed a miraculous sign in the sky that thousands of people witnessed and that was reported in the secular, anti-Christian newspapers of the time.

In 2000, the Prefect for the Congregation for the Doctrine of the Faith, Joseph Cardinal Ratzinger, explained the meaning of Fatima and Mary's words "my Immaculate Heart will triumph":

> The Heart open to God, purified by contemplation of God, is stronger than guns and weapons of every kind. The "fiat" of Mary, the word of her heart, has changed the history of the world, because it brought the Savior into the world. . . . The Evil One has power in this world, as we see and experience continually; he has power because our freedom continually lets itself be led away from God. But since God himself took a human heart and has thus steered human freedom toward what is good, the freedom to choose evil no longer has the last word. From that time forth, the word that prevails is this: "In the world you will have tribulation, but take heart; I have overcome the world" (Jn 16:33). The message of Fatima invites us to trust in this promise.

Mary taught this offering prayer to the children:

O Jesus, it is for love of you, for the conversion of sinners, and in reparation for the sins committed against the Immaculate Heart of Mary.

DAILY WORD: It is for love of you.

EVENING REVIEW: How did the Immaculate Heart triumph in and through me today?

May 14: St. Matthias

According to the Acts of the Apostles, during the time between Jesus' Ascension and the coming of the Holy Spirit at Pentecost, Peter told a group of 120 disciples that the apostle Judas, who had betrayed Jesus, ought to be replaced. Just as the ancient patriarch Jacob had 12 sons who became the 12 tribes of Israel, so the new Israel, the Church, ought to have 12 apostles who would be her pillars. In ancient times, the number 12 represented fullness as in 12 months making a full year. Thus, Matthias was chosen to be one of the 12 apostles. He was among those who had seen Jesus after his Resurrection and could witness to it.

Pope Benedict drew a lesson from this replacement. He said that the faithfulness of Matthias compensated for the betrayal of Judas. Every Christian is called to balance the evil in the world with good. "While there is no lack of unworthy or traitorous Christians in the Church, it is up to each of us to counterbalance the evil done by them with our clear witness to Jesus Christ, our Lord and Savior."

This is the meaning of reparation: to make up for the evil that has been done with good. The apostles of old did this, and contemporary apostles of prayer do so as well. Friends want to make up for the harm that is done to their friends.

Lord Jesus, through our sins we have betrayed you. You forgive me and now call me to make up for the harm sin has done to mankind. I offer you my day for this purpose. May I give clear witness to you.

DAILY WORD: With this good, I make up for what we've done wrong.

EVENING REVIEW: What acts of reparation did I do today?

May 15: St. Isidore the Farmer (1070–1130)

Isidore was a poor agricultural worker who labored for a wealthy landowner in Spain. He and his wife, Maria, who was also canonized, had one son, who died in infancy. Isidore went to Mass every morning before going to work, and this made him late. His fellow workers grumbled, but he was able to finish and even surpass his assigned work load with the assistance of angels who helped him plow. While he plowed and planted seeds he prayed. Isidore not only made an offering of his day by participating in the celebration of Mass, he prayed for people as he worked.

I offer God my day with its prayers and works. There are many opportunities to pray, especially if my work is routine. I can pray while driving or waiting in line at a store or for the internet. I can pray as I clean or walk from one place to another. There are many "empty" moments in my day where my mind wanders around with various thoughts. I can direct my thoughts in prayer for the many people who need God's help. In that way I can be a conduit for his love to enter their lives.

St. Isidore, a humble, hidden manual laborer, was canonized on March 12, 1622, along with some more famous and influential saints: St. Ignatius Loyola and St. Francis Xavier, St. Teresa of Ávila and St. Philip Neri. He is an example of one who did small things with great love.

Lord Jesus, the day I offer you may not seem very significant. It is filled with many "empty" moments. Help me to use them today for good as I pray while I work.

DAILY WORD: I pray as I work.

EVENING REVIEW: For whom did I pray during the "empty" times of my day?

May 16

At the Last Supper Jesus promised: "I will ask the Father, and he will give you another Counselor to be with you for ever, even the Spirit of truth" (Jn 14:16). He added: "it is to your advantage that I go away, for if I do not go away, the Counselor will not come to you; but if I go, I will send him to you" (16:7). This Counselor came at Pentecost and comes today in Baptism and Confirmation. The Spirit comes with seven gifts, which are listed in Isaiah 11:2.

One of these gifts is "fear of the LORD," which is "the beginning of wisdom" (Ps 111:10; Prov 9:10). According to Pope Francis, "it does not mean being afraid of God: we know well that God is Father, that he loves us and wants our salvation, and he always forgives, always; thus, there is no reason to be scared of him!"

What then is this fear of the Lord that is the basis for wisdom? According to Pope Francis, it

> is the gift of the Holy Spirit through whom we are reminded of how small we are before God and of his love and that our good lies in humble, respectful, and trusting self-abandonment into his hands. . . . When we are pervaded by fear of the Lord, then we are led to follow the Lord with humility, docility, and obedience. This, however, is not an attitude of resignation, passivity, or regret, but one of the wonder and joy of being a child who knows he is served and loved by the Father.

Holy Spirit, give me the awe of knowing I am a child of the Father of Jesus who loves me with an infinite love.

DAILY WORD: I am a child of God.

EVENING REVIEW: How did I experience humility, docility, and obedience today?

May 17: St. Pascal Baylon (1540–1592)

Today's saint was born on Pentecost Sunday and died on Pentecost Sunday fifty-two years later. He has been called "The Saint of the Blessed Sacrament", yet he was not ordained. From the age of seven until he was twenty-four, he helped his poor family as a shepherd. When he could not attend Mass because of his work, he would kneel and face the church where Mass was being celebrated. As a Franciscan Brother, he worked in his community's kitchen and as its doorkeeper. Whenever he took a break, he went to the chapel to pay a visit to Jesus present there. He died as the bell was being rung and the Host was being lifted up at Mass.

Eucharistic devotion can take many forms: a holy hour in a perpetual adoration chapel, a short visit to a church on the way home from work, making the sign of the cross when passing a church.

Pope St. John Paul II wrote:

> There is a particular need to cultivate a lively awareness of Christ's real presence, both in the celebration of Mass and in the worship of the Eucharist outside Mass. The presence of Jesus in the tabernacle must be a kind of magnetic pole attracting an ever greater number of souls enamored of him, ready to wait patiently to hear his voice and, as it were, to sense the beating of his heart.

Lord Jesus, on the Cross you offered yourself for me. In the Mass you continue to make present that world-changing offering, and in the Blessed Sacrament you show your love even further by remaining with me. I believe and I want to return love for love by offering myself and my day to you.

DAILY WORD: Thank you for your Eucharistic presence.

EVENING REVIEW: How was my day an act of thanksgiving?

May 18: Pope St. John I (d. 526)

Pope St. John XXIII was often called "Good Pope John", and when he died one newspaper's editorial cartoon depicted the world shrouded in mourning and the words "A Death in the Family". He was the last in a long line of popes named "John", and today the Church honors the first of them. When Pope St. John I lived, the Roman Empire was divided into East and West with the East ruled by Emperor Justinian and the West by King Theodoric who was an Ostrogoth, one of the many barbarian tribes that had invaded the empire. The Ostrogoths were Arians, followers of a heresy that believed Jesus was human but not divine. Theodoric sent Pope John I to Justinian to gain concessions for the Arians in the East. He obtained some but not all of the concessions, and when he returned he was arrested and thrown into prison where he died of starvation.

From John I to John XXIII and before and after them, popes have led the Church depending on the promise of Jesus to Peter that "the gates of Hades shall not prevail against it" (Mt 16:18). Holding fast to the truth, many of them have suffered and died. It is important to support the pope and all pastors with our prayers. For this reason, Morning Offering prayers often include mention of the pope and his intentions.

Lord Jesus, you called Peter, a simple fisherman, and declared him to be the rock on which you would build your Church. Throughout history you have called Peter's successors to lead your Church. As I offer my day to you, I pray especially for our present pope. Send your Spirit to guide him and keep him strong and courageous.

DAILY WORD: Bless the Holy Father.

EVENING REVIEW: What did I offer specifically for the pope today?

"Fear of the LORD is the beginning of wisdom" (Ps 111:10). Wisdom is the gift of the Holy Spirit that helps us know we are not God and thus not in control of everything. True wisdom includes humility.

Pope Francis said: "The Holy Spirit makes the Christian 'wise'. Not in the sense that he has an answer for everything, that he knows everything, but in the sense that he 'knows' about God, he knows how God acts, he knows when something is of God and when it is not of God; he has this wisdom that God places in our hearts."

Wisdom does not mean having a lot of scientific knowledge. Rather, it is the gift by which we know how to use that knowledge for our good, according to God's plan for man. Wisdom is not so much "head knowledge" as "knowledge of the heart".

Again, Pope Francis: "We have the Holy Spirit within us, in our heart; we can listen to him. If we listen to the Holy Spirit, he teaches us this way of wisdom, . . . which is seeing with God's eyes, hearing with God's ears, loving with God's heart, directing things with God's judgment."

Mary is called "Seat of Wisdom" because she saw, heard, and loved in this way.

Mother Mary, the Holy Spirit overshadowed you, and you received the Word into your heart so that he could take flesh in your womb. Pray that we may have hearts open to wisdom so that we will no longer live and use our knowledge in a way that is contrary to God's loving plan. I surrender myself today to the Holy Spirit's work in me and through me.

DAILY WORD: Spirit of Wisdom, fill me.

EVENING REVIEW: How did I see, hear, and love as God does?

May 20: St. Bernardine of Siena (1380–1444)

The Franciscan St. Bernardine was such a powerful preacher that he almost put a printer out of business. The man printed playing cards and, when Bernardine preached against gambling and playing card games to the neglect of one's spiritual life and family duties, people stopped buying cards from him. But his business picked up again when he began printing cards with "IHS"—the symbol for the Holy Name of Jesus. St. Bernardine was devoted to the Holy Name, and he used those cards to promote this devotion.

Card games are not wrong, and they can be a healthy form of recreation. But whether in a group or alone on a computer, games can become an obsession that takes us away from our duties to God and our neighbor. Moreover, it often happens that during games the Holy Name of Jesus is misused. This Name is itself a prayer. We can pray it throughout the day, remembering its meaning—"God saves."

Lord Jesus, as I offer you my day and especially its moments of play and recreation, I ask that I may reverence your Holy Name at all times. I do so now with the words of St. Bernardine: "Jesus, Name full of glory, grace, love, and strength! You are the refuge of those who repent, the medicine of souls, our banner of warfare in this life, the comfort of those who mourn, the delight of those who believe, the wages of those who toil, the healing of the sick. To you our devotion aspires, by you our prayers are answered. We delight in contemplating you. O Name of Jesus, you are the glory of all the saints for eternity. Amen."

DAILY WORD: Praised be the Name of Jesus!

EVENING REVIEW: How did my recreation give glory to God?

May 21: St. Cristobal Magallanes and Companions (20th Century)

"Viva Cristo Rey! Viva la Virgen de Guadalupe!" With these words, many of the twentieth-century martyrs of Mexico died, including Fr. Cristobal Magallanes, twenty-one other priests, and three lay people whom we honor today. In 1928, during its persecution of the Church, the government destroyed a statue of the Sacred Heart on Cubilete Hill, the geographical center of Mexico. The Church was able to rebuild the shrine in 1944. Pope Benedict XVI visited in 2012 and said:

> This monument represents Christ the King. But his crowns, one of a sovereign, the other of thorns, indicate that his royal status does not correspond to how it has been or is understood by many. His kingdom does not stand on the power of his armies subduing others through force or violence. It rests on a higher power that wins over hearts: the love of God that he brought into the world with his sacrifice and the truth to which he bore witness. This is his sovereignty which no one can take from him and which no one should forget.

Lord Jesus, because your throne on earth was the Cross, you now reign in heavenly splendor. Draw all people to yourself that they may know the love you have for them and your desire that your death for them may not be in vain. I dedicate myself to you for that purpose. Reign in my heart today and every day so that I may be an instrument of reconciliation in my family, in my community, in my church, and in a world that so desperately needs the justice and peace that only you, the King of Love, can bring it.

DAILY WORD: Viva Cristo Rey!

EVENING REVIEW: How did I foster or hinder Christ's reign in my life today?

May 22: St. Rita (1377–1457)

Rita of Cascia was born in answer to her parents' prayers for a child. As she grew up, she expressed her desire to become a nun, but her parents would have none of it. They wanted grandchildren and forced her to marry a man who turned out to be violent and unfaithful. For eighteen years she endured this, and even saw her two sons becoming like their father. She prayed intensely for their conversions. One day her husband was carried home on a stretcher, dying from wounds suffered in a fight. He asked for her forgiveness and died, but the sons began to plan revenge. Again Rita prayed. The sons died before they could carry out their plan. They died holy deaths, forgiving their father's murderers. Freed of family obligations, Rita could now follow her dream. She was refused entry by the Augustinian nuns three times because she had been married, but her perseverance over six years won out, and she was admitted. She served the sick Sisters and counseled lay people who came to the convent. Her devotion to Christ's Passion led to her receiving the mystical gift of a wound on her forehead in remembrance of the crown of thorns.

The story of St. Rita's life, with its many difficulties and trials, broken dreams and closed doors, led people to start asking her to intercede for them in their own difficult situations. She quickly became known as "The Saint of the Impossible" and "The Advocate of Desperate Cases".

Father, your daughter St. Rita was faithful in the midst of many difficulties. She did not give in to bitterness or discouragement. Help me with your grace to persevere in following your will for me today.

DAILY WORD: I will persevere.

EVENING REVIEW: How did I share in Christ's Passion today?

May 23

Two of the seven gifts that the Holy Spirit brings are knowledge and understanding. Like wisdom, these are not human but spiritual gifts. Pope Francis explained: "When we speak of knowledge, we immediately think of man's capacity to learn more and more about the reality that surrounds him and to discover the laws that regulate nature and the universe. The knowledge that comes from the Holy Spirit, however, is not limited to human knowledge; it is a special gift, which leads us to grasp, through creation, the greatness and love of God and his profound relationship with every creature." In this way, "everything speaks to us about Him and His love." We come to know God better through creation, which reflects his beauty and love.

Understanding is similar. "We are not dealing here with human understanding", Pope Francis said. "Rather, it is a grace which only the Holy Spirit can infuse and which awakens in a Christian the ability to go beyond the outward appearance of reality and to probe the depths of the thoughts of God and his plan of salvation."

According to St. Paul, only a person's deepest interior, or spirit, knows that person. And so, God gives us his own Spirit "that we might understand the gifts bestowed on us by God" (1 Cor 2:12). We know God and his plans for us through the knowledge and understanding the Spirit gives us.

Come, Holy Spirit! I surrender to you and your action in my life. May the events of this day help me grow in knowledge and understanding so that I may always live according to your loving will for me and the world.

DAILY WORD: Holy Spirit, give me knowledge and understanding.

EVENING REVIEW: How did I grow in true knowledge and understanding?

May 24: Mary, Help of Christians

In the early nineteenth century, the French Emperor Napoleon held Pope Pius VII a prisoner in France for almost six years. In 1814, Napoleon was defeated in battle and the pope was able to return to the Vatican. He entered Rome on this day to the cheers of the crowd that had gathered to welcome him back. In gratitude for his health and safe return, the pope instituted this feast of Mary. St. John Bosco said, "Spread devotion to Mary, Help of Christians, and you will see what miracles are."

Pope Benedict XVI asked us to pray for the Church in China on this day, which is also the feast of Our Mother of Sheshan in Shanghai. Our prayers, asking the intercession of Mary, are very powerful. She is a sister in Christ who, because she is with him in glory, continues to play a role in the life of every Christian. And so, we turn to her now with a prayer adapted from one written by St. John Bosco.

Most Holy Virgin Mary, Help of Christians, how sweet it is to come to your feet imploring your perpetual help. If earthly mothers never cease to remember their children, how can you, the most loving of all mothers, forget us? Grant then to us your help in all our necessities, in every sorrow, and especially in all our temptations. We ask for your unceasing help for all who are now suffering. Help the weak, cure the sick, convert sinners. Obtain for us, O Mary, Help of Christians, that having invoked you on earth we may love and eternally thank you in heaven. Amen.

DAILY WORD: Be with me, Mary, Help of Christians.

EVENING REVIEW: For what specific intentions did I pray today?

May 25: St. Bede (672–735), Pope St. Gregory VII (1020–1085), St. Mary Magdalene de Pazzi (1566–1607)

The Church honors three saints today with optional memorials.

St. Bede was a Benedictine monk who wrote a history of the English Church and whose holiness was so evident that shortly after his death he was called Bede the Venerable. Writing about Mary's Magnificat, he said: "She refers all her greatness to the gift of the one whose essence is power and whose nature is greatness, for he fills with greatness and strength the small and weak who believe in him."

Pope St. Gregory VII was a reformer who encountered much opposition from secular authorities. In a letter he wrote: "We are sure that you sympathize with our sufferings and that you pray for us. Do not doubt that we have the same mind toward you—and with good reason. For the Apostle [Paul] says: 'If one member suffers, the other members suffer with it.'"

St. Mary Magdalene de Pazzi was an Italian Carmelite who experienced both heights and depths. She received great consolations, the gift of healing, and other mystical gifts. She also experienced physical sufferings and terrible temptations to lust, gluttony, despair, and suicide. She joined her sufferings to the Cross and offered them for the salvation of all people.

I renew my offering, asking the Holy Spirit to touch me and all people today, with the following prayer of my Carmelite sister.

Come, Holy Spirit. Spirit of truth, you are the reward of the saints, the comforter of souls, light in the darkness, riches to the poor, comfort to those who are wandering. To sum up, you are the one in whom all treasures are contained. Come! As you descended upon Mary, that the Word might become flesh, work in us through grace as you worked in her through nature and grace.

DAILY WORD: Come, Holy Spirit!

EVENING REVIEW: What inspirations of the Holy Spirit did I receive today?

May 26: St. Philip Neri (1515–1595)

Philip pursued a career in business but ended up devoting himself to God's business. He worked so hard for the people of Rome that he was given the title "Second Apostle of Rome". As a priest, he founded the Congregation of the Oratory, which spread beyond Italy and included St. John Henry Newman as one of its members. He burned his writings before his death, but a few fragments survived, including this advice about prayer: "The best preparation for prayer is to read the lives of the saints, not from mere curiosity, but quietly and with recollection a little at a time. And to pause whenever you feel your heart touched with devotion."

His two favorite books were the New Testament and a joke book. He said: "A joyful heart is more easily made perfect than a downcast one." Pope St. John Paul II said that from St. Philip's faith "there arose spontaneously a life-style marked by joy, trust, serenity, healthy optimism. From this interior joy there sprang the extraordinary strength of his apostolate and his delicate and proverbial humor, for which he was called the 'saint of joy'."

Good friends share both their joys and their sorrows. When I offer my joys, I bring joy to God. The fact that much of religious art does not show Jesus smiling doesn't mean that he was always sad. I, as a member of the Body of Christ, am to be the smile that Jesus gives to the world today.

Jesus, you said that you wanted your joy in me and my joy to be complete (see Jn 15:11). I give myself to you so that your joy may radiate through me today.

DAILY WORD: I share my joys with you, Lord.

EVENING REVIEW: What joys did I experience and offer to-day?

May 27: St. Augustine of Canterbury (d. 604)

Augustine was a Benedictine monk in Rome whom Pope St. Gregory the Great sent along with thirty fellow monks to bring the Gospel to England. Waiting for a ship to take them across the English Channel, they heard stories of the fierce Anglo-Saxon people who lived there. Frightened, they stalled. Augustine returned to Rome to confer with the pope, who assured him that God would be with them. Thus, fear did not prevail, but God's grace and power did. The band of missionaries landed on English shores and quickly met King Ethelbert.

Augustine told him:

> Your everlasting peace, O king, and that of your kingdom, is the object we desire to promote in coming here. We bring you news of never-ending joy. Do not regard us as superstitious because we have been at pains to come from Rome to your dominions for the sake of your salvation and that of your subjects. Be assured that only a great love constrains us to do this. For we long, beyond all the desires and glory of the world, to have as many fellow citizens with us as we can in the kingdom of God.

King Ethelbert was persuaded and allowed the missionaries to preach. Within a short time, the king and thousands of his subjects were baptized.

Loving God, you create every person for heaven. You want all to know you and the love you have for them. I want what you want, and I offer myself and all I think, say, and do today for this intention—that I may be a fellow citizen with the saints and all those for whom I offer this day.

DAILY WORD: For the salvation of all souls.

EVENING REVIEW: How did my desire for the salvation of all affect the choices I made today? Where did fear hold me back?

May 28

It's common to think of piety in terms of externals: how we look when we pray or what we do. Or, as Pope Francis put it: "to close one's eyes, to pose like a picture and pretend to be a saint." But the piety that is a gift of the Holy Spirit is something much deeper.

Pope Francis said it is the Holy Spirit's gift that "touches the very heart of our Christian life and identity" because

> it indicates our belonging to God and our profound relationship with him. . . . When the Holy Spirit allows us to perceive the presence of the Lord and all his love for us, it warms the heart and moves us quite naturally to prayer and celebration. Piety, therefore, is synonymous with the genuine religious spirit, with filial trust in God, with that capacity to pray to him with the love and simplicity that belongs to those who are humble of heart. . . .
>
> It is *a relationship lived with the heart*: it is our friendship with God, granted to us by Jesus, a friendship that changes our life and fills us with passion, with joy. . . . [It] makes us gentle, makes us calm, patient, at peace with God, at the service of others with gentleness.

Lord Jesus, the Holy Spirit is the bond of love between you and the Father. At Baptism you gave me the Holy Spirit so that I would share the relationship you have with the Father, knowing that I am a beloved child of God. This knowledge frees me and fills my heart with love for the Father and for all his children, my brothers and sisters. May the gift of piety grow in me with each day I offer you.

DAILY WORD: Come, Spirit of Piety!

EVENING REVIEW: In what ways did I experience the gift of piety today?

May 29

At the Last Supper, Jesus promised to send the Paraclete, a legal term that means defense attorney or advocate. It includes the sense of comforter, consoler, counselor, spokesperson, mediator, and intercessor. Thus, one of the gifts of the Paraclete is counsel.

Pope Francis said: "We know how important it is in the most delicate moments to be able to count on the advice of people who are wise and who love us. Now, through the gift of counsel, it is God himself, through his Spirit, who enlightens our heart so as to make us understand the right way to speak and to behave and the way to follow."

This gift "begins to make us sensitive to his voice and to guide our thoughts, our feelings and our intentions according to the heart of God. . . . Counsel, then, is the gift through which the Holy Spirit enables our conscience to make a concrete choice in communion with God, according to the logic of Jesus and his Gospel."

"The essential condition for preserving this gift", according to Pope Francis, "is prayer" through which "we make space so that the Spirit may come and help us in that moment, that he may counsel us on what we all must do."

Holy Spirit, I live in a world of darkness, a world with many lights that are contrary to the light of the Gospel. I need my conscience to be formed through your teachings that come to me through Scripture and Tradition. I also need you to counsel me each day in the choices and decisions I face. I surrender myself to you so that you may guide me today.

DAILY WORD: Paraclete, give me counsel!

EVENING REVIEW: In what ways did I pray and open myself to the Spirit's guidance in the decisions I made?

May 30

The gifts of the Holy Spirit are specific ways in which the Spirit, given to us at Baptism, helps us on our journey through life. Fortitude is the gift that empowers us to act on the wisdom, knowledge, and counsel that are given, even in the face of opposition and the threat of death.

According to Pope Francis, fortitude "liberates" our heart and "frees it from sluggishness, from uncertainty, and from all the fears that can hinder it. . . . The gift of fortitude is a true help, it gives us strength." We often think of the martyrs, those who gave the ultimate witness to the faith by suffering and dying rather than giving up. But this is a gift that every Christian needs.

Pope Francis said:

> This gift must constitute the tenor of our Christian life, in the ordinary daily routine. As I said, we need to be strong every day of our lives, to carry forward our life, our family, our faith. The Apostle Paul said something that will benefit us to hear: "I can do all things in him who strengthens me" (Phil 4:13). When we face daily life, when difficulties arise, let us remember this.

Jesus, knowing how weak I am, I humbly come before you. I have many fears: rejection, suffering, and death. You faced those in your life on earth, and you had the strength not to give in to fear. You were so anxious you sweat blood in the Garden of Gethsemane, but, convinced of the Father's love for you, you surrendered yourself completely to his will. Give me the Spirit with the gift of fortitude today, so that I may overcome all that causes me fear.

DAILY WORD: "I can do all things in him who strengthens me."

EVENING REVIEW: How did I exercise fortitude?

May 31: Feast of the Visitation of Mary

On this last day of May, Mary's month, we celebrate an event in her life and at the beginning of the earthly life of her Son. According to the first chapter of Luke's Gospel, at the Annunciation, Mary told the Archangel Gabriel, "let it be done to me according to your word", and in that acceptance of God's will, she conceived the Son of God in her womb. The next thing she did was to think of her elderly kinswoman Elizabeth's need. She journeyed many miles south from Nazareth to Ein Karem, near Jerusalem. "When Elizabeth heard Mary's greeting, the infant leaped in her womb, and Elizabeth, filled with the holy Spirit, cried out in a loud voice and said, 'Most blessed are you among women, and blessed is the fruit of your womb.'" Elizabeth and her baby John, under the influence of the Spirit, recognized the presence of the Son of God in Mary's womb.

Pope St. John Paul II wrote: "When, at the Visitation, she bore in her womb the Word made flesh, she became in some way a 'tabernacle'—the first 'tabernacle' in history—in which the Son of God, still invisible to our human gaze, allowed himself to be adored by Elizabeth, radiating his light as it were through the eyes and the voice of Mary."

Lord Jesus, you were conceived and developed for nine months within Mary's womb. You come to me in the Eucharist and unite yourself to me. Remain with me always. As you are really present in the Eucharist, so you are truly present in me. Help me to live the Sacrament I receive by truly being your eyes, voice, hands—your Body—today.

DAILY WORD: Christ be within me.

EVENING REVIEW: How did I radiate Christ's light through my eyes and voice today?

JUNE

June 1: St. Justin (d. 165)

Justin was a pagan philosopher who, after Baptism, spent his life explaining the faith to non-Christians. He gave his life for the faith that he explained so well. In his writings we find the first postbiblical reference to the Heart of Jesus: "We Christians are the true Israel which springs from Christ, for we are drawn out of his heart as out of a rock." As Moses struck a rock in the desert to give water to save the people (Ex 17:1–6), so Jesus is the rock from whose Heart came blood and water, the source of salvation and the origin of the Church.

St. Justin wrote this about the Eucharist:

> The apostles, in their recollections, which are called Gospels, handed down to us what Jesus commanded them to do. They tell us that he took bread, gave thanks, and said: "Do this in memory of me. This is my Body." In the same way he took the cup, he gave thanks, and said: "This is my Blood." We do not consume the Eucharistic bread and wine as if it were ordinary food and drink, for we have been taught that as Jesus Christ our Savior became a man of flesh and blood by the power of the Word of God, so also the food that our flesh and blood assimilates for its nourishment becomes the flesh and blood of the incarnate Jesus by the power of his own words contained in the prayer of thanksgiving.

Lord Jesus, at every Mass, I believe you change bread and wine into your Body and Blood. In Holy Communion, you change me. Help me to live this change today by offering myself to the Father with you for the salvation of all.

DAILY WORD: Christ, live through me.

EVENING REVIEW: How did I consciously live as part of the Body of Christ today?

June 2: Sts. Marcellinus and Peter (d. 303)

Marcellinus, a priest, and Peter, an exorcist, were arrested in the last major persecution before Christianity was legalized. They were such powerful witnesses to the faith that they converted a number of fellow prisoners and their jailer and his family. Because of their popularity among the people of Rome, they were secretly taken from prison and beheaded in a nearby forest after being forced to dig their graves. Their executioner, who became a Christian, revealed the site of the grave, and the community brought their relics back for proper burial. As a boy, Pope St. Damasus (d. 384, see December 11) heard this story from the executioner's own lips. The Emperor Constantine built a church over their tomb and buried his mother, St. Helen, there.

Where did the martyrs get the courage to suffer and die for the faith? The word "courage" comes from the Latin word "cor" or "heart". When people are afraid, we tell them, "Take heart!" The martyrs "took heart." They lived with the new heart God promised through the prophet Ezekiel (11:19; 36:26). This new heart was the Heart of Jesus, which transformed their hearts, giving them the courage to give everything away, even their lives, for love of God and neighbor. I receive the new heart that God promised every time I receive the Eucharist—the Body and Blood, soul and divinity, of Jesus Christ, including his Sacred Heart.

Lord Jesus, out of love for me and for all people, you gave all of yourself. You continue to offer your Heart to me in the Eucharist. I offer my heart to you.

DAILY WORD: Eucharistic Heart of Jesus, transform me.

EVENING REVIEW: How did I live with a new heart today? How did the Heart of Jesus give me courage?

June 3: St. Charles Lwanga and Companions (d. 1886–87)

We honor twenty-two young African men who sacrificed their lives rather than give in to the immoral demands of the local king. One of them, Kizito, was only thirteen. Another, Matthew Malumba, had been a Muslim who became a Christian. Charles Lwanga and Joseph Mkasa were in charge of the young pages who served in the king's court. Joseph was beheaded, and Charles was roasted alive.

Living the new life of a Christian has never been easy. Each day we are faced with decisions that are either consistent or inconsistent with the life to which Jesus calls us. In 1993, Pope St. John Paul II went to the Ugandan Martyrs' shrine and said:

> They understood that "'faith is strengthened when it is given to others.'". . . Deepen your knowledge of the Church's faith, so that you can share its treasure ever more fully with others. . . . The effects of Christ's light must clearly be seen in the goodness of your lives! You must be examples of a faith that is rooted in a personal relationship to Jesus, lived in full communion with the Church. Your faith must be clearly seen in your obedience to the Gospel, in your lives of charity and service, and in your missionary zeal towards those who still do not believe or who no longer live the faith they received at Baptism. Take to heart St. Paul's lesson: be examples of patience and charity towards all people, mindful that if you have not love, then you are nothing at all.

Jesus, you told your followers to die to themselves and to live for you. I do this by offering myself so that God's will may be done in me. Make my offering perfect.

DAILY WORD: I treasure my faith.

June 4

The month of June, when the Solemnity of the Sacred Heart is usually celebrated, is dedicated to this mystery. Much more than a physical organ, the heart represents the deepest interior of a person, and it symbolizes love. Jesus experienced all the movements of a human heart, but, because he is divine as well as human, he experienced them with divine intensity.

As the physical heart gives life to the body, pumping blood to every corner, so the Heart of Jesus gives life to his Body, the Church. His physical heart was pierced on the Cross, and blood and water, symbolizing the Eucharist and Baptism, gushed forth. The eternal life that only the sacraments can give comes straight from the Heart of Jesus.

I am a cell within the Body of Christ, and I will only be spiritually alive and healthy insofar as I am one with Jesus. At the Last Supper, Jesus used the image of a vine and branches. A branch is dead unless the sap of the vine flows through it. So I am dead unless the Heart of Jesus pumps life into me. The Heart of Jesus is alive and beating with love for me. This Heart is contained in the Eucharist, from which I receive a continual flow of divine life.

Heart of Jesus, I want to live in union with you, for you said that apart from you I can do nothing. I need you as much as my body needs my heart. I give myself to you so that your Heart may beat within me, keeping me spiritually healthy. United to you, I shall live even after my own heart stops.

DAILY WORD: Heart of Jesus, give me life.

EVENING REVIEW: How did the love of Jesus' Heart touch me today?

June 5: St. Boniface (673?–754)

Many people look forward to their retirement, when they don't have to work and can take it easy. But there is one thing that we can never retire from—the practice of our faith. Serving God doesn't include a retirement plan, and we won't rest until we pass from this life and our relatives and friends pray for our eternal rest. Today's saint is an example of this.

Boniface was an English Benedictine who, as a missionary bishop, became known as the Apostle of Germany. At the age of eighty, he was still going strong, and, as he was preparing to administer the Sacrament of Confirmation, he was killed by a group of pagans who opposed Christianity.

In a letter, he wrote:

> In her voyage across the ocean of the world, the Church is like a great ship being pounded by the waves of life's different stresses. Our duty is not to abandon ship but to keep her on her course. Since this is the case, let us turn to the words of Solomon: 'Trust in the Lord with all your heart and do not rely on your own prudence. Think on him in all your ways, and he will guide your steps.' What we ourselves cannot bear let us bear with the help of Christ. For he is all-powerful, and he tells us: "My yoke is easy and my burden is light."

Lord Jesus, I am often tired as the burdens of life weigh me down. I bring them and offer them to you today. With you by my side, I can carry the burdens and face the trials that will come my way this day.

DAILY WORD: Sacred Heart of Jesus, I trust in you!

EVENING REVIEW: In what ways did Christ help me deal with the troubles of this day?

June 6: St. Norbert (1080–1134)

For his first thirty-five years, Norbert lived a carefree and worldly life, thinking only of himself. Then one day, as he was riding, a storm came up, lightning struck, and his horse reared up. He was thrown to the ground where he lay unconscious. When he came to, he prayed in gratitude that he was still alive, and then, perhaps feeling that he'd been given a second lease on life, he asked God: "What do you want me to do?" He sensed the answer within him: "Turn away from evil and do good. Seek peace and pursue it." Thus began the conversion that led him to become the founder of a religious order (the Premonstratensions, or Norbertines), a bishop, and a reformer in the Church.

Norbert had a deep love for the Eucharist. He said: "Reverence around the altar demonstrates the liveliness of one's faith and the fervor of one's love." At the time, the Blessed Sacrament was reserved in a room outside the main body of the church so that Holy Communion could be brought to the sick and dying. According to tradition, Norbert brought the tabernacle into the main body of the church in one of his monasteries so that our Lord could be worshipped throughout the day.

Lord Jesus, I believe that you are truly present in the Blessed Sacrament. I cannot receive you now, but I pray that you come to me spiritually. As I pause to offer myself to you this day, I ask the same question Norbert asked of you—"What do you want me to do?" May I turn from evil, do good, and seek peace, so that this day may be an offering pleasing to you.

DAILY WORD: I will do what you want.

EVENING REVIEW: What made my day pleasing to God?

June 7

On this day in 1925, an alcoholic by the name of Matt Talbot died at the age of sixty-nine. He had not taken a drink in forty-one years, not because he relied on willpower, but because he relied on God's power to keep him sober one day at a time.

Matt lived in Ireland, where he began working at the age of twelve in a wine-bottling shop. It didn't take long before he had his first of many drinks. When he was twenty-eight, he'd had enough. He was sick and tired of being sick and tired. He went to confession and promised the priest that he would not drink for three months, though he didn't know how he could ever fulfill his pledge. With much prayer and God's help, he did and pledged another three months until one day he pledged that he would not take a drink for the rest of his life.

Matt didn't have the benefit of Alcoholics Anonymous. Their first three of the twelve steps to recovery involve surrendering oneself to God. Whether or not I battle addictions, I need to admit that I am not in control of my life. I must admit that I am not God and that God is God of my life. The following is the Third Step Prayer from AA:

God, I offer myself to Thee—To build with me and to do with me as Thou wilt. Relieve me of the bondage of self, that I may better do Thy will. Take away my difficulties, that victory over them may bear witness to those I would help of Thy Power, Thy Love, and Thy Way of life. May I do Thy will always!

DAILY WORD: I surrender to your care.

EVENING REVIEW: How did I try to be in control today?

In 1673, Jesus appeared to a Visitation nun, St. Margaret Mary Alacoque. As she spent time in Eucharistic adoration, she sensed Jesus holding her to his chest just as he held, at the Last Supper, the apostle John to his chest. She wrote that Jesus "revealed the wonders of his love and the mysterious secrets of his Sacred Heart."

Then, he told her: "My divine Heart is so passionately fond of the human race, and of you in particular, that it cannot keep back the pent-up flames of its burning charity any longer. They must burst out through you and reveal my Heart to the world, so as to enrich mankind with my precious treasures." She continues: "Next, he asked for my heart. I begged him to take it; he did, and placed it in his own divine Heart. He let me see it there—a tiny atom being completely burned up in that fiery furnace. Then, lifting it out—now a little heart-shaped flame—he put it back where he had found it."

This profound and mystical experience inspires me. Jesus wants me also to give my heart to him so that, enflamed with his burning love, I, too, will reveal to everyone I meet today the "precious treasures" of the love of God revealed in the Heart of the Son of God.

Jesus, I give you today the deepest center of my being—my heart. Fill it with your love. Enflame it with the love that burns in your Heart and that wants every person to know how much you love them. May each person I meet today know your love a little more through me.

DAILY WORD: Make my heart like yours.

EVENING REVIEW: How did God's love, like a flame, warm the hearts of those I met?

June 9: St. Ephrem (306–373)

Ephrem was a musician, composer, and deacon who lived in Syria. At the time, many heretical groups, knowing how lyrics of catchy songs stay with the listener, used music to spread their teachings. Ephrem countered with songs of his own, earning him the title "Harp of the Holy Spirit". Pope Benedict XV named him a Doctor of the Church in 1920. The following passage of his speaks of the importance of not just saying prayers but living with a prayerful spirit:

> It is good, then, to pray always and not to lose heart, as the Lord says, and again the Apostle [Paul] says, "Pray without ceasing", that is, by night and by day and at every hour, and not only when coming into the church. But whether you are working, lying down to sleep, travelling, eating, drinking, sitting at table, do not interrupt your prayer, for you do not know when he who demands your soul is coming. Don't wait for Sunday or a feast day, or a different place, but, as the Prophet David says, "in every place of his dominion". Whether you are in church, in your house, or in the country; whether you are guarding sheep, constructing buildings, or present at parties, do not stop praying. Prayer is conversation with God, equal honor with the angels, progress in good things, averting of evils. See what strength prayer has. There is no possession more precious than prayer in the whole of human life. Never be parted from it; never abandon it.

Holy Spirit, I am your temple. I belong to you. You are as close to me as my breath. With each breath I take today, fill me with your inspiration and love.

DAILY WORD: Every moment, a prayer.

EVENING REVIEW: How was I conscious of the Holy Spirit?

During one of Jesus' appearances to St. Margaret Mary while she prayed in front of the Blessed Sacrament, he was, in her words, "a blaze of glory". His wounds were like suns, and flames shot forth from his body, "especially from his divine breast, which was like a furnace and which he opened to disclose his utterly affectionate and lovable heart, the living source of all those flames".

She continues the account of this apparition: "It was at this moment that he revealed to me the indescribable wonders of his pure love for mankind: the extravagance to which he'd been led for those who had nothing for him but ingratitude and indifference. He said: 'Do me the kindness, then—you, at least—of making up for all their ingratitude, as far as you can.'"

One way that she was asked to do this was to promote a feast in honor of the Sacred Heart of Jesus. It was a way in which people, moved by the knowledge of God's love revealed in the Pierced Heart of Jesus, would return love for love, their love for God's love.

This is not something I do just once a year. It's something I ought to do every day and at every moment. That's the meaning of the daily offering that I renew now.

Jesus, yours is the greatest love the world has ever known. You love me as though I were the only person in the world, and you died for me. You love me so much that you would rather die than ever to live without me. I accept your love and now return love for love by offering you every moment of my day as an act of love.

DAILY WORD: I return love for love.

EVENING REVIEW: How did I show my love for Jesus?

June 11: St. Barnabas (1st Century)

In the early Christian community of Jerusalem was a man named Joseph. He "sold a piece of property that he owned, then brought the money and put it at the feet of the apostles", who named him "Barnabas", which means "Son of encouragement" (Acts 4:36–37). Barnabas helped the former persecutor Saul, known as Paul, to be accepted by the community (Acts 9:26–27). Barnabas was sent to Antioch to confirm the work of the Holy Spirit there, and he spent a year teaching with Paul (Acts 11:19–26). In Antioch, Paul and Barnabas were called to go forth as missionaries (Acts 13:1–3).

But not everything went smoothly. One of the other missionaries, John Mark, a cousin of Barnabas, left the ministry and returned to Jerusalem (Acts 13:13). Later, when Paul began a second mission trip, Barnabas wanted to take John Mark along. Paul refused, and "there arose a sharp contention, so that they separated from each other" (Acts 15:36–41).

Not everything in the early Church was as peaceful and idyllic as we often think. Reflecting on Barnabas, Pope Benedict XVI said:

> Hence there are also disputes, disagreements, and controversies among saints. And I find this very comforting, because we see that the saints have not 'fallen from Heaven'. They are people like us, who also have complicated problems. Holiness does not consist in never having erred or sinned. Holiness increases the capacity for conversion, for repentance, for willingness to start again and, especially, for reconciliation and forgiveness.

Lord Jesus, throughout history you call sinners to follow you. That means not everything will run smoothly in your Church. I offer myself to you with my weaknesses. Help me to be a sign of encouragement for others.

DAILY WORD: As you encourage me, so I encourage others.

EVENING REVIEW: How did I encourage people?

June 12

Traditional images of the Sacred Heart of Jesus show his Heart on the outside of his body. This may seem odd, but it's a way that he says to us: "My Heart goes out to you. My Heart always goes out to you. My Heart is there for you."

In the Gospel of Matthew, there are three places where the Heart of Jesus is "moved" to go out to suffering people. First, as Jesus travels, proclaiming the good news and healing people, "when he saw the crowds, he had compassion for them, because they were harassed and helpless, like sheep without a shepherd" (9:36). Another time, "as he went ashore [from a boat] he saw a great throng; and he had compassion on them, and healed their sick" (14:14). Lastly, before a miracle in which he fed four thousand, Jesus told his disciples: "I have compassion on the crowd, because they have been with me now three days, and have nothing to eat" (15:32).

The Heart of Jesus is compassionate, which comes from the Latin *cum* and *passio*—to suffer with. Jesus sees suffering and shares in it. He wants me to have a heart that is moved as his Heart is. What moves my heart with pity for others?

Jesus, your merciful and compassionate Heart saw the pain of mankind and each individual and was moved to give yourself completely to us. You shared our suffering and even our death. As I offer myself to you today, help me to see others as you see them and to be moved by their sufferings as your Heart is moved.

DAILY WORD: May the love of Jesus move me.

EVENING REVIEW: How was my heart moved with pity today?

June 13: St. Anthony of Padua (1195–1231)

One of the most popular saints in the calendar is the Franciscan St. Anthony. Most people know him as the patron saint of lost articles, and various prayers have resulted:

"St. Anthony, St. Anthony, please come down, something's lost and can't be found."

"Something's lost and can't be found, please, St. Anthony, look around."

Such prayers may seem childish, but Jesus said that unless we become like little children, we will not enter the Kingdom of Heaven. Asking Anthony to help us when something is lost is a way that we show our dependence on God, who is happy to show his glory through the intercession of the saints. But how did Anthony become the saint of the lost?

There were no printing presses in his time, and so manuscripts were especially valuable. One day, the story goes, a younger member of his community ran off with part of the Bible in order to sell it. Anthony prayed for its safe return, and soon the thief returned, telling Anthony that as he was on his way, he saw a terrible vision that so frightened him that he decided he had better return the stolen manuscript.

Through Baptism, I too am a member of the Communion of Saints. I have a role to play in helping others. It may be small, like helping someone find a lost article, or it may be big, like helping people who have lost their way in life to return to God.

Loving God, I offer myself to you. Use me, as you use St. Anthony, to help others, especially those who are lost. And if I lose my way today through sin, help me to get back on track quickly.

DAILY WORD: I once was lost, but now am found.

EVENING REVIEW: How did I lose or find my way today?

June 14

On June 14, 1777, in the middle of thirteen British colonies' war for independence, a flag with thirteen alternating white and red stripes and a blue field in the top left corner with thirteen stars, was adopted by the Second Continental Congress as the official flag of the United States.

A flag represents a nation and its people. It should be treated respectfully. The citizens of a country have a moral obligation to love their country. The *Catechism of the Catholic Church* states: "It is the *duty of citizens* to contribute along with the civil authorities to the good of society in a spirit of truth, justice, solidarity, and freedom. The love and service of *one's country* follow from the duty of gratitude and belong to the order of charity" (no. 2239).

What does the U.S. flag mean? It clearly represents unity—that from thirteen colonies came thirteen states in one nation. "*E pluribus unum*"—"Out of many, one"—is the motto that appears on the Seal of the United States. This, too, is the Church about which St. Paul wrote: "Just as the body is one and has many members, and all the members of the body, though many, are one body, so it is with Christ" (1 Cor 12:12).

As a citizen of both an earthly nation and a heavenly kingdom (see Phil 3:20), I am called to promote harmony and unity in a nation and world divided by sin.

Loving God, the Sacred Heart has been called the emblem or sign of your love. Your Son told St. Margaret Mary to carry a picture of this sign over her heart. As I offer myself to you today, configure my heart to your Son's.

DAILY WORD: One Heart for me and for all.

EVENING REVIEW: How did I fulfill my duties as a citizen?

On May 15, 2006, Pope Benedict XVI wrote a letter for the fiftieth anniversary of an encyclical letter that Pope Pius XII wrote about the Sacred Heart—*Haurietis Aquas*. He said that after fifty years, "it is still a fitting task for Christians to continue to deepen their relationship with the Heart of Jesus, in such a way as to revive their faith in the saving love of God and to welcome him ever better into their lives." In this way, he continued, "we will be able to understand better what it means *to know* God's love in Jesus Christ, *to experience* him, keeping our gaze fixed on him to the point that we *live* entirely on the experience of his love, so that we can subsequently *witness* to it to others."

He concluded by saying that this devotion "has an irreplaceable importance for our faith and for our life in love". He added that it "cannot be considered a transitory form of worship or devotion" but "remains indispensable for a living relationship with God."

Lord Jesus, as I renew the offering of myself to you, striving to return love for the love with which you have loved me, I ask you to revive my faith in your saving love. Help me to be "sure that neither death, nor life, nor angels, nor principalities, nor things present, nor things to come, nor powers, nor height, nor depth, nor anything else in creation, will be able to separate" (Rom 8:38–39) me from the love God revealed in your Heart. Help me today to keep my gaze fixed on you so that I live entirely on the experience of your love and show it to others.

DAILY WORD: I keep your Heart before me always.

EVENING REVIEW: How did the knowledge of God's love help me today?

Pope Francis described the Solemnity of the Sacred Heart of Jesus as "the feast of love". He said:

> Jesus wanted to show us his heart as the heart that loved so deeply. This is why we have this commemoration today, especially of God's love. God loved us, he loved us with such great love. I am thinking of what St. Ignatius [Loyola] told us. . . . He pointed out two criteria on love. The first: love is expressed more clearly in actions than in words. The second: there is greater love in giving than in receiving. These two criteria are like the pillars of true love: deeds, and the gift of self.

Since Jesus is so devoted to me, not only telling me in the Gospels of his love but showing it in the great deed of his death on the Cross and Resurrection, offering himself for my salvation and then making a gift of himself to me in the Eucharist—how can I not want to return his love in deeds and the gift of myself?

Lord Jesus, I know that love is not ultimately a feeling and not simply a matter of words. Action. Love, as it's been said, is a verb. Feelings come and go. I can say one thing but then do another, so words are not a reliable sign of love. Deeds. I want to show you my love today in all that I do. Take my thoughts and feelings today, and, where they are not worthy of you, transform them so that only deeds of love will flow from me. Love for you that is shown by my love for my neighbor and even my enemies.

DAILY WORD: Love in deeds today.

EVENING REVIEW: How did my actions show or not show my love for Jesus?

Speaking to the crowd gathered in St. Peter's Square to pray the Angelus on June 9, 2013, Pope Francis said: "The month of June is traditionally dedicated to the Sacred Heart of Jesus, the greatest human expression of divine love. Popular piety highly values symbols, and the Heart of Jesus is the ultimate symbol of God's mercy. But it is not an imaginary symbol; it is a real symbol which represents the center, the source from which salvation flowed for all of humanity."

He mentioned Gospel references to the Heart of Jesus, beginning with "Come to me, all who labor and are heavy laden, and I will give you rest. Take my yoke upon you, and learn from me; for I am gentle and lowly in heart" (Mt 11:28–29). Then he told how a soldier pierced Jesus' Heart after he died on the Cross (Jn 19:33–34), adding, "from the Heart of Jesus, the Lamb sacrificed on the Cross, flow forgiveness and life for all people."

Finally, he said: "The mercy of Jesus is not only an emotion; it is a force which gives life! . . . Today let us not forget the love of God, the love of Jesus: he watches us, he loves us, he waits for us. He is all heart and all mercy." When we see people who show great love, we say, they are "all heart." This is most true for Jesus.

Jesus, you are all heart, so much so that you allowed your Heart to be pierced, and from it flowed blood and water. Water for Baptism and blood for the Eucharist—the total gift of yourself to me. In response, I give myself to you.

DAILY WORD: May I be all heart.

EVENING REVIEW: In what ways did I put my whole heart into what I did for God?

In a message he wrote for Lent in 2015, Pope Francis contrasted the Heart of Jesus with the sin-hardened heart of the world that is indifferent to others' suffering. He wrote: "God does not ask of us anything that he himself has not first given us. . . . He is not aloof from us. Each one of us has a place in his heart. . . . He is interested in each of us; his love does not allow him to be indifferent to what happens to us. Usually, when we are healthy and comfortable, we forget about others. . . . Our heart grows cold."

We need the fire of love in the Heart of Jesus to warm, purify, and transform our hearts. Pope Francis invited us to engage "in what Benedict XVI called a formation of the heart. . . . A merciful heart does not mean a weak heart. Anyone who wishes to be merciful must have a strong and steadfast heart, closed to the tempter but open to God. A heart which lets itself be pierced by the Spirit so as to bring love along the roads that lead to our brothers and sisters."

He concluded with a prayer from the Litany of the Sacred Heart of Jesus: "let us all ask the Lord: . . . 'Make our hearts like yours'. . . . In this way we will receive a heart which is firm and merciful, attentive and generous, a heart which is not closed, indifferent or prey to the globalization of indifference."

Jesus, as I offer my heart to you, I ask: Make my heart like yours. Then I will see others as you see them—people so important to you, so beloved by you, that you were willing to die for them.

DAILY WORD: Make my heart like yours.

EVENING REVIEW: How was my heart "firm and merciful, attentive and generous today"?

June 19: St. Romuald (951–1027)

Romuald lived a very worldly life until one day he saw his father kill another man in a duel over some property. He was so shaken that he fled to a Benedictine monastery to pray and do penance for his father. For three years, his example so aroused the jealousy and anger of the other monks, who were more laid back, that the abbot gave Romuald permission to leave and place himself under the direction of a saintly hermit. In time he went around Italy founding monasteries of a stricter observance of the Rule of St. Benedict, the most famous one being at Camaldoli, from which his reformed group of Benedictines takes its name.

On the 1000th anniversary of their founding, Pope Benedict XVI addressed the Camaldolese monks. Quoting a verse from the Letter to the Colossians—"whatever you do, in word or deed, do everything in the name of the Lord Jesus" (3:17), he said that "the Apostle [Paul] exhorts his listeners to live according to the high measure of Christian life that is holiness."

How is this possible? Pope Benedict answers:

> At the root of everything is the grace of God. . . . But this grace demands a response from those who have been baptized: it requires the commitment to be reclothed in Christ's sentiments: tenderness, goodness, humility, meekness, magnanimity, mutual forgiveness, and above all, as a synthesis and a crown, . . . the love that God has given us through Jesus, the love that the Holy Spirit has poured into our hearts.

Father, at my Baptism, I was clothed in Christ. Refresh my clothing so that I may live this day with the sentiments, the movements of Jesus' Heart.

DAILY WORD: I put on Christ.

EVENING REVIEW: How did I exhibit the sentiments of Christ?

June 20

On June 1, 2008, Pope Benedict XVI said: "I am pleased to recall that this month is traditionally dedicated to the Heart of Christ, symbol of the Christian faith, particularly dear to the people, to mystics and theologians because it expresses in a simple and authentic way the 'good news' of love."
He continued:

> Every person needs a "centre" for his own life, a source of truth and goodness to draw from in the daily events, in the different situations and in the toil of daily life. Every one of us, when he/she pauses in silence, needs to feel not only his/her own heartbeat, but deeper still, the beating of a trustworthy presence, perceptible with faith's senses and yet much more real: the presence of Christ, the heart of the world.

The love of Jesus keeps me, keeps the entire world, in existence. As I pause and quiet myself, I try to sense Jesus' Heart beating with love. With this awareness, I offer myself, returning love for love.

Pope Benedict said that one of the ways we express our devotion to the Sacred Heart is through the elements that form the program of the Pope's Worldwide Prayer Network (Apostleship of Prayer): "I invite each one of you to renew in the month of June his/her own devotion to the Heart of Christ, also using the traditional prayer of the daily offering and keeping present the intentions I have proposed for the whole Church."

O Jesus, through the Immaculate Heart of Mary, I offer you all my prayers, works, joys, and sufferings of this day in union with the Holy Sacrifice of the Mass throughout the world. In particular I offer them for the pope's monthly intention.

DAILY WORD: Heart of Jesus, I give myself to you.

EVENING REVIEW: What prayers, works, joys, and sufferings were in this day?

June 21: St. Aloysius Gonzaga (1568–1591)

The father of Aloysius had big plans for his oldest son. To prepare him to be the heir in the powerful house of Gonzaga, he was sent to a royal court in Spain. There, Aloysius was drawn to spiritual things more than material, and as a teenager he asked his father's permission to renounce his inheritance in order to serve Christ the King rather than an earthly king. At first his father opposed him but eventually relented, allowing him to enter the Jesuits when he was seventeen. He shared his dreams of being a missionary and martyr with his spiritual director, St. Robert Bellarmine. When a plague broke out in Rome, he traversed the city looking for the sick and carrying them to hospitals where he bathed them and prepared them for death. He contracted the disease and died before fulfilling his dreams, but he attained the best dream—becoming a saint in a short time.

Aloysius had a deep devotion to the Blessed Virgin Mary, which is an integral part of devotion to the Heart of Christ. The heart that most resembles Jesus' Heart is the Immaculate Heart of Mary. I offer myself now to Jesus through Mary as I pray in the words of St. Aloysius:

Holy Mary, my Queen, I commend myself to your blessed protection and special keeping, and to the bosom of your mercy, this day and every day of my life and the hour of my death. I entrust to you all my hopes and consolations, all my trials and miseries, my life and the end of my life, that through your most holy intercession and your merits, all my actions may be ordered and directed according to your will and that of your Son.

DAILY WORD: To Jesus, through Mary.

EVENING REVIEW: In what ways was Mary part of my offering?

June 22: Sts. Thomas More and John Fisher (d. 1535)

Bishop John Fisher and Sir Thomas More—lawyer, husband, father, and Lord Chancellor of England—were imprisoned and then executed for refusing to recognize King Henry VIII as the Supreme Head of the Church in England. Thomas More is the patron saint of lawyers, statesmen, and politicians.

In his book *Render unto Caesar*, Archbishop Charles Chaput wrote:

> More's humanity is what draws us. He is not a plastic saint. He urgently wanted to live; but not at the cost of selling his soul. . . . More became the saint God wanted not by dramatic words or gestures. He did it by the simple daily habit of examining his actions in the light of his faith. He fed his conscience with prayer. He submitted himself to the routine of seeking and choosing what his Catholic formation knew to be right. This same path to God is open to anyone who sincerely seeks it.

The following is a prayer of St. Thomas More used daily by Pope Francis:

Grant me, O Lord, good digestion, and also something to digest. Grant me a healthy body, and the necessary good humor to maintain it. Grant me a simple soul that knows to treasure all that is good and that doesn't frighten easily at the sight of evil, but rather finds the means to put things back in their place. Give me a soul that knows not boredom, grumblings, sighs and laments, nor excess of stress, because of that obstructing thing called "I." Grant me, O Lord, a sense of good humor. Allow me the grace to be able to take a joke, to discover in life a bit of joy, and to be able to share it with others.

DAILY WORD: Give me good humor, Lord.

EVENING REVIEW: How did I live St. Thomas More's prayer today?

June 23

Another saint who was included in yesterday's calendar is Paulinus of Nola (353–431). He was born in France to a wealthy, aristocratic family and spent his youth traveling and serving various local governments. After marriage and the death of a child, he and his wife became Christians and gave their wealth to the poor. In time Paulinus became bishop of Nola, a village near Naples, Italy.

Paulinus wrote many letters and poems. The following excerpt is from one that he wrote to parents who had just lost a child:

> It is right for us to strengthen our spirits, raise our minds, and thrust cowardly fears from our hearts. For, as you see, the Son of God laid down his life for us and took it up again, while remaining God in every way. God victoriously celebrated a victory over our death and conveyed our human body with him to the stars. He considered it insufficient to have drained the entire cup of mortal life for us, removing our wounds by means of his own. He also rose again with the body in which he fell, so that the troubled anxiety of a hesitant mind should not keep me in uncertainty.

God of life, I believe that my life on earth is not the only life for which you created me. You promise me the fullness of life in heaven. I believe that in surrendering my life to you one day at a time and at the hour of my death, you will receive it and give back to me the eternal life that Jesus won for me through his death and Resurrection. Keep this faith of mine strong today and always.

DAILY WORD: I believe in eternal life

EVENING REVIEW: How did my faith in the resurrection help me to offer myself?

June 24: Birth of St. John the Baptist

Today is a birthday celebration, one of only three in the liturgical calendar. We celebrate the birth of our Savior and his Mother and today, his cousin John. Mary was conceived without original sin, and John, according to tradition, was freed of it when his mother, Elizabeth, "filled with the Holy Spirit," greeted Mary at the Visitation and he "leaped for joy" in her womb (Lk 1:39–44).

Sanctified in the womb, John is a great example of humility. Crowds flocked to see him, hear him, and be baptized in a purification ritual. He could have had a great following for himself. Instead, he pointed to Jesus and told people to follow him because he was the Lamb of God. He said: "You yourselves bear me witness, that I said, I am not the Christ, but I have been sent before him. He who has the bride is the bridegroom; the friend of the bridegroom, who stands and hears him, rejoices greatly at the bridegroom's voice; therefore this joy of mine is now full. He must increase, but I must decrease" (Jn 3:28–30).

Humble people seek not their own glory but the glory of others. Like John the Baptist, my joy is not in shining but in helping others to shine, in drawing attention to others.

Jesus is the bridegroom of the Church and of each member of the Church. I am made for union with God. That's the goal of my life and the reason I offer myself and my day to him.

Jesus, I want to point to you in all I do. I want you to have all the glory. I follow John's example and offer myself to you and your plan.

DAILY WORD: "He must increase; I must decrease."

EVENING REVIEW: How did I point to Jesus? How did I let others shine?

June 25

Consecration means setting something apart as sacred or dedicating something for a sacred purpose. Each of us was consecrated at Baptism with sacred chrism. Periodically, people consecrate themselves in other ways. "Consecrated persons" deepen their baptismal consecration by pronouncing vows as members of a religious congregation. In 1899, in what he called "the greatest act of my pontificate," Pope Leo XIII consecrated the human race to the Sacred Heart. Dioceses and parishes have made a similar solemn consecration. Families and individuals can also consecrate themselves.

In such a consecration, I am saying to Jesus, "You've given me everything. You've given me my very self. By dying and rising you give me eternal life. Now I give myself back to you."

This consecration must then be lived in daily life so that it is not just a matter of pious words but a reality. As the end of this month dedicated to the Sacred Heart draws near, I offer this day and renew my baptismal consecration with a consecration prayer to the Sacred Heart of Jesus.

Lord Jesus Christ, I want to give myself to you completely. When I see your Sacred Heart, I reflect upon your love. You taught us to love God with all our hearts. I now consecrate myself to your Sacred Heart, Jesus. You are the Son of God whom I love with all my heart. I offer you my body, my soul, my mind, and my heart. Receive me, make me holy, make my heart like your Heart, and guide me in the way of perfect love today and every day of my life. Amen.

DAILY WORD: My day is consecrated to you, Jesus.

EVENING REVIEW: How did Jesus make the heart that I gave him today to be more like his Heart?

June 26

On this day in 1975, a Spanish priest named Josemaria Escrivá died. He was born in 1902 and in 1928 founded a religious association called "Opus Dei", or "The Work of God". At his canonization in 2002, Pope St. John Paul II quoted him: "The ordinary life of a Christian who has faith, when he works or rests, when he prays or sleeps, at all times, is a life in which God is always present."

One current member named Michael describes his experience this way: "I stumble out of bed, shut off the alarm, and then I kneel and say '*Serviam!*'—I will serve you, God. Then, still kneeling, I make a morning offering. The '*Serviam!*' echoes St. Michael's valiant pledge of allegiance to God, in contrast to Satan's 'I will not serve.' It reminds us that our vocation is one of service to God, to the Church, and to our fellow man."

This word—"*Serviam*"—also brings to mind the Blessed Virgin Mary, who offered herself entirely to God that his will would be done in and through her. Her "yes" contrasts with the "no" of our ancestral parents, Adam and Eve, who thought they had a better way than God's way. The following offering prayer is one that St. Josemaria learned as a child and recited every day for the rest of his life.

O my Lady, O my Mother, I offer myself entirely to you, and in proof of my filial affection I offer to you this day my eyes, my ears, my tongue, my heart, in a word, my whole self. Now that I am entirely yours, Mother of goodness, keep me and defend me as your own property and possession. Amen.

DAILY WORD: *Serviam!* I will serve you, God.

EVENING REVIEW: How did I choose to serve or not to serve God today?

June 27: St. Cyril of Alexandria (370–444)

Cyril of Alexandria in Egypt, bishop and Doctor of the Church, played an important role at the Council of Ephesus (431), which declared that because Jesus is fully human and fully divine, and because Mary gave birth to him, she can rightly be called "Mother of God".

He also emphasized how the Eucharist and the Holy Spirit make all Christians one Body. He wrote:

If, in Christ, all of us, both ourselves and he who is within us by his own flesh, are members of the same body, is it not clear that we are one, both with one another and with Christ? With regard to our unity in the Spirit, we may say, following the same line of thought, that all of us who have received one and the same Spirit, the Holy Spirit, are united intimately, both with one another and with God. Just as Christ's sacred flesh has power to make those in whom it is present into one body, so the one, indivisible Spirit of God, dwelling in all, causes all to become one in spirit.

God of Love, Holy Trinity, Father, Son, and Holy Spirit, I believe that I am made in your image. I am not an individual separated from others but part of the human family and, through Baptism, part of the Body of Christ. I belong to you. I offer myself to you. May every moment of this day strengthen the union that is ours through Baptism and the Eucharist. May all my actions foster greater unity among all the members of the Church, the Body of Christ. I ask this through the powerful intercession of Mary, Mother of God.

DAILY WORD: We are one in Christ.

EVENING REVIEW: How did I foster my union with God and with my brothers and sisters in Christ?

June 28: St. Irenaeus (d. 202/203)

Each of us has a spiritual genealogy. We could trace our faith back through history, beyond the first in our family to be baptized and through the ancestors of the one who did the baptizing. In that way our faith can be traced back to the apostles who were the first to baptize as Jesus directed them to do.

Irenaeus was a third-generation Christian. He lived in Asia Minor, where he met St. Polycarp, who was a disciple of the apostle John. In time he migrated to France, where he became the bishop of Lyons and passed the faith on to the people of that part of the world. Irenaeus was a brilliant theologian who wrote against the dangerous heresies of his time.

In his writings about the Eucharist, he reminds us that the Mass not only makes present the perfect offering of Jesus on the Cross, but also draws us into that "oblation". He wrote: "We must make an offering to God and show ourselves in everything grateful to him who made us, in the purity of our thoughts, the sincerity of our faith, and the firmness of our hope and our burning charity, as we offer him the first fruits of the creatures that are his."

God, Creator of all that exists, I am nothing without you. Thank you for the gift of life and all the ways that you have sustained me to this very moment. Thank you for the gift of eternal life that comes to me through Jesus and his perfect offering of himself for my salvation. In gratitude, I offer myself to you. I offer you this day and those to come.

DAILY WORD: I offer the fruits of my day.

EVENING REVIEW: How were my thoughts pure, my faith sincere, my hope firm, and my charity burning?

June 29: Solemnity of Sts. Peter and Paul

Today's saints are considered the founders or pillars of the Church in Rome. Peter was the leader of the apostles to whom Jesus gave a great promise, telling him after he professed his faith in Jesus as "the Christ, the Son of the living God, . . . 'you are Peter, and on this rock I will build my Church, and the gates of Hades shall not prevail against it" (Mt 16:16–18). Tradition has it that Peter left Jerusalem, went to Antioch, and finally to Rome, where he was crucified upside down.

Paul was known as Saul, a strict Pharisee and persecutor of Christians. But after Jesus appeared to him, he experienced a profound conversion and became one of the greatest missionaries of all time. He, too, ended up in Rome where he was beheaded.

On this feast, Pope Francis said:

How many forces in the course of history have tried, and still do, to destroy the Church, from without as well as within, but they themselves are destroyed and the Church remains alive and fruitful! . . . Everything passes, only God remains. Indeed, kingdoms, peoples, cultures, nations, ideologies, powers have passed, but the Church, founded on Christ, notwithstanding the many storms and our many sins, remains ever faithful to the deposit of faith shown in service; for the Church does not belong to Popes, bishops, priests, nor the lay faithful; the Church in every moment belongs solely to Christ. Only the one who lives in Christ promotes and defends the Church by holiness of life, after the example of Peter and Paul.

Lord Jesus, thank you for calling Peter and Paul to serve you. Thank you for calling me to serve you. I offer you my service today.

DAILY WORD: I am your servant.

EVENING REVIEW: How would I rate my service today?

June 30: First Martyrs of the Church of Rome

On the night of July 18 in the year 64, a terrible fire broke out in Rome. Some say that the emperor Nero ordered the fire in order to clear out parts of the city—a gruesome form of urban renewal. Nero fixed the blame on Christians. The Roman historian Tacitus wrote about their fate: "Covered with the skins of beasts, they were torn by dogs and perished, or were nailed to crosses, or were doomed to the flames and burnt, to serve as a nightly illumination, when daylight had expired."

Speaking about these martyrs, Pope Benedict XVI said: "Where does the strength to face martyrdom come from? From deep and intimate union with Christ. . . . If we read the lives of the Martyrs we are amazed at their calmness and courage in confronting suffering and death: God's power is fully expressed in weakness, in the poverty of those who entrust themselves to him and place their hope in him alone." He went on to say that most of us won't be called to martyrdom, but each of us is called to die to ourselves. "All of us, especially in our time when selfishness and individualism seem to prevail, must take on as a first and fundamental commitment the duty to grow every day in greater love for God and for our brothers and sisters, to transform our own lives and thereby transform the life of our world, too."

Jesus, I don't know where or how my life will end. I may not be a martyr, but I am called to be a witness in all I say and do. I offer this day to you. Give me the grace to be your witness.

DAILY WORD: Calmness and courage at all times.

EVENING REVIEW: How did my day give witness that I belong to Christ?

JULY

July 1: St. Junipero Serra (1713–1784)

Junipero, a Spanish Franciscan, received a doctorate in theology in 1738 and became a renowned professor of philosophy. His missionary heart led him to the Americas in 1750, and he became famous for founding the California missions, where, in Pope Francis' words, he "defended the indigenous peoples against abuses by the colonizers".

When Pope St. John Paul II visited his tomb in 1987, he said:

> Like Father Serra and his Franciscan brethren, we too are *called to be evangelizers*. . . . The way in which we fulfill that mission will be different from theirs. But their lives speak to us still because of their sure faith that the Gospel is true, and because of their passionate belief in the value of bringing that saving truth to others at great personal cost. . . . This *single-mindedness* is not reserved for great missionaries in exotic places.

He went on to speak about the special Christian witness of lay people:

> If couples cease believing in their marriage as a sacrament before God, or treat religion as anything less than a matter of salvation, then the Christian witness they might have given to the world is lost. Those who are unmarried must also be steadfast in fulfilling their duties in life if they are to bring Christ to the world in which they live. "In him who is the source of my strength I have strength for everything" (Phil 4:13). These words . . . remind us that our strength is not our own. . . . It is the strength that inspired Father Serra's motto: "always forward, never back".

Jesus, I want everyone to know your love. Give me strength today to show your love to all those I meet.

DAILY WORD: "Always forward, never back."

EVENING REVIEW: To whom did I show the love of Jesus to-day? Who showed me his love?

July 2

After the month of May, Mary's month, we have a month dedicated to the Sacred Heart of Jesus. Mary's "yes" to God led to Jesus' conception and birth. The Sacred Heart of Jesus comes to us from Mary. But we might ask, what comes to us through Jesus' Heart? The Blood that saved the world. Thus, July has traditionally been celebrated as a month dedicated to the Precious Blood of Jesus.

For the Israelites, the blood of any creature was sacred. Blood is life and belongs to God. And so, in the Law of Moses, the people could not eat any food product that contained blood in it. The first time that human blood was shed—when Cain killed his own brother Abel (see Gen 4:8–11)—the blood of Abel cried out from the earth for justice. The Blood of Jesus is different. When it was shed on the Cross and fell to the earth, it cried out, not for vengeance, but for mercy. Jesus gave his Blood, his life, so that we could be free from sin and death and have eternal life.

St. Peter wrote in his first letter: "conduct yourselves with fear. . . . You know that you were ransomed from the futile ways inherited from your fathers, not with perishable things such as silver or gold, but with the precious blood of Christ" (1:17–19). Therefore, I am precious to God!

Jesus, I believe that you suffered and died for me so that I might be freed from sin, which leads to eternal death. You rose, and your Sacred Heart beats with love for me always. In the Eucharist you offer yourself—Body and Blood—to me. I offer myself to you.

DAILY WORD: I am precious to God.

EVENING REVIEW: How did this day confirm the knowledge that I am precious to God?

July 3: St. Thomas the Apostle

Poor Thomas. For centuries his name has been synonymous with doubt. "Doubting Thomas". He questioned the Resurrection of Jesus, and ever since he's been known that way. But, after seeing Jesus and touching the wounds on his risen and glorified body, Thomas made a profound act of faith, exclaiming, "My Lord and my God!" (Jn 20:28). Thomas touched and knew Jesus was risen and alive. In this case, seeing wasn't believing but knowing. Yet Thomas did believe something more. He believed that the man in front of him was no mere man but his Lord and God.

Then Jesus told Thomas: "Blessed are those who have not seen and yet believe." Jesus blessed us and all people who, without seeing and touching Jesus as Thomas did, have placed their faith in him.

The risen body of Jesus still had the wounds of his Passion. They are there for my belief. When I look upon a crucifix or picture of Jesus crucified and touch the wounds of Jesus with my eyes, I am called to make an act of faith that this is the Son of God who died for me. I am challenged to believe he has the power to heal my doubt and wounds. Then, others can look at me and see that healing and new life are possible.

Jesus, I believe in the power of your love and your Resurrection. I believe that you are truly human and truly God and therefore have the power to heal all my wounds. I offer myself to you with my wounds—physical, emotional, and spiritual. Give me strength to carry them. Bring all of me, including my wounds, to the ultimate healing of new life in heaven.

DAILY WORD: By his wounds I am healed.

EVENING REVIEW: How did I deal with my wounds today?

July 4: St. Elizabeth of Portugal (1270–1336)[1]

As a young girl of twelve, Elizabeth was given in marriage to the King of Portugal, who was unfaithful to her. She raised the two children they had together as well as her husband's illegitimate children. When he died, she became a secular Franciscan and gave her wealth away for the care of the poor and sick. At various times, she interceded in conflicts and brought about reconciliation and peace.

When he visited Portugal in 2010, Pope Benedict XVI said "that today's pastoral priority is to make each Christian man and woman a radiant presence of the Gospel perspective in the midst of the world, in the family, in culture, in the economy, in politics." This is what it means to be, as Jesus said in the Sermon on the Mount, salt and light for the world (Mt 5:13–16).

Pope Benedict went on:

> Christ is always with us and always walks with his Church, accompanies her and guards her, as he has told us: "I am with you always, to the close of the age." Never doubt his presence! . . . Learn to listen to his word and also to recognize him in the poor. Live your lives with joy and enthusiasm, sure of his presence and of his unconditional, generous friendship, faithful even to death on the cross. Bear witness to all of the joy that his strong yet gentle presence evokes, starting with your contemporaries. Tell them that it is beautiful to be a friend of Jesus and that it is well worth following him.

---

[1] In the United States, the Feast of St. Elizabeth of Portugal has been transferred to July 5.

Jesus, I believe that you are with me, walking with me today. I want to stay close to you throughout this day. I want nothing to separate us.

DAILY WORD: Make me salt and light.

EVENING REVIEW: How did I sense Jesus' presence with me?

July 5: St. Anthony Zaccaria (1502–1539)

Anthony's mother was widowed when she was eighteen, and she devoted her life to the care of her only son. He graduated from the University of Padua with a degree in medicine but felt called to focus on the care of souls rather than bodies. He founded the Congregation of the Clerks Regular of St. Paul, also known as the Barnabites, which was dedicated to reforming society by means of preaching, prayer, and penance.

Jesus sent the apostles of his time into the world to carry on his work of reconciliation. This work continues. It begins with me as I deal with the conflicts and hurts that come my way. I will not "fight fire with fire" unless that fire is that which burns in the Heart of Jesus. I will see in persecution and opposition an opportunity to enter into a closer union with Jesus who suffered in that way.

St. Anthony Zaccaria offered the following advice:

We should love and feel compassion for those who oppose us, rather than abhor and despise them, since they harm themselves and do us good, and adorn us with crowns of everlasting glory. And even more than this, we should pray for them and not be overcome by evil, but overcome evil by goodness. We should heap good works "like red-hot coals" of burning love "upon their heads," as our Apostle [Paul] urges us to do, so that when they become aware of our tolerance and gentleness they may undergo a change of heart and be prompted to turn in love to God.

Jesus I offer myself to you so that with your grace I will be an instrument of reconciliation today and every day.

DAILY WORD: I forgive as I've been forgiven.

EVENING REVIEW: How did I practice reconciliation?

July 6: St. Maria Goretti (1890–1902)

Maria's father died when she was ten, and her mother carried on the hard agricultural work of the family with other relatives and neighbors. One day, as Maria was baby-sitting, nineteen-year-old Alessandro came to seduce her, and when she resisted, telling him it was a sin, he tried to rape her. As she fought him off, he took a knife and stabbed her fourteen times. She died the next day, forgiving him and saying, "I hope that he too will join me in Paradise."

Alessandro was sentenced to thirty years of hard labor in prison. At first, he expressed no remorse, but one night, in 1910, he had a dream in which Maria handed him a bouquet of lilies. He had a conversion, and when he was released, he went to ask the forgiveness of Maria's mother. She was present at Maria's canonization in 1950, when Pope Pius XII said, "Not all of us are expected to die a martyr's death, but we are all called to the pursuit of Christian virtue."

As a youth, Alessandro had fed his imagination with suggestive pictures and sexual stories, the equivalent of today's pornography. Archbishop Charles Chaput once wrote: "Citizens need to stop the pornography industry because it poisons the human heart, imagination, and soul just as steel mills once poisoned our air and water, only worse. Pornography is poison. It should be controlled like any other toxic waste."

Jesus, you said "Blessed are the pure in heart, for they shall see God" (Mt 5:8). I give my heart to you. Make it clean so that I will see all people today as images of you and not objects for my pleasure.

DAILY WORD: Blessed are the pure of heart.

EVENING REVIEW: How pure was my heart today?

July 7

On this day in 1977, Blessed Maria Romero Meneses was on vacation along the ocean in Nicaragua. Those who were with her report her saying, "I see God in every drop of water in this sea. How beautiful it would be to die facing the ocean." Her desire was fulfilled when she suffered a fatal heart attack two hours later.

Maria was a Salesian Sister who had spent most of her life working in Costa Rica among the poor and homeless. When he beatified her in 2002, Pope St. John Paul II highlighted her "passionate love for God and an unlimited confidence in the assistance of the Blessed Virgin Mary."

When she was seventy-five, celebrating her golden jubilee of religious profession, she wrote in her journal:

> O happy exchange. In place of my father, you have given me yourself; in place of my mother, the Blessed Mother; in place of my brothers and sisters, the saints; in place of my friends, the angels, in place of my country, the whole world, and after that, heaven; in place of my will, your will; in place of my comforts, rest and peace in your heart; in place of material riches, spiritual riches; in place of my earthly satisfactions, spiritual delights. Embracing the cross, I have encountered you, and live and die with you, to praise you eternally.

Loving God, it's been said that you won't be outdone in generosity. You have showered blessings upon me. All I am and have comes from you. What can I give you in return? I give you myself, one day at a time. Offering my earthly life to you, I trust that one day, because my hands are open, I will receive eternal life.

DAILY WORD: O happy exchange!

EVENING REVIEW: How did I return love for love?

July 8

On June 30, 1960, Pope St. John XXIII issued an encyclical which began:

> From the very outset of our pontificate, in speaking of daily devotions we have repeatedly urged the faithful . . . to cherish warmly that marvelous manifestation of divine mercy toward individuals and Holy Church and the whole world redeemed and saved by Jesus Christ: we mean devotion to his Most Precious Blood. From infancy this devotion was instilled in us within our own household. Fondly we still recall how our parents used to recite the Litany of the Most Precious Blood every day during July.

He went on to say: "Unlimited is the effectiveness of the God-Man's Blood—just as unlimited as the love that impelled him to pour it out for us."

Then, quoting St. John Chrysostom about the Eucharist, he wrote:

> Let us, then, come back from that table like lions breathing out fire. . . . This Blood, when worthily received, drives away demons and puts them at a distance from us, and even summons to us angels and the Lord of angels. . . . This Blood, poured out in abundance, has washed the whole world clean. . . . This is the price of the world; by it Christ purchased the Church. . . . Let us remember what privileges God has bestowed on us, let us give thanks, let us glorify him, not only by faith, but also by our very works.

Lord Jesus, I thank you that before I was born I was precious to you, so precious that you shed your Blood and died for love of me. In gratitude I offer myself to you.

DAILY WORD: Blood of Christ, fill me with love.

EVENING REVIEW: In what ways did I see other people as precious because Jesus shed his Precious Blood for them?

July 9: St. Augustine Zhao Rhong and the Chinese Martyrs

Today we remember 120 Catholics who were martyred in China between the years 1648 and 1930. They include foreign missionaries and eighty-seven native Chinese—lay people and four diocesan priests—ranging in age from nine to seventy-two.

In 2000, when he canonized them, Pope St. John Paul II spoke about some of the younger martyrs: "The testimonies which have come down to us allow us to glimpse in them a state of mind marked by deep serenity and joy. . . . Young Ann Wang, a 14-year-old, withstood the threats of the torturers who invited her to apostatize. Ready for her beheading, she declared with a radiant face: 'The door of heaven is open to all', three times murmuring: 'Jesus'. And 18-year-old Chi Zhuzi, cried out fearlessly to those who had just cut off his right arm and were preparing to flay him alive: 'Every piece of my flesh, every drop of my blood will tell you that I am Christian.'"

In 2007, Pope Benedict XVI wrote a letter to the Church in China. Quoting the First Letter of Peter, he wrote: "Rejoice, though now for a little while you may have to suffer various trials, so that the genuineness of your faith, more precious than gold which though perishable is tested by fire, may redound to praise and glory and honor at the revelation of Jesus Christ" (1:6-7).

Loving God, you gave the martyrs courage and strength to endure suffering and death rather than give up their precious faith. They offered every piece of their bodies and every drop of their blood as an act of love for you. Accept the offering of my day and give me courage and strength to live as a faithful Christian.

DAILY WORD: All of me is yours, God.

EVENING REVIEW: How did my actions tell all that I am Christian?

July 10

On July 9, 1926, the daughter of the famous American writer Nathaniel Hawthorne died. Rose was born in 1851, married George Lathrop in 1871, had a son who died at the age of five, and became Catholic in 1891. George died seven years later, and Rose began living among the poor in New York City and caring for those with cancer.

At the time, cancer was thought to be contagious, and those who could not hire nurses to care for themselves at home were sent to Blackwell's Island in the middle of the East River. Seeing their plight, Rose took out an ad: "Let the poor, the patient, the destitute, and the hopeless receive from our compassion what we would give to our own families." In time, Alice Huber joined her, and together they founded a new religious community called "Servants of Relief for Incurable Cancer" and who are known today as the Hawthorne Dominican Sisters.

She once wrote: "The distance up Fifth Avenue sometimes seems as far and as frozen as the road to the famous mines of Alaska. Or so it seems when I stand in my little room very nearly at the end of my money for the time being and ask myself, what am I doing down here among the poor?" She answered: "To take the lowest class we know, both in poverty and suffering, and put them in such a condition, that if our Lord knocked on the door we should not be ashamed to show what we have done."

Jesus, you knock at the door of my heart every day. As I renew my offering, help me to be more attentive to you in my suffering brothers and sisters.

DAILY WORD: Are you knocking, Lord?

EVENING REVIEW: How did Jesus come to me today?

July 11: St. Benedict (480–550)

Benedict spent his youth in Rome, where the worldliness and unhappiness he saw led him to flee and become a hermit. A community formed around him, and Benedict wrote a Rule that became the basis for monasticism in Western Europe.

In his Rule, Benedict, whose motto was "Ora et Labora"— Pray and Work—wrote: "Whenever you begin any good work, you should first of all make a most pressing appeal to Christ our Lord to bring it to perfection; that he who has honored us by counting us among his children may never be grieved by our evil deeds." He also wrote: "Girded with faith and the performance of good works, let us follow in the Lord's paths by the guidance of the Gospel."

I renew my daily offering with St. Benedict's "Prayer of Firm Purpose of Amendment":

O Lord, I place myself in your hands and dedicate myself to you. I pledge to do your will in all things: to love the Lord God with all my heart, all my soul, all my strength. To honor all persons. . . . Not to do to another what I would not wish done to myself. . . . To prefer nothing to the love of Christ. Not to give way to anger. Not to foster a desire for revenge. . . . To put my trust in God. To refer the good I see in myself to God. . . . To keep constant watch over my actions. To remember that God sees me everywhere. . . . To desire eternal life with spiritual longing. To keep death before my eyes daily. . . . To call upon Christ for defense against evil thoughts that arise in my heart. . . . Never to despair of your mercy, O God of Mercy. Amen.

DAILY WORD: I prefer nothing to Christ's love.

EVENING REVIEW: How did I put St. Benedict's prayer into practice today?

July 12: Sts. Louis and Zélie Martin (19th Century)

Today, the day before their wedding anniversary, is the feast of the first married couple in history to be canonized together—Louis and Zélie Martin, the parents of St. Thérèse of Lisieux. Louis was a watchmaker and jeweler, and Zélie ran a lace-making business. They had nine children, four of whom died in childhood. The surviving five daughters became nuns; four as Carmelites and one as a Visitation Sister. Zélie died of breast cancer at the age of forty-six, and in his later years Louis suffered from cerebral arteriosclerosis, dying when he was seventy.

Zélie, quite busy running her business, still found time to write beautiful letters that reveal her deep faith. She wrote: "God protects all who trust in Him. Not a single person has ever been abandoned by Him. When I think of what God, in whom I've put all my trust and in whose hands I've put the care of my whole life, has done for me and my husband, I don't doubt that His Divine Providence watches over His children with special care."

Convinced of God's providential care, so much greater than her own concern for her children, she wrote: "Let's abandon ourselves to His goodness and His mercy, and He'll arrange everything for the best." When her children were small, she taught them to pray the following prayer: "Good Jesus, I give you my heart. Take it, please, so that no creature may possess it, but only you, my good Jesus."

Good Jesus, I give you my heart and all the love that is in it. I offer myself to you with great confidence that you will "arrange everything for the best." May the peace that comes from my trusting surrender touch all those whom I meet today.

DAILY WORD: Providence watches over me.

EVENING REVIEW: Did I try to take my heart back anytime?

July 13: St. Henry (973–1024)

Henry II was Duke of Bavaria and Holy Roman Emperor. He established schools, worked to bring peace to the vast territory he ruled, and promoted the reform of the Church at a time when many clerics, appointed by secular authorities, were more interested in power and wealth than in serving God's people.

He wrote the following in a letter:

> By the instructions of sacred eloquence [the Gospels] we are taught and advised to abandon temporal riches, to lay aside earthly goods, and to strive to reach the eternal and everlasting dwelling places in heaven. For present glory is fleeting and meaningless, while it is possessed, unless in it we can glimpse something of heaven's eternity. Not turning a deaf ear to the Lord's commandments and obediently following divine urgings, we desire to take the treasures of divine generosity bestowed upon us by his bounty and store them in heaven, where thieves cannot dig them up or steal them and rust or moth may not destroy them.

Lord God, my loving Maker, you created me not just for this life, which is passing, but for eternal life. All you have given me is designed to help me on my journey to you. I do not want the goods of this world to weigh me down on this journey through life or to distract me from you. I know that I can take nothing of what I possess with me after I die. I can only take what I have lovingly given to you as I have tried to serve your other children. Help me to keep my eyes fixed on my goal—heaven—as I offer myself in your service today.

DAILY WORD: This too shall pass.

EVENING REVIEW: What have I given away today—time, talent, treasure—that I can take with me into eternity?

July 14: St. Kateri Tekakwitha (1656–1680)

Kateri, born in upstate New York, was the daughter of an Algonquin mother who was Christian and an Iroquois father who would not allow her to be baptized. Her parents died when she was four from a small pox epidemic that left Kateri disfigured and almost blind. Escaping harsh treatment from other relatives, she eventually took refuge at a Jesuit mission near Montreal and was baptized at the age of twenty.

When he canonized her in 2012, Pope Benedict XVI said: "Her greatest wish was to know and to do what pleased God. She lived a life radiant with faith and purity. Kateri impresses us by the action of grace in her life in spite of the absence of external help and by the courage of her vocation. . . . In her, faith and culture enrich each other! May her example help us to live where we are, loving Jesus without denying who we are."

Jesuit missionary, Fr. Pierre Cholenec, a contemporary of hers, wrote: "To keep alive her devotion for the mystery of Our Savior's Passion, and to have it always present to her mind, she carried on her breast a little crucifix which I had given her."

Pope St. John Paul II, when he beatified Kateri in 1980, said: "Her last words, simple and sublime, whispered at the moment of her death, sum up, like a noble hymn, a life of purest charity: 'Jesus, I love you.'"

Loving God, you want all people to know you and your love. As I offer myself to you, send your Holy Spirit to make me a sign of your love just as you made Kateri such a sign for Native Americans and all people.

DAILY WORD: "Jesus, I love you."

How did the culture in which I live help or hinder me today in loving God with all my heart, mind, and strength?

July 15: St. Bonaventure (1218–1274)

When he was baptized, today's saint was named Giovanni (John). According to tradition, St. Francis of Assisi healed him of a serious childhood illness, and when he joined the Franciscans, he was given the name Bonaventure, "Good Fortune". In time he became a noted professor of theology and head of the Franciscan order.

Bonaventure's writings reveal a burning love for God, and so he has been called the "Seraphic Doctor", after the fiery choir of angels. The following is part of his "Act of Love" that is often used as a prayer of thanksgiving after Communion.

Most loving Lord Jesus, pierce the depths of my soul with the blessed and life-giving wound of your love, with serenity of spirit and a holy, apostolic charity, that my heart may ever languish and melt with love and longing for you. . . . May it ever thirst after you, the fountain of life, the fountain of wisdom and knowledge, the fountain of eternal light, the torrent of pleasure, the richness of the house of God. May it ever aspire after you, seek you, find you, run to you, attain you, meditate on you, speak of you, and do all things to the praise and glory of your Name, with humility and discretion, with ease and affection, with love and satisfaction, and with perseverance unto the end. May you alone ever be my hope, my entire assurance, my riches and delight, my pleasure and joy, my rest and tranquility, my sweetness and peace, my fragrance and savor, my food and refreshment, my refuge and help, my wisdom and possession, my portion and treasure, in whom may my mind and heart be fixed and firm and rooted immovably for all eternity. Amen.

DAILY WORD: All for the glory of your Name, Jesus.

EVENING REVIEW: How was or wasn't my day an act of love for God?

July 16: Our Lady of Mount Carmel

At Mt. Carmel, the prophet Elijah displayed God's power as he called the Israelites to return to God after they had wandered away (1 Kings 18:16–40). There, a monastic community of Carmelites had formed, but violence in that volatile region forced them to emigrate to England.

According to tradition, on this day in 1251, as a sign of favor and protection, the Blessed Virgin Mary appeared to St. Simon Stock and gave him the brown scapular. Since then, Carmelites and lay people have worn the scapular as they dedicate themselves to Mary.

Pope St. John Paul II said the following on the 750th anniversary of this gift:

> The scapular is essentially a "habit". Those who wear the Scapular are thus brought into the land of Carmel . . . and experience the loving and motherly presence of Mary in their daily commitment to be clothed in Jesus Christ and to manifest him in their life for the good of the Church and the whole of humanity. . . . [They have] the awareness that devotion to her cannot be limited to prayers and tributes in her honor on certain occasions, but must become a "habit", that is, a permanent orientation of one's own Christian conduct, woven of prayer and interior life, through frequent reception of the sacraments and the concrete practice of the spiritual and corporal works of mercy. In this way the Scapular . . . concretely translates the gift of his Mother, which Jesus gave on the Cross to John and, through him, to all of us, and the entrustment of the beloved Apostle and of us to her, who became our spiritual Mother.

Jesus, clothe me with yourself today (Rom 13:14) so that I, like you and your Mother, may do God's will at all times.

DAILY WORD: All yours, Jesus, through Mary.

EVENING REVIEW: In what ways was I clothed in Christ today?

July 17

Three days ago was Bastille Day, commemorating the beginning of the French Revolution in 1789, when a medieval fortress in Paris was stormed by a mob intent on overthrowing the monarchy. Yesterday we celebrated the feast of Our Lady of Mt. Carmel. Today, in 1794, a group of over a dozen Carmelite Sisters were guillotined during the Reign of Terror that followed the storming of the Bastille.

In the trial preceding their execution, the prosecutor accused them of being fanatics. Sister Mary asked him what he meant, and he replied, "I mean by that your attachment to childish beliefs and your silly religious practices." Turning to the other nuns, Sister Mary said, "You see! We are being condemned for clinging to our holy religion. We have the happiness to die for God."

As they were transported to the execution site, they sang the Salve Regina, Hail Mary, and the Te Deum, a hymn of thanksgiving. They knelt before going to the guillotine and sang the Veni Creator, Come Holy Spirit, as they had done when they offered themselves to God when they professed their vows. When they finished, they renewed both their baptismal promises and their religious vows.

Their bodies were thrown into a large sand pit along with over 1,200 other victims of the revolution that was intended to bring fraternity, equality, and liberty.

Lord Jesus, even today Christians are being persecuted and killed throughout the world. You predicted this would happen: that as you were hated, so would your followers be hated. I offer my day to you. Take each thing that I do, and make it a prayerful offering for my suffering brothers and sisters.

DAILY WORD: It is happiness to live and die for you, God.

EVENING REVIEW: During the day, how did I renew the offering I made for persecuted Christians?

July 18: St. Camillus de Lellis (1550–1614)

Camillus was a giant—six feet, six inches—but his holiness was greater. Yet, knowing him as a youth, no one would have predicted it. A soldier who lived a wild life, addicted to gambling, he developed an infection in his leg and was hospitalized. Shocked at the way he and the other patients were treated, he experienced a profound conversion at the age of twenty-five. He tried to enter the Capuchin Franciscans twice but was rejected because of his ulcerated leg. Providence had other plans. His confessor, St. Philip Neri, helped him to be ordained when he was thirty-four and encouraged him to found a new religious congregation—the Servants of the Sick.

An early biography tells of his love for the sick:

> To enkindle the enthusiasm of his religious brothers, he used to impress upon them the consoling words of Jesus Christ: "I was sick and you visited me." He seemed to have these words truly graven on his heart. In the sick he saw the person of Christ. His imagination was so vivid that, while feeding them, he perceived his patients as other Christs. His reverence in their presence was as great as if he were really and truly in the presence of his Lord.

Jesus, you said that whatever we did or didn't do for the least of our brothers and sisters, we did or didn't do for you. You said that if we visited the sick, we visited you. As I offer myself to you today, help me to see you in all the people that I will meet today. Help me to treat them with reverence for you who shed your Precious Blood for them.

DAILY WORD: Whatever I do to others, I do to Christ.

EVENING REVIEW: Who are the people who were Christ for me today?

July 19: St. Macrina the Younger (d. 379)

It shouldn't be surprising that sanctity can run in families for, as the saying goes, "the apple doesn't fall far from the tree." That was certainly the case with St. Macrina, whose name appears in the Church's roll of saints today. She was the granddaughter of St. Macrina the Elder, the eldest child of Saints Emmelia and Basil the Elder, and the sister of Saints Basil the Great (see January 2), Peter of Sebastea, and Gregory of Nyssa.

Taught by her mother to read, it is said that the Wisdom of Solomon and the Psalms were her constant companions. When she was twelve, her fiancé died suddenly, and Macrina helped her mother raise and educate her nine siblings. Basil relates that when he returned from school a very conceited young man, Macrina taught him humility. When her mother died, she gave her inheritance to the poor and lived on what she earned spinning and weaving wool.

According to St. Gregory of Nyssa's biography of his sister, this is part of a prayer she said before dying:

O Lord, You have freed us from the fear of death; You have made the end of life here the beginning of a true life for us. O God everlasting, toward whom I have directed myself, whom my soul has loved with all its strength, to whom I have dedicated my body and my soul, prepare for me a shining angel to lead me to the place of refreshment. Do You who have power on earth to forgive sins forgive me so that I may be refreshed. May my soul be taken into Your hands as an offering before Your face.

DAILY WORD: Receive me as an offering now and at the hour of death.

EVENING REVIEW: How did today's sacrifices prepare me for my final offering?

July 20: St. Apollinaris (1st Century)

Apollinaris was a disciple of St. Peter who sent him to Ravenna as its first bishop. There he became famous for healing people in the Name of Jesus. As a result, more and more people became Christian to the dismay of the pagan authorities. Three times he was flogged and banished but returned each time until finally Emperor Vespasian issued a decree against Christians. Apollinaris was beaten by a mob and, according to tradition, died as a result of his wounds.

The word "martyr" means witness, and whether or not we are persecuted and threatened with death, we must be ready to witness to our faith. St. Peter wrote: "Always be prepared to make a defense to any one who calls you to account for the hope that is in you, yet do it with gentleness and reverence; and keep your conscience clear, so that, when you are abused, those who revile your good behavior in Christ may be put to shame. For it is better to suffer for doing right, if that should be God's will, than for doing wrong" (1 Pet 3:15–17).

Sometimes the explanation we give is not heard but seen through our actions. At the Last Supper, Jesus told his disciples, "By this all men will know that you are my disciples, if you have love for one another" (Jn 13:35). A challenging question I can ask myself today is, if it were against the law to be a Christian, would there be enough evidence to convict me?

Jesus, as you worked miracles of healing through St. Apollinaris, you drew people to yourself. I give myself to you so that my own works of charity may draw people to you.

DAILY WORD: Draw people to you through me.

EVENING REVIEW: How did I silently witness to Jesus through my acts of love?

July 21: St. Lawrence of Brindisi (1559–1619)

Named Caesar at birth, Lawrence received a new name when he joined the Capuchin Franciscans at the age of sixteen. Fluent in at least eight languages, he went on to become one of the greatest preachers of his time. The pope himself sent Lawrence as a personal emissary to convince some warring Christians to seek peace. This excerpt from a sermon demonstrates his practical eloquence:

> When Christ decided to give sight to a man blind from birth, he placed mud on the man's eyes, an action that was much more suited to blinding those who see than to giving sight to the blind who could not see. So, too, the Passion and death of Christ was more likely to destroy the faith of those who believed than to commend faith to nonbelievers. Christ came into this world to do battle with Satan and to turn the world to faith. He could have accomplished this by using the weapons of his might. Who would not then have believed in Christ? But in order that his victory might be the more glorious, he willed to fight Satan in our weak flesh. It is as if an unarmed man, right hand bound, were to fight with his left hand alone against a powerful army; if he emerged victorious, his victory would be regarded as all the more glorious. So Christ conquered Satan with the right hand of his divinity bound and using against him only the left hand of his weak humanity.

Jesus, even my weakness can give you glory as you make clear that it is not human power that prevails, but divine. Accept me with all my weaknesses, and use them to bring glory to yourself today.

DAILY WORD: "My power is made perfect in weakness" (2 Cor 12:9).

EVENING REVIEW: How did God work through my weakness?

July 22: St. Mary Magdalene

Mary of Magdala, according to the Gospel of Luke, followed Jesus after he exorcised her of "seven demons" (8:2). Her devotion to him gave her the courage to stand under the Cross as he died and to stay near the tomb on Easter morning. The risen Jesus appeared to her there and sent her to the apostles to tell them the good news of his Resurrection (Jn 20:1–18). As a result, she has been called "the apostle to the apostles".

St. Gregory the Great wrote:

> We should reflect on Mary's attitude and the great love she felt for Christ; for though the disciples had left the tomb, she remained. She was still seeking the one she had not found, and while she sought she wept; burning with the fire of love, she longed for him who she thought had been taken away. And so it happened that the woman who stayed behind to seek Christ was the only one to see him. For perseverance is essential to any good deed. At first she sought but did not find, but when she persevered, it happened that she found what she was looking for. Anyone who succeeds in attaining the truth has burned with such a love.

Jesus, I want the same love that St. Mary Magdalene had—a love that makes me want to be close to you always, a love that gives me courage to stand by you, a love that makes me persevere in prayer even when you seem far away from me. Though I may not sense your presence, I believe that you are with me in the people and events of my day. Receive each moment of my day as an act of love for you.

DAILY WORD: It is for love of you.

EVENING REVIEW: How did I practice perseverance?

July 23: St. Bridget of Sweden (1303–1373)

When she was fourteen, Bridget married Ulf Gudmarsson, who was eighteen. They had eight children, one of whom, Catherine, is also recognized as a saint. Ulf died in 1340, and Bridget founded a monastery for both men and women, who lived separately but came together for common worship. Today, the Bridgettine Order has no male members. In 1350 she made a pilgrimage to Rome for the second Jubilee Holy Year in history. She remained in Rome for the rest of her life except for a pilgrimage to the Holy Land in 1371. She was deeply devoted to the Passion of Jesus, and in one mystical encounter she sensed him saying: "O my friends, I love my sheep so tenderly that were it possible I would die many other times for each one of them that same death I suffered for the redemption of all."

Moved by such love, I offer myself and my day with this prayer of St. Bridget:

O Jesus! True and fruitful Vine! Remember the abundant outpouring of blood which you so generously shed from your sacred body as juice from grapes in a wine press. From your side, pierced with a lance by a soldier, blood and water issued forth until there was not left in your body a single drop. Through this bitter Passion, and through the outpouring of your Precious Blood, I beg you, sweet Jesus, to pierce my heart so that I may be entirely converted to you. May my heart be your perpetual habitation, may my conversation be pleasing to you, and may the end of my life be so praiseworthy that I may merit heaven and there with your saints praise you forever. Amen.

DAILY WORD: You died for love of me.

EVENING REVIEW: How did the thought of Jesus' love inspire me today?

July 24: St. Sharbel Makhlouf (1828–1898)

As a Maronite Catholic youth in Lebanon, Sharbel's favorite book was *The Imitation of Christ*. Thus, it was no surprise when he left home at twenty-three to enter a monastery and imitate the Desert Fathers of the early Church. He became a hermit and dedicated himself to prayer and fasting in solitude. He died on Christmas Eve repeating the names of Jesus, Mary, and Joseph. For over forty days after his burial, a bright light shone around his grave, and when his body was exhumed, it was found to be incorrupt. People flocked to his grave seeking his intercession.

Bishop Francis Zayek attests:

> From April 22 to July 14, 1950, three hundred and fifty cases of cures, which were considered to be miraculous, have been recorded at Saint Maron's Monastery of Annaya. In detail, they consist of curing thirty-one blind, one hundred and sixty-three paralytic and lame, and one hundred and nineteen incurable diseases. Twenty Moslem recipients are included in the last cases.

When he beatified him shortly before the end of the Second Vatican Council, Pope St. Paul VI said:

> This holy monk reminds us of the indispensable role of prayer, hidden virtues, and mortification. In a world that is largely fascinated with riches and comfort, he helps us understand the irreplaceable value of poverty, penance, and asceticism to liberate the soul in its ascent to God. Of course, the practice of these virtues varies according to the state of life and the responsibilities of each, but no Christian can exempt himself from them if he wants to follow Our Lord.

Jesus, you continue to perform miracles through your Body, the living and deceased members of the Church. I offer myself: use me however you wish today.

DAILY WORD: Make me your instrument.

EVENING REVIEW: How did I practice "prayer, hidden virtues, and mortification"?

July 25: St. James the Greater, Apostle

The sons of Zebedee, James whom we celebrate today and John, were, with Peter, part of an inner circle of apostles. Either because of this or because he was older, he was called "greater". These brothers certainly aspired to greatness, approaching Jesus and asking for places of honor, one on the left and the other on the right, when he came into his "glory" (Mk 10:35–37). We also see them acting like their nickname, "Sons of Thunder", when they asked Jesus if he wanted them "to bid fire come down from heaven and consume" the Samaritan village that did not welcome them (Lk 9:51–54). James was the first apostle to "drink the chalice" that Jesus drank (Mk 10:38) when King Herod had him "killed . . . with the sword" (Acts 12:1–2).

Pope Benedict XVI said:

> We can learn much from St. James: promptness in accepting the Lord's call even when he asks us to leave the "boat" of our human securities, enthusiasm in following him on the paths that he indicates to us over and above any deceptive presumption of our own, readiness to witness to him with courage, if necessary to the point of making the supreme sacrifice of life. . . . In following Jesus, like St. James, we know that even in difficulties we are on the right path.

Jesus, you invited James, along with his brother John and Peter, the Rock on which you said you would build your Church, to see you transfigured in glory on Mt. Tabor and to keep you company during your agony in the Garden of Gethsemane. Keep me close to you every minute of this day which I offer to you.

DAILY WORD: May I stay with you forever.

EVENING REVIEW: In what ways did Jesus ask me to follow him and to "drink his cup"?

July 26: Sts. Joachim and Anne, Grandparents of Jesus

Little is actually known about the parents of the Blessed Virgin Mary, but in the eighth century, St. John Damascene honored them with these words:

> Joachim and Anne, how blessed a couple! All creation is indebted to you. For at your hands the Creator was offered a gift excelling all other gifts: a chaste mother, who alone was worthy of him. Joachim and Anne, how blessed and spotless a couple! You will be known by the fruit you have borne, as the Lord says: "By their fruits you will know them." The conduct of your life pleased God and was worthy of your daughter. While leading a devout and holy life in your human nature, you gave birth to a daughter nobler than the angels, whose queen she now is.

According to tradition, Joachim and Anne were elderly and childless when God blessed them with a daughter. No one is too old to "bear fruit". According to Pope Francis, our "throwaway culture" has little room for the elderly, but God has room for everyone in his heart. Each precious moment of life can be made into a powerful prayer when joined to Jesus' perfect offering. Every time, like Jesus and Mary, I join my will to God's loving will, great, though perhaps hidden, things will happen. Pope Francis wrote: "No single act of love for God will be lost, no generous effort is meaningless, no painful endurance is wasted. All of these encircle our world like a vital force."

God, help me to believe that every moment of this day that I offer you can "encircle our world like a vital force" and contribute to your plan for me and the world.

DAILY WORD: I believe I am important to God.

EVENING REVIEW: Where were my "generous effort", "act of love for God", and "painful endurance" today?

July 27

God speaks to us through the grandeur and beauty of nature. When we slow down and become quiet, we grow in the awareness of God's presence in creation. As God is present to us, we want to be present to God at all times.

In his encyclical *Laudato Si*, Pope Francis wrote: "Nature is filled with words of love, but how can we listen to them amid constant noise, interminable and nerve-wracking distractions, or the cult of appearances? Many people today sense a profound imbalance which drives them to frenetic activity and makes them feel busy, in a constant hurry which in turn leads them to ride rough-shod over everything around them."

What shall we do? Pope Francis answered:

We are speaking of an attitude of the heart, one which approaches life with serene attentiveness, which is capable of being fully present to someone without thinking of what comes next, which accepts each moment as a gift from God to be lived to the full. Jesus taught us this attitude when he invited us to contemplate the lilies of the field and the birds of the air, or when seeing the rich young man and knowing his restlessness, "he looked at him with love" (Mk 10:21).

He was completely present to everyone and to everything, and in this way he showed us the way to overcome that unhealthy anxiety which makes us superficial, aggressive, and compulsive consumers.

Loving God, creation is your gift. Help me not to ignore your gift or treat it as anything less than a revelation of your beauty and love. I offer myself to be a steward of creation as you called mankind to be.

DAILY WORD: Let all creation give praise to God!

EVENING REVIEW: When was I "fully present" to the people and events of my day?

July 28

One of the greatest tragedies is to think that one's life is insignificant. Especially in a world that wants to "super-size" everything, we can feel very small. We look at the problems in our world and say, "I'm just one person. What can one person do?" And then we resign ourselves to the way things are. Discouragement is a favorite tactic of God's enemy and ours.

The story is told that St. Teresa of Kolkata was once asked how she ever got started helping so many poor people in India. She responded that she saw a man dying in a gutter, picked him up, and cared for him. She said that if she had not done that, she would never have cared for the millions of others that she and the Missionaries of Charity have helped over the years since then.

In speaking about caring for creation, Pope Francis reminded us in *Laudato Si* that every action, no matter how large or small, fosters our relationship with God, with one another, and with creation. He wrote: "Saint Thérèse of Lisieux invites us to practise the little way of love, not to miss out on a kind word, a smile, or any small gesture which sows peace and friendship. An integral ecology is also made up of simple daily gestures which break with the logic of violence, exploitation, and selfishness."

Lord God, help me not to give in to discouragement when I hear about the crises and problems in the world. Help me to live today as an offering to you. Take this offering that seems so small, and make of it something beautiful for yourself.

DAILY WORD: No to discouragement.

EVENING REVIEW: How did I practice "the little way of love"? With what kind words, smiles, and other small gestures did I sow peace and friendship?

July 29: Sts. Martha, Mary, and Lazarus

These two sisters and their brother were some of Jesus' closest friends. A few days before his death, Jesus went to their house to spend time with them. Just like an earlier encounter (Lk 10:38–42), "Martha served" and Mary sat near Jesus' feet (Jn 12:1–3). Martha is often criticized for being active while Mary represents the ideal of a contemplative life. But most of us are not called to be cloistered contemplative monks and nuns. We are actively engaged in the world.

Jesus did not criticize the fact that Martha was busy. Rather, he criticized the attitude she brought to her activity, saying, "Martha, Martha, you are anxious and troubled about many things" (Lk 10:41). Anxiety and worry are negatives that sap our energy and actually get in the way of our work. They usually arise when we are concerned about ourselves—looking good in front of others, getting others' approval and praise, being successful. Jesus confronts this self-centered attitude by telling Martha to keep her eyes on him.

There is a quote that goes: "If you worry, why pray, and if you pray, why worry?" Worry is a common temptation, and, like any temptation, it has an opposite virtue—trust that leads to surrender. This is where prayer comes into play. Daily prayer helps me to focus more and more on Jesus and less and less on myself. In that context, I can trustingly surrender my day with all its concerns.

Jesus, when I worry, I put myself in the center. As you challenged Martha, so you challenge me to keep you at the center of my life. I trust you and surrender myself to you.

DAILY WORD: No to worry, yes to trust.

EVENING REVIEW: How did I handle worry today?

July 30: St. Peter Chrysologus (380–451)

Peter was such a good preacher that he was given the nickname "Chrysologus" or "Golden-Worded". In Sermon 148, he challenges us to believe in our sacred dignity: "Why do you think so little of yourself when God thinks so highly of you? Why dishonor yourself when God so honors you? All visible creation is your home. More than this, the Creator made you his image. Then, what he had made in you he took to himself and decided to make himself visible in human form. Christ raises man wholly to God."

Moreover, through Baptism, Christians are joined to Christ and share in his dignity as priest, prophet, and king. Our daily offering is how we exercise our priesthood, as St. Peter shows in Sermon 108:

How marvelous is the priesthood of the Christian, for he is both the victim that is offered on his own behalf, and the priest who makes the offering. Truly it is an amazing sacrifice in which a body is offered without being slain and blood is offered without being shed. Paul says: "I appeal

to you by the mercy of God to present your bodies as a
sacrifice, living and holy" [Rom 12:1]. The prophet said
the same thing: "Sacrifices and offering you did not desire,
but you have prepared a body for me" [Ps 40:5; Heb 10:5].
Each of us is called to be both a sacrifice to God and his
priest. Do not forfeit what divine authority confers on you.
Let your heart be an altar. Then, with full confidence in
God, present your body for sacrifice. God desires not death,
but faith; God thirsts not for blood, but for self-surrender.

I offer myself as a living sacrifice.

DAILY WORD: I sacrifice myself for you.

EVENING REVIEW: How did I exercise my priesthood today?

July 31: St. Ignatius Loyola (1491–1556)

Ignatius aspired to a worldly life of romance and military
exploits, but his dreams were shattered by a cannon ball.
During a long recovery, he read about the saints and was
inspired. He traded service of an earthly king for the service
of Christ the King and founded the Society of Jesus, the
Jesuits, whose motto is "For the Greater Glory of God".

His "Spiritual Exercises", the fruit of a long period of
solitary prayer, end with a reflection that culminates in a
wholehearted gift of oneself to God. I ask for "an intimate
knowledge of the many blessings received, that filled with
gratitude for all, I may in all things love and serve the Divine Majesty." Then, "I will ponder with great affection
how much God our Lord has done for me, and how much
He has given me of what He possesses, and finally, how
much, as far as He can, the same Lord desires to give Himself to me."

Knowing that the Son of God made a total gift of himself on the Cross for my salvation and how he continues

to give himself to me in the Eucharist where he is present "Body and Blood, soul and divinity", I am moved to return love for love and make a total gift of myself. I do that now with the prayer that St. Ignatius offers at this point in the "Exercises":

Take, Lord, and receive all my liberty, my memory, my understanding, and my entire will, all that I have and possess. You have given all to me. To you, O Lord, I return it. All is yours. Dispose of it wholly according to your will. Give me only your love and your grace. With these I am rich enough and want for nothing more.

DAILY WORD: "All is yours."

EVENING REVIEW: What gifts did God give me?

AUGUST

August 1: St. Alphonsus Liguori (1696–1787)

Alphonsus was only seventeen when he was awarded doctorates in both civil and Church law. He founded the Redemptorists to work as missionaries in rural areas and is the patron saint of confessors, moral theologians, and those with arthritis.

He said the following about prayer:

> To pray, it is not necessary always to be on bended knee, or in church, or even in some quiet corner at home. You can pray while at work, you can pray while walking the street, under all circumstances, by raising your mind to God, and thinking of the Passion of Christ, or any other pious subject. Whenever you feel disturbed by trials or adversities, consider them as coming from God. Say with love and humility, 'God wills it thus', and be at peace. Direct all your thoughts and prayers to this end: that God may accomplish His Adorable Will in your regard.

He also said: "All holiness lies in our love for Jesus Christ. It is in this vein that he speaks to us: 'O beloved, consider carefully that I first loved you. You had not appeared in the light of day, nor did the world yet exist, but already I loved you. From all eternity I have loved you.'"

Moved by this eternal love, I offer myself with this prayer of St. Alphonsus:

My Jesus, I love You with all my heart. I am sorry that I have so often offended Your infinite goodness. With the help of Your grace, I resolve to offend You no more. I consecrate myself to You without reserve. I give You my will, my affections, my desires, and all that is mine. *Henceforth do with me whatsoever You please. I ask for nothing but You and Your holy love, final perseverance, and a perfect fulfillment of Your will.*

DAILY WORD: "God wills it thus."

EVENING REVIEW: How did God love me today?

August 2: St. Eusebius of Vercelli (283–371) and St. Peter Julian Eymard (1811–1868)

Bishop Eusebius defended the doctrine of the divinity of Christ against the heretical Arians and suffered exile from his diocese as a result. In a letter, he wrote: "I beg you to keep the faith with all vigilance, to preserve harmony, to be earnest in prayer, so that the Lord may grant freedom to his Church, which is suffering throughout the world."

Peter, known as the "Apostle of the Eucharist", said: "One idea haunted me: that Jesus in the Blessed Sacrament had no religious institute to glorify His mystery of love, whose only object was entire consecration to Its service. There ought to be one." His devotion led him to start two religious congregations dedicated to Eucharistic adoration. He wrote:

> It would indeed be unfortunate if we could be in touch with the Eucharistic Jesus only in His churches. The light of the sun envelops and illumines us even when we do not stand directly beneath its rays. In the same way, from His Host, our Lord will find the means to send some rays of His love into your home to bring you warmth and strength. It would be a sad thing were Jesus to receive adoration from us only when we come to visit Him in church. No, no! He sees everywhere, He blesses everywhere, He unites Himself everywhere to those who want to communicate with Him. Adore Him therefore everywhere; turn in spirit toward His tabernacle.

Jesus, present in the Blessed Sacrament, I adore you! I offer myself to you! Shine the rays of your love into me and through me today.

DAILY WORD: Eucharistic Jesus, fill me!

EVENING REVIEW: Jesus is hidden under the appearance of bread and wine and, as St. Teresa of Kolkata said, under the "distressing disguise" of those in need. How did I meet him there today?

August 3

In 2013, Pope Francis canonized Peter Faber (1506–1546), whose feast was celebrated yesterday. At the University of Paris, St. Ignatius Loyola became Peter's roommate, and in time the two were joined by St. Francis Xavier. Peter was the first of the early Jesuits to be ordained, and he traveled throughout Europe on foot, preaching and leading people in St. Ignatius' "Spiritual Exercises". He had a great devotion to the angels and often conversed with them as he walked along. Pope Paul III appointed him to be one of the papal theologians at the Council of Trent, but he died on his way there as he visited in Rome with his good friend Ignatius, whom he had not seen in seven years.

St. Ignatius said that Peter had "a gift for guiding people's souls toward God" and that he was "someone who can squeeze water from a rock". He had, in the words of a contemporary, "a wonderfully winning personality." Another early Jesuit spoke of his "gentleness and cordiality". Peter said, "Time is God's messenger", and he strove to find God in the events and people of his life, writing, "If you keep your heart wide open to God, he will quickly show you that everything else is open to you and that you can welcome it." He also said, "If only you take things as you find them and set out to improve and develop them, there will be an abundant harvest."

The following is an offering prayer of his:

May my most intimate self, and above all my heart, be surrendered to Christ, who has entered into me, and may he occupy the center of my heart.

DAILY WORD: "Occupy my heart", Lord.

EVENING REVIEW: How did God touch people today through my "gentleness and cordiality"?

August 4: St. John Vianney (1786–1859)

Pope Benedict XVI wrote the following about today's saint, the patron of all priests:

> He arrived in Ars, a village of 230 souls, warned by his Bishop beforehand: . . . "There is little love of God in that parish; you will be the one to put it there." As a result, he was deeply aware that he needed to go there to embody Christ's presence and to bear witness to his saving mercy. . . . Saint John Mary Vianney taught his parishioners primarily by the witness of his life. It was from his example that they learned to pray. . . . "One need not say much to pray well. . . . We know that Jesus is there in the tabernacle: let us open our hearts to him, let us rejoice in his sacred presence. That is the best prayer."

Word of this holy priest spread, and people came great distances to receive from him the Sacrament of Reconciliation.

Pope Benedict also said:

> At a close look, what made the Curé of Ars holy was his humble faithfulness to the mission to which God had called him; it was his constant abandonment, full of trust, to the hands of divine Providence. . . . He won over even the most refractory souls by communicating to them what he himself lived deeply, namely, his friendship with Christ. He was "in love" with Christ.

The following prayer of his shows the love that I also desire to have today as I offer myself to God:

I love you, O my God, and my only desire is to love you until my last breath. If my tongue is not able to say at every opportunity that I love you, I want at least my heart to repeat it to you as many times as I take a breath.

DAILY WORD: "I love you, O my God."

EVENING REVIEW: How did I abandon myself to the hands of Providence?

August 5: Dedication of the Basilica of St. Mary Major

The Church celebrates the anniversaries of important churches. Today we celebrate the consecration anniversary of one of the four major basilicas in Rome. It was built in the year 366 and restored and dedicated to the Blessed Virgin Mary shortly after the Council of Ephesus (431), which affirmed Mary's title, "Mother of God". More recently, popes have gone there to ask Mary's intercession as they begin or return from their worldwide trips.

Pope Benedict XVI said: "This Basilica was the first in the West to be dedicated to the Virgin Mother of God. Mary is the model: it is she who holds out the mirror in which we are invited to recognize our identity. The dispositions of her heart—the listening, welcome, humility, the faithfulness, praise, and waiting—correspond to the inner attitude and gestures that shape Christian life."

On the day after he was elected pope, Francis brought a bouquet of flowers to St. Mary Major and prayed there. He returned a few months later to pray a rosary during Mary's month of May. At that time, he said:

The mother takes care that her children develop better, that they grow strong, capable of accepting responsibilities, of striving for great ideals. Mary's whole life is a hymn to life: she generated Jesus in the flesh and accompanied the birth of the Church on Calvary and in the Upper Room. The mother teaches us how to be fruitful, to be open to life and to always bear good fruit, and never to lose hope, to give life to others, physical and spiritual life.

Father, make me like your Son's mother, so that my openness to your Spirit may bear good fruit today.

DAILY WORD: Let your will be done in me.

EVENING REVIEW: What fruit did I bear today?

August 6: Feast of the Transfiguration of the Lord

Jesus took his three closest friends—Peter, James, and John —and went up Mt. Tabor where he was "transfigured". About this event, St. Peter wrote:

> We did not follow cleverly devised myths when we made known to you the power and coming of our Lord Jesus Christ, but we were eyewitnesses of his majesty. For when he received honor and glory from God the Father and the voice was borne to him by the Majestic Glory, "This is my beloved Son, with whom I am well pleased," we heard this voice borne from heaven, for we were with him on the holy mountain. (2 Pet 1:16–18)

Pope Benedict XVI spoke about two other figures who appeared on the mountain:

> Elijah and Moses appeared beside Jesus, meaning that the Sacred Scriptures were in concordance with the proclamation of his Paschal Mystery; that, in other words, Christ had to suffer and die in order to enter into his glory. At that moment Jesus saw silhouetted before him the Cross, the extreme sacrifice necessary in order to free us from the dominion of sin and death. And in his heart, once again,

he repeated his "Amen." He said yes, here I am, may your loving will be done, O Father.

Jesus, as you taught your disciples that the Son of Man would suffer and die, you knew how discouraged and afraid they would be. So you gave them a taste of glory, showing them that death was not the end of your story or theirs. I want to follow you by saying my own "Amen" to the Father's will for me this day. I believe that in this way I will follow you into glory.

DAILY WORD: "May your loving will be done, O Father."

EVENING REVIEW: How was God's will accomplished or not accomplished in me?

August 7: St. Sixtus II and Companions (d. 258) and St. Cajetan (1480–1547)

Pope Sixtus II was seized while celebrating Mass in a catacomb and beheaded immediately, along with several of his deacons.

Cajetan received a doctorate in Church law, was ordained, and served the sick and poor. He founded a new congregation called the Theatines, dedicated to the renewal of the Church. On Christmas Day 1517, as he venerated a relic of Jesus' crib in the Basilica of St. Mary Major, he was gifted with a mystical experience: Mary appeared to him and placed the Christ Child in his arms.

Cajetan's total trust in Jesus is revealed in this excerpt from a letter he wrote:

You know, of course, that we are pilgrims in this world, on a journey to our true home in heaven. The man who becomes proud loses his way and rushes to death. While living here, we should strive to gain eternal life. Yet of ourselves we cannot achieve this since we have lost it through sin; but Jesus Christ has recovered it for us. For this reason, we must always be grateful to him and love him. We must always obey him and as far as possible remain united with him. He has offered himself to be our food. To us has been given the opportunity to receive Christ, son of the Virgin Mary. I want you to surrender to him, that he may welcome you and, as your divine Savior, do to you and in you whatever he wills.

Jesus, I know that I am nothing without you. I cannot guarantee one moment of my earthly life or a future eternal life in heaven. You are my guarantee. As you offered yourself for my salvation, I offer myself for love of you.

DAILY WORD: Do to me and in me what you will.

EVENING REVIEW: How was I able to remain united with Christ?

August 8: St. Dominic (1170–1221)

Religious art often depicts Dominic with a dog carrying a blazing torch in its mouth. This is because of a tradition that when she was pregnant with her son, Dominic's mother had a dream with that image. In a sense, it was prophetic, for Dominic did indeed set the world on fire through the Order of Preachers that he founded shortly after St. Francis of Assisi, who became his friend, founded his Order. The motto of the Dominicans is "To contemplate the truth and to share with others the fruit of contemplation."
Pope Benedict XVI said that Dominic

always spoke *with* God and *of* God. Love for the Lord and for neighbor, the search for God's glory and the salvation of souls in the lives of Saints always go hand in hand. . . . This great Saint reminds us that in the heart of the Church a missionary fire must always burn. It must be a constant incentive to make the first proclamation of the Gospel and, wherever necessary, a new evangelization. Christ, in fact, is the most precious good that the men and women of every time and every place have the right to know and love!

Lord Jesus, St. Paul wrote: "Indeed I count everything as loss because of the surpassing worth of knowing Christ Jesus my Lord" (Phil 3:8). Echoing his words, I tell you that all I want is to know you. Then, with this "surpassing worth", I want to go forth from my prayer and bring the knowledge of you to everyone I meet today. As I offer myself to you in this prayer, so I want to offer you to everyone.

DAILY WORD: To know you and share you.

EVENING REVIEW: In what ways did Jesus reveal himself and his love through me?

August 9: St. Teresa Benedicta of the Cross (1891–1842)

Edith Stein was the youngest child in a German Jewish family who earned a doctorate in philosophy at the age of twenty-five. Her search for truth led her to St. Teresa of Ávila's autobiography, which in turn led her to be baptized in 1922. She continued her academic career until 1933, when the Nazi government forced her to resign and she decided to become a Carmelite nun in Cologne. In 1938, for her safety, she was smuggled to a convent in the Netherlands.

In 1942, the Dutch bishops publicly condemned Nazi racism. Within a week, the Nazis ordered the arrest of all Jewish Christians. On August 2, Edith, now known as Sister Teresa Benedicta of the Cross, and her sister Rosa were arrested with over 240 other Jews who had been baptized. Transported to the Auschwitz concentration camp, they were gassed on this day.

She once wrote: "I have an ever deeper and firmer belief that nothing is merely an accident when seen in the light of God, that my whole life down to the smallest details has been marked out for me in the plan of Divine Providence and has a completely coherent meaning in God's all-seeing eyes. And so I am beginning to rejoice in the light of glory wherein this meaning will be unveiled to me." She also wrote: "Learn from St. Thérèse [of Lisieux] to depend on God alone and serve Him with a wholly pure and detached heart. Then . . . you will be able to say 'I do not regret that I have given myself to Love.'"

I renew my offering with this prayer of hers:

I surrender myself entirely to Your divine will, O Lord. Make my heart grow greater and wider, out of itself into the Divine Life.

DAILY WORD: I depend on God alone.

EVENING REVIEW: How was God present in "the smallest details"?

August 10: St. Lawrence (d. 258)

Lawrence was one of the seven deacons captured with Pope Sixtus II on August 6, 258. Knowing that Lawrence was in charge of distributing alms to the poor, the governor postponed his execution and demanded that the Church's riches be handed over. Lawrence responded:

"The Church is indeed rich. The emperor does not have any treasure that compares. I will show you a valuable part, but allow me a little time to get everything in order and to make an inventory." The governor happily agreed and gave him three days to gather the Church's treasures. On August 10, Lawrence presented to him the Church of Rome's riches— the blind, the lame, lepers, orphans, widows, and the poor.

The governor was furious, but Lawrence responded: "Why are you displeased? These are the treasures of the Church."

As a result, the governor ordered that Lawrence be killed, not with a swift beheading, but by being roasted alive on a gridiron. God strengthened Lawrence to endure this torture and tradition has it that at one point he joked to the executioner: "Let my body be turned. This side is broiled enough!" Pope St. Leo the Great called Lawrence an "illustrious hero" and said: "The flames could not overcome Christ's love, and the fire that burned outside was less keen than that which blazed within." St. Augustine, referring to Christ's gift of self on the Cross and the altar, said: "Just as he had partaken of a gift of self at the table of the Lord, so he prepared to offer such a gift."

Jesus, may your love burn within me as it burned within the heart of St. Lawrence. May it give me strength to offer my sufferings to you today.

DAILY WORD: Heart of Jesus, inflame me with your love.

EVENING REVIEW: How did I keep my sense of humor?

August 11: St. Clare (1194–1253)

Clare was so impressed by the example and teaching of Francis of Assisi that she resolved to follow his way of life herself. Against her family's wishes, she gave away all her possessions and received a poor religious habit from St. Francis in 1212. As other women joined her in a life of prayer, penance, and witness to simplicity—including two of her sisters and eventually her mother—the Order of Poor Clares was formed.

In 1244, an army attacked Assisi. Though she was sick, Clare asked to be carried with the Blessed Sacrament to the wall of the convent. She prostrated herself and prayed: "Does it please Thee, O God, to deliver into the hands of these beasts the defenseless children whom I have nourished with Thy love? I beseech Thee, good Lord, protect these whom I am now not able to protect." As she finished, she heard the voice of a little child say: "I will have them always in my care." At that moment the attacking soldiers were seized with terror and fled.

With trust like Clare's, I offer myself in her words:

Glory and praise be to You, most loving Jesus Christ! Having redeemed me by Baptism, so may You now, by Your Precious Blood, which is offered and which is received throughout the world, deliver me from all evils, past, present, and to come! By Your most bitter death, give me a lively faith, firm hope, a perfect charity, so that with my whole heart I may love You—with all my soul, with all my strength. Make me firm and steadfast in good works, and in Your service make me persevere, so that I may be able always to please You, Lord Jesus Christ.

DAILY WORD: Make me firm.

EVENING REVIEW: What good works did I offer? What opportunities did I miss?

August 12: St. Jane Frances de Chantal (1572–1641)

Jane Frances married at twenty-one and began raising a family of six children. After only seven years, her husband was tragically killed in a hunting accident, and she was left to raise and educate the children herself. When they were grown, she met St. Francis de Sales, who became her spiritual director. Together they founded the Sisters of the Visitation of Mary, of which St. Margaret Mary, the great apostle of the Sacred Heart, was a member.

Finding God's will in the events of her life, Jane lived in peaceful confidence. She said: "The soul that is happy to repose in God's hands by entire confidence is never shaken by anything. Everything turns out well for it. In everything good or ill that befalls us, see only the Will of God. Then whatsoever the event we shall always be tranquil because we shall have no love, no desire other than that of his adorable Will."

She also saw each moment of the day as an opportunity to offer something as an act of love for God. She said: "We must live in the present moment without forecast and care for ourselves. We cannot always offer God great things, but at each moment we can offer him little things with great love. Look to God, forget self and all else to please him."

Loving God, I want to trust in you and your love so much that I live totally at peace even as I encounter unexpected challenges and disturbing news. Thank you for the ways you have formed me, using the events and people of my daily life, to be the person I am. In gratitude I offer each moment of this day as an act of love for you.

DAILY WORD: Live, Jesus, in me.

EVENING REVIEW: How did I embrace or struggle with God's will?

August 13: St. Pontian and St. Hippolytus (d. 235)

Hippolytus was a major theologian of his time, and Pontian was pope from 230–235. Unfortunately, they were enemies. For a number of years, Hippolytus disagreed with several popes because he thought they were too lenient with heretics and with people who had fallen away from the faith under the threat of torture and death. He allowed himself to be elected as the first "anti-pope" in history. However, both men were exiled to hard labor in the mines of Sardinia where they were reconciled and then died from the mistreatment they received.

Jesus Christ came into the world to reconcile us with God and one another. He gave his life for this, and the Church now continues his mission. Appearing to the apostles in the Upper Room after his Resurrection, he said: "Peace be with you. As the Father has sent me, even so I send you" (Jn 20:21). Each member of the Body of Christ is now sent to continue the work of reconciliation.

Announcing the Jubilee Year of Mercy, Pope Francis wrote:

> Jesus affirms that mercy is not only an action of the Father, it becomes a criterion for ascertaining who his true children are. In short, we are called to show mercy because mercy has first been shown to us. Pardoning offences becomes the clearest expression of merciful love, and for us Christians it is an imperative from which we cannot excuse ourselves. At times how hard it seems to forgive! And yet pardon is the instrument placed into our fragile hands to attain serenity of heart. To let go of anger, wrath, violence, and revenge are necessary conditions to living joyfully.

Jesus, I accept my mission. I offer myself to you. Make me your instrument of reconciliation.

DAILY WORD: Be merciful!

EVENING REVIEW: How did my actions overcome conflicts or add to them?

August 14: St. Maximilian Kolbe (1894–1941)

When he was twelve, Raymond Kolbe had a vision of Mary that he described this way: "I asked the Mother of God what was to become of me. Then she came to me holding two crowns, one white, the other red. She asked if I was willing to accept either of these crowns. The white one meant that I should persevere in purity, and the red that I should become a martyr. I said that I would accept them both."

He joined the Conventual Franciscans, received the name

Maximilian, and promoted devotion to Mary, "the Immaculata", in Poland and as a missionary in Japan. Back in Poland, he was arrested by the Nazis on February 17, 1941, and sent to the Auschwitz concentration camp. There he became "a martyr of charity" because he offered to take the place of a man who had been selected to die in the starvation bunker as punishment for another prisoner's escape. He once said: "The real conflict is the inner conflict. Beyond armies of occupation and the extermination camps, there are two irreconcilable enemies in the depth of every soul: good and evil, sin and love. And what use are the victories on the battlefield if we ourselves are defeated in our innermost personal selves."

It is there, on the battlefield of our own hearts, that we must sacrifice ourselves in the same way that Jesus did and for the same reason—the salvation of others. Maximilian said: "Let us remember that love lives through sacrifice and is nourished by giving. Without sacrifice, there is no love."

Lord, I give myself to you. Dwell in my heart and conquer sin. May I share your victory with all people today.

DAILY WORD: "Without sacrifice, there is no love."

EVENING REVIEW: How did I experience "the inner conflict" today?

August 15: The Assumption of the Blessed Virgin Mary

We celebrate the mystery that Jesus would not allow corruption to touch the body of his Mother, who carried him in her womb. Rather, at the end of her earthly life, he raised her up body and soul into heaven.

Pope Benedict XVI spoke of this:

The Feast of the Assumption is a day of joy. God has won. Love has won. It has won life. Love has shown that it is stronger than death, that God possesses the true strength and that his strength is goodness and love. Mary was taken up body and soul into Heaven: there is even room in God for the body. . . . We have a mother in Heaven.

Precisely because she is with God and in God, she is very close to each one of us. While she lived on this earth she could only be close to a few people. Being in God, who is close to us, actually, "within" all of us, Mary shares in this closeness of God. Being in God and with God, she is close to each one of us, knows our hearts, can hear our prayers, can help us with her motherly kindness and has been given to us, as the Lord said, precisely as a "mother" to whom we can turn at every moment. She always listens to us, she is always close to us, and being Mother of the Son, participates in the power of the Son and in his goodness. We can always entrust the whole of our lives to this Mother, who is not far from any one of us.

I entrust myself to you, Jesus, through Mary, your Mother and mine.

DAILY WORD: God has won!

EVENING REVIEW: How did I see the victory of love?

August 16: St. Stephen of Hungary (969–1038)

Stephen was the first king of the Magyar people of Hungary, and he showed himself an able leader. He had a special concern for the poor and often walked the streets in disguise as he gave alms to people in need.

His advice to his son is good advice for everyone:

I pray that you may show favor not only to relations and kin, or to the most eminent, be they leaders or rich men or neighbors or countrymen, but also to foreigners and to all who come to you. Be merciful to all who are suffering violence, keeping always in your heart the example of the

Lord who said: "I desire mercy and not sacrifice." Be patient with everyone, not only with the powerful, but also with the weak. Finally, be strong lest prosperity lift you up too much or adversity cast you down. Be humble in this life, that God may raise you up in the next. Be truly moderate and be gentle. Be honorable so that you may never bring disgrace upon anyone. All these virtues I have noted above make up the royal crown, and without them no one is fit to rule here on earth or attain to the heavenly kingdom.

Jesus, through Baptism, you share your kingship, your royal identity with me. Make me worthy of it, and may I bring no disgrace to it today. I know that I am weak and prone to seek my own good rather than the common good, the good of others. Therefore, I need your grace to be true to my deepest identity. I offer myself to you that you may transform me and my world as you desire.

DAILY WORD: I am a royal son/daughter.

EVENING REVIEW: How did I live the virtues that St. Stephen enumerated?

August 17

From July to November, 1916, one of the bloodiest battles of World War I raged. About 140,000 Allied soldiers were killed, including an Irish Jesuit who served as chaplain and fell on August 16—Fr. William Doyle.

Sergeant T. Flynn wrote in a letter home: "We had the misfortune to lose our chaplain, Fr. Doyle, the other day. He was a real saint and would never leave his men. He did not know what fear was, and everybody in the battalion, Catholic and Protestant alike, idolized him. He was asked not to go into action with the battalion, but he would not stop behind, and I am confident that no braver or holier man ever fell in battle than he."

He himself wrote:

I have long had the feeling that, since the world is growing so rapidly worse and worse and God has lost His hold,
as it were, upon the hearts of men, He is looking all the
more earnestly and anxiously for big things from those who
are faithful to Him still. He cannot, perhaps, gather a large
army round His standard, but He wants everyone in it to
be a hero, absolutely and lovingly devoted to Him. If only
we could get inside that magic circle of generous souls, I
believe there is no grace He would not give us to help on
the work He has so much at heart, our personal sanctification. Every day you live means an infallible growth in holiness which may be multiplied a thousand times by a little
generosity.

*Jesus, I often feel I am a coward. I give myself to you so that you
may make me a hero in the great battle you are still waging against
evil.*

DAILY WORD: Overcome evil with good.

EVENING REVIEW: What battles did I win or lose?

August 18: St. Alberto Hurtado (1901–1952)

On this day in 1952, at the age of fifty-one, Fr. Alberto Hur-
tado died of pancreatic cancer. He had joined the Jesuits in
Chile in 1922 after obtaining a law degree. To meet the
needs of the homeless children of Santiago, he started "El
Hogar de Cristo", "The Home of Christ". Pope Benedict
XVI canonized him in 2005.

Shortly after his ordination in 1933, he wrote:

The secret is in devotion to the Sacred Heart of Jesus, to
the overflowing love of our Lord, the love that Jesus as God
and as man has for us, a love that shone clearly throughout
his life. If we could only realize this ideal in our lives: What

does the Heart of Jesus think of this or that? And endeavor to think and feel as he does, how this would enlarge our hearts and transform our lives! In this pervasive atmosphere of skepticism in which we live, I do not think there are any other means, humanly speaking, to preach Jesus Christ among those who will only believe the example of a charity like that of Christ.

He also said: "Devotion to the Sacred Heart cannot content itself with savoring the love of God but must repay it with concrete love in return. Christianity is summed up in the word love: an ardent desire for the happiness of our brothers, not only the eternal happiness of heaven, but also everything that will make them better and happier in this life, everything worthy of a son of God."

Jesus, St. Alberto said, "The Mass is my life, and my life is a prolonged Mass." Help me to live the Mass so that my life may become a perfect offering like yours.

DAILY WORD: "My life is a prolonged Mass."

EVENING REVIEW: How did I help make others better and happier?

August 19: St. John Eudes (1601–1680)

John founded the Congregation of Jesus and Mary to meet the need for better seminary formation. Devoted to the Hearts of Jesus and Mary, he composed the prayers that were later used at Masses in honor of the Sacred Heart.

He wrote: "You are one with Jesus as the body is one with the head. The mysteries of Jesus are not yet completely perfected and fulfilled. They are complete, indeed, in the person of Jesus, but not in us, who are his members, nor in the Church, which is his Mystical Body." As a result, we are called to make up, in St. Paul's words, "what is lacking in Christ's afflictions for the sake of his body" (Col 1:24). St. John also wrote:

> The Heart of Christ is a temple of divine love. It is an eternal temple, the altar of divine love. It is on this altar that the sacred fire of that same love is burning night and day. It is on this altar that our High Priest Jesus offers and sacrifices himself as a victim of love, the holiest and most perfect that ever was or ever will be. He sacrifices Himself entirely, His body, His soul, His blood, all His life, all His thoughts, all His actions, and all that He has suffered on earth. He makes this offering ceaselessly and with an immense and infinite love. Let us then offer ourselves to Him and ask Him to consume us entirely, as holocausts of His love, in the divine flames that ceaselessly burn on the altar of His Heart.

Jesus, out of love for you and all mankind, I offer myself with you to the Father.

DAILY WORD: I offer this for love of you.

EVENING REVIEW: How did I imitate Jesus' perfect offering?

August 20: St. Bernard (1090–1153)

When he was twenty-two, Bernard, with five of his brothers and twenty-five other young noblemen, entered a Cistercian monastery in France. Three years later, he was sent to start a new monastery at Clairvaux, which soon became the center of monastic renewal throughout Europe. He is known as the "Mellifluous Doctor" from the Latin "mel" (honey) because of his attractive personality and desire to bring harmony to the Church.

He wrote:

> Of all the movements, sensations, and feelings of the soul, love is the only one in which the creature can respond to

the Creator and make some sort of similar return, however unequal though it be. For when God loves, all he desires is to be loved in return; the sole purpose of his love is to be loved, in the knowledge that those who love him are made happy by their love of him. The Bridegroom asks in return nothing but faithful love. Let the beloved, then, love in return. Could it be that Love not be loved?

I offer myself now in these words of St. Bernard:

O Lord, I willingly offer You my sacrifice, since You freely offered Yourself, not through any need on Your part, but for my salvation. I have only two poor possessions, O Lord: my body and my soul. How I wish I could worthily offer You these two pittances in a sacrifice of praise! It would be better, much better, for me to offer myself to You than to be left to myself. In fact, if I remain alone, my soul is troubled, but in You my spirit is exultant as soon as it offers itself to You in complete dedication. In very truth, that is an offering which pleases You, a living offering.

DAILY WORD: I want Love to be loved.

EVENING REVIEW: How did I attract people to Christ?

August 21: St. Pius X (1835–1914)

Pius X is called the "Pope of the Eucharist" because of his decrees encouraging frequent reception of Holy Communion and for lowering the age at which children could receive.

He saw the world heading toward worldwide conflict, and in 1903, in his first encyclical, entitled "On the Restoration of All Things in Christ", he called man back to God in these words:

Who can avoid being appalled and afflicted when he beholds, in the midst of a progress in civilization which is justly extolled, the greater part of mankind fighting among themselves so savagely as to make it seem as though strife were universal? The desire for peace is certainly harbored in every breast, and there is no one who does not ardently invoke it. But to want peace without God is an absurdity, seeing that where God is absent thence too justice flies, and when justice is taken away it is vain to cherish the hope of peace. "Peace is the work of justice" (Is 22:17). There are many, we are well aware, who, in their yearning for peace, that is for the tranquility of order, band themselves into societies and parties, which they style parties of order. Hope and labor lost. For there is but one party of order capable of restoring peace in the midst of all this turmoil, and that is the party of God. It is this party, therefore, that we must advance, and to it attract as many as possible, if we are really urged by the love of peace.

Jesus, make me an instrument of your peace today. I offer myself to you so that through me you may attract others to yourself—the Justice of God, the True Reconciler, the Prince of Peace.

DAILY WORD: "To restore all things in Christ."

EVENING REVIEW: How did I work for justice and peace?

August 22: The Queenship of Mary

Eight days after the feast of the Assumption of Mary into heaven, we celebrate her coronation as Queen of heaven and earth. Raised body and soul into heaven, she shares in the glory of Jesus Christ the King.

When he instituted this feast in 1954, Pope Pius XII wrote:

> Certainly, in the full and strict meaning of the term, only Jesus Christ, the God-Man, is King; but Mary, too, as Mother of the divine Christ, as His associate in the redemption, in His struggle with His enemies and His final victory over them, has a share, though in a limited and analogous way,

in His royal dignity. For from her union with Christ she attains a radiant eminence transcending that of any other creature; from her union with Christ she receives the royal right to dispose of the treasures of the Divine Redeemer's Kingdom. . . . Let all, therefore, try to approach with greater trust the throne of grace and mercy of our Queen and Mother, and beg for strength in adversity, light in darkness, consolation in sorrow; above all let them strive to free themselves from the slavery of sin and offer an unceasing homage, filled with filial loyalty, to their Queenly Mother.

Honoring the royal dignity of Mary today, we are reminded that through Baptism we, too, have become royalty, for Scripture says: "you are a chosen race, a royal priesthood, a holy nation, God's own people" (1 Pet 2:9).

Jesus, one with you in Baptism, I believe that I am part of your royal family. I offer myself to you so that I may live today conscious of the dignity that is mine.

DAILY WORD: I serve as my King and Queen did.

EVENING REVIEW: How did I live out my royal dignity and responsibility?

August 23: St. Rose of Lima (1586–1617)

As a child, Rose, the first canonized saint of the Western Hemisphere, wanted to become a nun, but her parents opposed her. She ended up vowing not to marry and to live a single life as a lay Dominican, dedicating herself to prayer, penance, and works of charity. Rose shows us that even when our desires are not fulfilled, God will help us attain our goal of holiness in other ways.

The Second Vatican Council spoke of "the universal call to holiness". In 2001, Pope St. John Paul II wrote:

Since Baptism is a true entry into the holiness of God through incorporation into Christ and the indwelling of his Spirit, it would be a contradiction to settle for a life of mediocrity, marked by a minimalist ethic and a shallow religiosity. To ask catechumens: "Do you wish to receive Baptism?" means at the same time to ask them: "Do you wish to become holy?" It means to set before them the radical nature of the Sermon on the Mount: "Be perfect as your heavenly Father is perfect" (Mt 5:48). As the Council itself explained, this ideal of perfection must not be misunderstood as if it involved some kind of extraordinary existence, possible only for a few "uncommon heroes" of holiness. The ways of holiness are many, according to the vocation of each individual.

Through the events and opportunities of each day, I can grow in holiness. When my plans are disrupted, I have an opportunity to exercise total and trusting surrender to the will of God in the moment.

Father, I am your child. I give you my day so that you can make me perfectly holy as you are holy.

DAILY WORD: I want to be holy.

EVENING REVIEW: How was God making me holy as I tried to be faithful to my vocation?

August 24: St. Bartholomew, Apostle

According to Pope Benedict XVI, Bartholomew, also known as Nathanael, met Jesus in an unexpected place (see Jn 1:45 – 51). He said:

> Philip told this Nathanael that he had found "him of whom Moses in the law and also the prophets wrote, Jesus of Nazareth, the son of Joseph" (Jn 1:45). As we know, Nathanael's retort was rather strongly prejudiced: "Can anything good come out of Nazareth?". . . But at the same

time Nathanael's protest highlights God's freedom, which baffles our expectations by causing him to be found in the very place where we least expect him. . . . Nathanael's reaction suggests another thought to us: in our relationship with Jesus we must not be satisfied with words alone. In his answer, Philip offers Nathanael a meaningful invitation: "Come and see!" (Jn 1:46). Our knowledge of Jesus needs above all a first-hand experience.

We see here the importance of the personal experience of Jesus that prayer gives us. A privileged place for meeting him is the Scriptures, because "the word of God is living and active" (Heb 4:12). Prayerful reading of Scripture helps me to know the ways of God. Then, as I go about my daily life, I am more attentive to the Lord's presence in its events and in the people I meet.

Jesus, before you met Nathanael, you said "Behold, an Israelite indeed, in whom there is no guile" (Jn 1:47). Make me like him. I give myself to you so that you may make of me a person of integrity. May I never lead a double life, saying one thing and doing another. Make the witness of my life today consistent with the fact that I am your friend and follower.

DAILY WORD: "No guile!"

EVENING REVIEW: How did I live my day with integrity and not duplicity?

August 25: St. Louis (1214–1270)

Husband, father, king of France—Louis found holiness in the midst of the world. He showed concern for the poor and especially enjoyed helping blind people who could not recognize him. Louis knew that true glory is found, not in earthly power, but in being a servant king like Christ.

Through Baptism we are joined to Christ and share in his kingly mission. In a 1988 Apostolic Exhortation, Pope St. John Paul II wrote:

> Through charity towards one's neighbor, the lay faithful exercise and manifest their participation in the kingship of Christ, that is, in the power of the Son of man who 'came not to be served but to serve' (Mk 10:45). They live and manifest such a kingship in a most simple yet exalted manner, possible for everyone at all times because charity is the highest gift offered by the Spirit for building up the Church . . . and for the good of humanity.

St. Louis wrote the following to his son:

> My dearest son, my first instruction is that you should love the Lord your God with all your heart and all your strength. Keep yourself from everything that you know displeases God, that is to say, from every mortal sin. If the Lord has permitted you to have some trial, bear it willingly and with gratitude, considering that it has happened for your good and that perhaps you well deserved it. If the Lord bestows upon you any kind of prosperity, thank him humbly and see that you become no worse for it, either through vain pride or anything else, because you ought not to offend him in the matter of his gifts.

Father, I give myself to you "for building up the Church and for the good of humanity."

DAILY WORD: Keep me from sin.

EVENING REVIEW: How did I deal with adversity and prosperity?

August 26

Yesterday was also the optional memorial of St. Joseph Calasanz (1557–1648). He was a Spanish priest who, while serving as personal theologian to a cardinal in Rome, was appalled at the abandoned children he saw there. He began schools for them and founded a congregation, the Piarists, who take a fourth vow dedicating themselves to the education of poor youth.

He wrote about the importance of education:

> Everyone knows the great merit and dignity attached to that holy ministry in which the young, especially the poor, receive instruction for the purpose of attaining eternal life. This ministry is directed to the well-being of body and soul; at the same time it shapes behavior, it also fosters devotion and Christian doctrine. Like the twigs of plants the young are easily influenced, as long as someone works to change their souls. But if they are allowed to grow hard, we know well that the possibility of one day bending them diminishes a great deal and is sometimes utterly lost.

He also gave this advice:

> All who undertake to teach must be endowed with deep love, the greatest patience, and, most of all, profound humility. They must perform their work with earnest zeal. Then, through their humble prayers, the Lord will find them worthy to become fellow workers with him in the cause of truth. He will console them in the fulfillment of this most noble duty, and, finally enrich them with the gift of heaven.

Christ the Teacher, I offer myself to you today so that all my words and actions may teach others of your love. In particular, I offer my day as a prayer for all teachers and students as they begin a new school year.

DAILY WORD: My day is a prayer.

August 27: St. Monica (332–387)

Pope Benedict XVI said:

> Today . . . we commemorate St Monica and tomorrow we will be commemorating St Augustine, her son: their witnesses can be of great comfort and help to so many families also in our time. Monica, who was born into a Christian family [in North Africa], lived her mission as a wife and mother in an exemplary way, helping her husband Patricius to discover the beauty of faith in Christ and the power of evangelical love, which can overcome evil with good. After his premature death, Monica courageously devoted herself to caring for her three children, including Augustine, who initially caused her suffering with his somewhat rebellious temperament.

For thirty years, Monica prayed with great intensity for Augustine, who put off being baptized because he did not want to change his immoral life-style and followed the Manichean heresy. A bishop told her to persevere, saying: "Let him be, and continue to pray for him; it's impossible that a son of so many tears should be lost." In time, Augustine was converted and went on to become a great bishop and Doctor of the Church.

Augustine reports that shortly before Monica's death, the two of them talked about "what it would be like to share the eternal life enjoyed by the saints". As they talked, "the world and its pleasures lost all their attractions." Monica wondered why she was still alive because she had fulfilled her mission.

I, too, have a mission. It may not seem as dramatic as Monica's, but it is. My own prayers, tears, and sacrifices can play a role in others' conversion.

Loving God, I offer you my day for the conversion of all who do not know you or have rejected you.

DAILY WORD: My offering can help someone.

EVENING REVIEW: For whom did I consciously offer myself?

August 28: St. Augustine (354–430)

We customarily honor saints on the day of their death, their birth into heaven. Forty-three years and one day after the death of his mother, Monica, Augustine died, ensuring that their feasts would be celebrated one after the other.

Regarding the son, Pope Benedict XVI said:

> His whole life was a passionate search for the truth. In the end, not without a long inner torment, he found in Christ the ultimate and full meaning of his own life and of the whole of human history. In adolescence, attracted by earthly beauty, he "flung himself" upon it . . . with selfish and possessive behavior that caused his pious mother great pain. But through a toilsome journey and thanks also to her prayers, Augustine became always more open to the fullness of truth and love until his conversion, which happened in Milan under the guidance of the Bishop, St Ambrose.

With the following prayer of St. Augustine, I acknowledge God's love for me and return that love by offering myself:

Late have I loved you, O Beauty ever ancient, ever new, late have I loved you! You were within me, but I was outside, and it was there that I searched for you. In my unloveliness I plunged into the lovely things which you created. You were with me, but I was not with you. Created things kept me from you; yet if they had not been in you they would not have been at all. You called, you shouted, and you broke through my deafness. You flashed, you shone, and you dis-

pelled my blindness. You breathed your fragrance on me; I drew in breath, and now I pant for you. I have tasted you, now I hunger and thirst for more. You touched me, and I burned for your peace.

DAILY WORD: I burn for your peace.

EVENING REVIEW: How did God touch me?

August 29: The Passion of John the Baptist

In addition to a feast for the birth of John (June 24), we also have a feast to honor his martyrdom. According to the Gospels and the "Antiquities" written by the early Jewish historian Josephus, John was imprisoned by King Herod because he challenged the immorality of Herod's taking his brother's wife Herodias as his own. When Salome, daughter of Herodias, thrilled Herod with a dance, he promised her "whatever you ask me, . . . even half of my kingdom" (Mk 6:23). Prompted by her mother, Salome asked for John's head on a platter.

We might wonder how this was a martyrdom—a witness to Jesus. St. Bede the Venerable answered: "There is no doubt that blessed John suffered imprisonment and chains as a witness to our Redeemer, whose forerunner he was, and gave his life for him. His persecutor had demanded, not that he should deny Christ, but only that he should keep silent about the truth. Nevertheless, he died for Christ. Does Christ not say: I am the truth? Therefore, because John shed his blood for the truth, he surely died for Christ."

We live in a world that Pope Francis, quoting Pope Benedict XVI, called "a dictatorship of relativism". It's a world that denies there is an objective truth that can be known. Witnessing to the truth requires courage, just as it did for John the Baptist and millions afterward who were threatened by those who deny the truth of the human person and God.

Jesus, you told the apostles that you are "the truth" (Jn 14:6), and you told Pilate, "For this I was born, and for this I have come into the world, to bear witness to the truth" (Jn 18:37). I give myself to you. Make me a witness to the truth.

DAILY WORD: Truth at all times.

EVENING REVIEW: Was I truthful? Did my day witness to truth?

August 30: St. Jeanne Jugan (1792–1879)

As a youth, Jeanne rejected marriage proposals, saying, "God wants me for himself, he is keeping me for a work that is not yet founded." In 1839, she met an elderly, half-paralyzed, blind woman whom she carried home and placed in her own bed while she slept in the attic. This was the humble beginning of the Little Sisters of the Poor.

Jeanne was canonized in 2009 by Pope Benedict XVI, who said:

> "Come, follow me." This is the Christian vocation which is born from the Lord's proposal of love and can only be fulfilled in our loving response. Jesus invites his disciples to give their lives completely, without calculation or personal interest, with unreserved trust in God. Saints accept this demanding invitation and set out with humble docility in the following of the Crucified and Risen Christ. Their perfection . . . consists in no longer putting themselves at the center but in choosing to go against the tide, living in line with the Gospel.
>
> Jeanne Jugan was concerned with the dignity of her brothers and sisters . . . whom age had made more vulnerable, recognizing in them the Person of Christ himself. . . . Jeanne focused upon the elderly a compassionate gaze drawn from her profound communion with God in her joyful, disinterested service, . . . desiring herself to be poor among the poor. Jeanne lived the mystery of love,

peacefully accepting obscurity and self-emptying until her death. . . . In the Beatitudes [she] found the source of the spirit of hospitality and fraternal love, founded on unlimited trust in Providence.

Jesus, by offering you my day, I place you at the center of my life. Help me live "in line with the Gospel" today.

DAILY WORD: "God wants me for himself."

EVENING REVIEW: Who was at the center of the hours of my day?

August 31: St. Raymond Nonnatus (1204–1240).

St. Raymond Nonnatus died on this day in 1240. "Nonnatus" is Latin for "not born", and this name was given to Raymond because of the way in which he came into the world in 1204. His mother died during labor, and he was cut from his mother's womb. In time Raymond joined the recently founded Mercedarian Order, a religious congregation with the mission of ransoming Christian slaves. Mercedarians went so far as to take their place until enough money could be collected to pay the ransom. This is what Raymond did, and while he was in prison, he preached the Gospel so convincingly that some of his Muslim captors became Christian. This infuriated the governor, who, according to tradition, had a red-hot spike driven through Raymond's lips and a padlock inserted to prevent his preaching. Eventually Raymond was ransomed, returned to Europe, and was made a cardinal adviser to the pope, who had heard about his courageous witness. On his way to Rome, he died.

I might ask myself today: Are there invisible locks on my lips that prevent me from speaking the truth with love?

What prevents me from sharing my faith? Is it fear of what others will think of me? Is it fear of conflict? Is it laziness?

Holy Spirit, you came at Pentecost and gave the apostles courage to preach in a way that all who heard them understood. I offer myself to you today so that I might be your voice. Come to me with your gift of fortitude. May I speak the truth in a way that shows others my love for them and promotes the harmony that you bring.

DAILY WORD: Truth with love.

EVENING REVIEW: How did fear and courage play a role in what I said and did?

SEPTEMBER

September 1: World Day of Prayer for the Care of Creation

Pope Francis instituted an annual day to pray for the care of creation in order to give "to individual believers and to the community a precious opportunity to renew our personal participation in this vocation as custodians of creation, raising to God our thanks for the marvelous works that He has entrusted to our care, invoking His help for the protection of creation and His mercy for the sins committed against the world in which we live."

Made in God's image, I am called to work with God, who loves and cares for creation. I offer my day for the care of God's gift of creation with part of Pope Francis' prayer at the end of his encyclical *Laudato Si*:

Triune Lord, wondrous community of infinite love, teach us to contemplate you in the beauty of the universe, for all things speak of you. Awaken our praise and thankfulness for every being that you have made. Give us the grace to feel profoundly joined to everything that is. God of love, show us our place in this world as channels of your love for all the creatures of this earth, for not one of them is forgotten in your sight. Enlighten those who possess power and money that they may avoid the sin of indifference, that they may love the common good, advance the weak, and care for this world in which we live. The poor and the earth are crying out. O Lord, seize us with your power and light, help us to protect all life, to prepare for a better future, for the coming of your Kingdom of justice, peace, love, and beauty. Praise be to you! Amen.

DAILY WORD: All your works speak of your glory, Lord (see Ps 145:10–11).

EVENING REVIEW: How did my actions show care or disrespect for creation?

September 2

The Bible speaks of creation as God's handiwork. After each "day", as new wonders were created, God looked on creation and "saw that it was good" (Gen 1:4, 10, 12, 18, 21, 25). The climax of God's creative efforts was man, for then God "saw everything that he had made, and behold, it was very good" (1:31). God now had a partner in the work of caring for his beautiful creation.

The *Catechism of the Catholic Church* (no. 2427) highlights the value of work:

> *Human work* proceeds directly from persons created in the image of God and called to prolong the work of creation by subduing the earth, both with and for one another. . . . Work honors the Creator's gifts and the talents received from him. It can also be redemptive. By enduring the hardship of work in union with Jesus, the carpenter of Nazareth and the one crucified on Calvary, man collaborates in a certain fashion with the Son of God in his redemptive work. He shows himself to be a disciple of Christ by carrying the cross, daily, in the work he is called to accomplish. Work can be a means of sanctification and a way of animating earthly realities with the Spirit of Christ.

Loving Creator, I accept my call to work with you in caring for creation. I want my work today to give you glory and to make the world a better place for all your children. I join the difficult and unpleasant tasks of the day to the Cross of your Son so that they may play a role in the building of your Kingdom.

September 3: St. Gregory the Great (540–604)

Gregory, the son of a Roman senator, was the city's prefect from 573 to 578. After his father's death, he became a monk and turned his home into a monastery. In 579, Pope Pelagius II sent him as his personal representative to the Eastern Emperor in Constantinople. Seven years later, he was called back to be papal advisor, and when the pope died, Gregory was elected to succeed him on this day in 590. Thus began the work that led to his being called "Great". He wrote many theological and pastoral books and sent missionaries to a distant island—England. He promoted a form of Church music that bears his name and helped the city of Rome, rebuilding it after natural disasters, feeding the hungry through charitable programs, and protecting it from barbarian invaders.

He wrote:

"Blessed are those who have not seen and have believed" (Jn 20:29). There is here a particular reference to ourselves; we hold in our hearts one we have not seen in the flesh. We are included in these words, but only if we follow up our faith with good works. The true believer practices what he believes. But of those who pay only lip service to faith, Paul has this to say: "They profess to know God, but they deny him in their works" (Tit 1:16). Therefore James says: "Faith without works is dead" (2:17).

We see Gregory's emphasis on deeds in these words as well: "The proof of love is in the works. Where love exists, it works great things. But when it ceases to act, it ceases to exist."

Jesus, I love you, and I want this entire day to be proof of my love.

DAILY WORD: For you, Jesus.

EVENING REVIEW: How deep was the love I showed?

September 4

Work is often viewed as a punishment. This idea comes from the Bible, where Genesis shows God telling Adam after the first sin: "Cursed is the ground because of you; in toil shall you eat of it all the days of your life. . . . In the sweat of your face you shall eat bread" (3:17, 19). Work can be difficult, but it is not a punishment. Work makes us like God, who invites us to share in the work of caring for creation.

St. Ignatius reflected on this in his "Spiritual Exercises", writing: "Consider how God works and labors for you in all creatures upon the face of the earth, that is, he conducts himself as one who labors. Thus, in the heavens, the elements, the plants, the fruits, the cattle, etc., he gives being, conserves them, confers life and sensation, etc." (no. 236).

Moreover, Jesus came to carry on the work of the Father. He said: "My food is to do the will of him who sent me, and to accomplish his work" (Jn 4:34). "Truly, truly, I say to you, the son can do nothing of his own accord, but only what he sees the Father doing" (Jn 5:19). "If I am not doing the works of my Father, then do not believe me" (Jn 10:37).

God works for the good of creation, and Jesus works with the Father. As one of Jesus' followers, joined to him through Baptism, I also work.

Lord Jesus, I give myself to you so that the works of the Father may be accomplished through me as they were accomplished through you. Work with me today and every day.

DAILY WORD: This work is God's work.

September 5: St. Teresa of Kolkata (1910–1997)

Born in what is now Macedonia, Mother Teresa felt called to consecrated life. She went to Ireland and joined the Sisters of Our Lady of Loreto. She was sent to India, where, in 1948, she experienced a special call and founded the Missionaries of Charity. In the years that followed, she experienced terrible interior darkness, but she persevered, demonstrating that the love of God is not so much a feeling as an act of the will and action.

She wrote:

> Total abandonment consists of giving oneself fully to God because God has given himself to us. If God, who owes us nothing, is willing to give us nothing less than himself, can we respond by giving him only a part of ourselves? Renouncing myself, I give myself to God that he might live in me. How poor we would be if God had not given us the power to give ourselves over to him! Instead, how rich we are right now! How easy it is to conquer God! We give ourselves to him, and God becomes ours, and now we have nothing but God. The prize with which God rewards our self-abandonment is himself.

The following was a daily prayer of Mother Teresa:

Dear Jesus, help me to spread Thy fragrance everywhere I go. Flood my soul with Thy spirit and love. Penetrate and possess my whole being so utterly that all my life may only be a radiance of Thine. Shine through me and be so in me that every soul I come in contact with may feel Thy presence in my soul. Let them look up and see no longer me but only Jesus. Stay with me, and then I shall begin to shine as you shine, so to shine as to be a light to others.

DAILY WORD: I am Christ's fragrance.

EVENING REVIEW: How did I shine?

September 6

The word "labor" means "work", but it also refers to the process of giving birth. Not all labor, whether it's the work one does or the process of birthing, is easy. It can be painful. But in both cases, labor is designed to bring new life. All human work should be directed toward respecting and fostering human life with an eye toward eternal life.

Both work and childbirth involve sacrifice. This is not a popular word in a world that wants more not less. Yet sacrifice is a key element of love. True love is willing to sacrifice everything for the beloved.

St. Paul shows us the proper attitude toward work when he gives this advice: "Slaves, be obedient to those who are your earthly masters, with fear and trembling, in singleness of heart, as to Christ; not in the way of eye-service, as men-pleasers, but as servants of Christ, doing the will of God from the heart, rendering service with a good will as to the Lord and not to men, knowing that whatever good any one does, he will receive the same again from the Lord, whether he is a slave or free" (Eph 6:5-8). He repeats this to the Colossians: "Whatever your task, work heartily, as serving the Lord and not men, knowing that from the Lord you will receive the inheritance as your reward; you are serving the Lord Christ" (3:23-24).

In other words, our work and the sacrifice it often involves has purpose and meaning no matter what it is because it can be done for God, as an act of love.

Father, thank you for my skills and talents. Thank you for the time you give me to use them to show you my love.

DAILY WORD: God is my master.

EVENING REVIEW: How did my activities show my love for God?

September 7

Tomorrow is the anniversary of the death of Bl. Frédéric Ozanam (1813–1853), who earned both a law degree and a doctorate in literature and became, at the age of twenty-seven, the youngest professor at the prestigious and very secular Sorbonne in Paris. He started a discussion group among the students where one of them challenged him, saying "The Church is hypocrisy. What are you doing for the poor?" In response, Frédéric and several friends started the Conference of Charity, which soon became known as the St. Vincent de Paul Society.

In 1997, at his beatification, Pope St. John Paul II said:

> Frédéric Ozanam believed in love, the love of God for every individual. He felt himself called to love, giving the example of a great love for God and others. He went to all those who needed to be loved more than others, those to whom the love of God could not be revealed effectively except through the love of another person. There Ozanam discovered his vocation, the path to which Christ called him. He found his road to sanctity. And he followed it with determination. . . . He understood that charity must lead to efforts to remedy injustice. Charity and justice go together.

I renew my offering with part of a prayer from the St. Vincent de Paul Society:

> *Lord Jesus, make us responsive to the Christian calling to seek and find the forgotten, the suffering, or the deprived so that we may bring them your love. Help us to be generous with our time, our possessions, and ourselves in this mission of charity. Perfect in us your love, and teach us to share more fully in the Eucharistic Sacrifice offered for all.*

DAILY WORD: God is love.

EVENING REVIEW: How did I show the love of God for all?

September 8: The Nativity of Mary

Because the Blessed Virgin Mary was conceived and born without sin, we celebrate her birth as well as her Assumption into heaven.

St. Alphonsus Liguori wrote the following:

> Before the birth of Mary, the world was lost in the darkness of sin. "Mary was born, and the dawn arose", says a holy father. Of Mary it had already been said, "Who is she that comes forth as the morning rising?" As the earth rejoices when the dawn appears, because it is the precursor of the sun, so also when Mary was born, the whole world rejoiced because she was the precursor of Jesus Christ, the Sun of Justice, who being made her son, came to save us by His death. The Church sings, "Your nativity, O Virgin Mother of God, announced joy to the whole world; for from you arose the Sun of Justice, who has given us life eternal."

I ask Mary to take my offering and to purify it so that I may be a blessing for others. My prayer is from Pope Benedict XVI:

Holy Mother of the Lord, at the decisive hour in your life, you said: "Here I am, the servant of the Lord" (Lk 1:38). Teach us to carry out our responsibilities in the same way. Help us to become patient and humble, but also free and courageous, just as you were at the hour of the Cross. In your arms you hold Jesus, the Child who blesses, the Child who is also the Lord of the world. By holding the Child who blesses, you have yourself become a blessing. Show us Jesus, the blessed fruit of your womb! Pray for us sinners, now and at the hour of our death. Amen!

DAILY WORD: Here I am, Lord!

EVENING REVIEW: How did God bless others through me?

September 9: St. Peter Claver (1580–1654)

When he was twenty-five and a Jesuit seminarian, Peter met and was befriended by a seventy-two-year-old Jesuit Brother, St. Alphonsus Rodriguez, who encouraged him to become a saint by going to the New World as a missionary. Peter set sail from Spain and arrived in Cartagena, Colombia, where he was ordained in 1616. Cartagena was the port of entry for the Africans who were kidnapped, transported across the ocean, and sold into slavery. It's estimated that 10,000 slaves a year passed through this port. The conditions on the slave ships were so terrible that it was considered a successful trip if only one-third of the "cargo" died.

Peter, who called himself "the slave of black slaves forever", ran to greet the ships and to care for the slaves. He wrote: "We spoke to them, not with words but with deeds; and for people in their situation who were convinced that they had been brought there to be eaten, any other form of address would have been pointless." When he beatified Peter Claver in 1851, Pope Blessed Pius IX said that he had never read a biography of a saint that so moved him as his. In 1888, Pope Leo XIII canonized both Peter and his mentor, Alphonsus.

Lord God, you called St. Peter Claver to serve the poorest of the poor of his time. He offered himself to your service, persevering in extremely difficult circumstances. His heroic example of sacrificial love inspires me to offer myself in your service. But I am weak. I am afraid of discomfort and pain. Please, give me the same courage that Peter Claver had so that I may show your love in word and deed.

DAILY WORD: Love and sacrifice.

EVENING REVIEW: How did I persevere in loving even when it was unpleasant or difficult?

In 1985, Pope St. John Paul II beatified a humble Jesuit Brother whose primary apostolic work was to serve as the doorkeeper of a Spanish Jesuit college. Bl. Francis Garate, who died on September 9, 1929, is an example of how simple work that appears insignificant in the eyes of the powerful of the world can play a role in the world's salvation when it is joined to the perfect offering of Jesus Christ.

The Jesuit cardinal archbishop of Genoa, Italy, wrote the following about Brother Francis:

> I must say that the most precious memory of my time in Spain is that of the excellent Brother Doorkeeper of our University College of Bilbao. There was nothing remarkable in his outward appearance, but it was enough to exchange words with him even for a short time to realize that he was a man of deep spirituality, endowed with outstanding virtues. During my stay, I would often stop in the porter's lodge. That entrance hall was a place of ceaseless activity: parents wanting to speak to their sons, all kinds of visitors asking to see the Fathers or the professors, tradesmen delivering their goods, beggars asking for alms. For everyone he had a courteous and friendly word and all this with truly remarkable serenity and calm.
>
> One day I asked him, "How are you able, Brother, to be involved in so many things and yet remain so calm, never losing your patience?" His reply was, "Father, I do what I can, and leave the rest to the Lord, who can do everything. With his help all is easy and pleasant, because we serve a good master."

Jesus, Good Master, I offer you all I do. Take it and make up for anything that is lacking.

DAILY WORD: The Lord can do everything.

EVENING REVIEW: In what ways did I exercise serenity and patience, trusting God alone?

September 11

Today is the anniversary of the terrorist attack on the United States in 2001. On that day, Archbishop José Gomez said:

> A friend of mine asked me, "How can we keep our faith when a tragedy like this occurs?" I answered him: What do we expect God to do—be available when we need Him and then go away when we don't? Because that's the way many of us act. We ignore Him, or we pay Him lip service—and then we expect Him to show up like a paramedic when we dial 911. That's not "loving" God. That's just using Him.
>
> It's hard to believe Gospel words like "Do not be distressed or fearful", when murderers crash a plane carrying children into a skyscraper. When the towers of the World Trade Center caved in today, what collapsed with them was any illusion that we can create our own gods out of money or technology, or find safety in our own power and ingenuity.
>
> Tonight is a crossroad in each of our lives. Our only security is God; the way to God is Jesus Christ; and the only way to follow Jesus Christ is to share in His work of redemption, which means sharing the cross, turning away from vengeance and anger, and loving others no matter what the cost. St. Paul asks us to "live according to what you have learned and accepted." Living as disciples, living as people of love rather than hate, is the only road to peace —real peace, the peace that frees us from fear.

Loving God, you want peace for your children. "Let there be peace on earth, and let it begin with me." I offer you my day for the conversion and healing that our world desperately needs.

DAILY WORD: Let there be peace.

EVENING REVIEW: What were my thoughts, words, and works of peace?

September 12: The Most Holy Name of Mary

We honor the name of Mary for several reasons. First, we are following the example of the Archangel Gabriel, who came to Mary announcing that she would be the Mother of God and addressing her with "Hail Mary!" Secondly, Mary spoke prophetically at the Visitation when she said "henceforth all generations will call me blessed" (Lk 1:48). If Mary is called blessed by all, then her name is also blessed. Lastly, Jesus, who is without sin, would have followed the Ten Commandments perfectly, one of which is "Honor your father and your mother." Jesus would have honored his Mother by honoring her name. As Christians, we follow his example. When we honor the name of a person, we honor that person, and Mary, as the Mother of God, deserves such honor.

Pope St. John XXIII wrote:

> It is a name that moves heaven and earth. We pray to Mary continually, and call upon her name. We have the holy rosary: a summary of the whole story of Redemption. These are not events of yesterday—they go back two thousand years—yet they have preserved intact their meaning, their power, and their lesson for every day. That is why we ask you all to recite the rosary, pondering each individual mystery. By so doing we shall have unending peace in our hearts and the hope, nay, the certainty, that Mary hears us, blesses us, and guides us to salvation.

Jesus, Mary is your Mother and the Mother of the Church, your Body. I am happy to call upon my Mother and to ask her help. I do so now as I offer myself so that the will of the Father may be done in me today.

DAILY WORD: "Hail Mary!"

EVENING REVIEW: How did my speech bring honor or dishonor to my Mother Mary?

September 13: St. John Chrysostom (347–407)

John was such an outstanding preacher that he was called "Chrysostom", or "golden-mouthed". He served the Church in Antioch, where the followers of Jesus were first called "Christians". Then he was named the bishop of Constantinople, center of the Eastern Roman Empire. According to Pope Benedict XVI,

> He was tireless in denouncing the contrast that existed in the city between the wasteful extravagance of the rich and the indigence of the poor. . . . He was so persistent in defending the poor and reproaching those who were excessively wealthy that he inspired displeasure and even hostility to himself among some of the rich as well as among those who wielded political power in the city.

He was exiled to Armenia in 404, but after three years was sent even farther away because of his challenging letters.

He wrote:

> Prayer and converse with God is a supreme good: it is a partnership and union with God. I do not mean the prayer of outward observance but prayer from the heart, not confined to fixed times or periods but continuous throughout the day and night. Our spirit should be quick to reach out toward God, not only when it is engaged in meditation; at other times also, when it is carrying out its duties, caring for the needy, performing works of charity, giving generously in the service of others, our spirit should long for God and call Him to mind, so that these works may be seasoned with the salt of God's love and, so, make a palatable offering to the Lord of the universe.

Jesus, as I offer myself, I ask that you help me to pray throughout the coming day so that all I do "may be seasoned with the salt of God's love".

DAILY WORD: Make me salt.

EVENING REVIEW: How mindful of God was I?

September 14: The Exaltation of the Holy Cross

Today's feast commemorates several events. First, the discovery of Jesus' Cross by St. Helen, mother of the Roman emperor Constantine, who legalized Christianity. Second, the dedication of the Church of the Holy Sepulchre, which was built on the site of Jesus' crucifixion, burial, and Resurrection. Third, the return and display of the Cross after it had been taken and held for fifteen years by Persians. All these events, however, are not as important as what made the Cross holy. As Pope Benedict XVI put it: "The Cross is the moving manifestation of the act of infinite love with which the Son of God saved mankind and the world from sin and death. . . . The Church invites us proudly to lift up this glorious Cross so that the world can see the full extent of the love of the Crucified one for mankind, for every man and woman."

St. Andrew of Crete said:

> Had there been no cross, Christ could not have been crucified. Had there been no cross, life itself could not have been nailed to the tree. And if life had not been nailed to it, there would be no streams of immortality pouring from Christ's side, blood and water for the world's cleansing. Had there been no cross, death would not have been trodden underfoot. Therefore the cross is something wonderfully great and honorable. The cross is honorable because it is both the sign of God's suffering and the trophy of his victory.

Jesus, when I look upon a cross, I see how much you loved me. I return love for love. I adore you, O Christ, and I praise you, for by your holy Cross you have redeemed the world.

DAILY WORD: The Cross is my salvation.

EVENING REVIEW: How did I live with hope in Christ's victory?

September 15: Our Lady of Sorrows

After honoring the Cross of Jesus, we honor the one who shared most intimately in the suffering he underwent. Mary suffered as only a mother could as she watched her own flesh and blood die on the Cross. She joined her sufferings to his. Pope Benedict XVI said: "we contemplate Mary sharing her Son's compassion for sinners. As Saint Bernard declares, the Mother of Christ entered into the Passion of her Son through her compassion."

Mary did not scream or try to stop the soldiers. She shared in her Son's faith that this act of violence would not be the end, that somehow God would bring great good from it, that God was saving the world through it. She had great faith, but it didn't take away her own pain and sorrow.

I am called, like Mary, to unite my own sufferings to the Cross of Jesus and in that way participate, as part of his Body, in the salvation of the world. Pope Benedict XVI said:

> Dear brothers and sisters, spiritually united to Our Lady of Sorrows, let us also renew our "yes" to God, who chose the Way of the Cross in order to save us. This is a great mystery which continues and will continue to take place until the end of the world, and which also asks for our collaboration. May Mary help us to take up our cross every day and follow Jesus faithfully on the path of obedience, sacrifice, and love.

Dear Jesus, your Mother shared in your work of saving the world. All suffering, when it is joined to your Cross, becomes a source of grace for the world. Give me faith to believe this as I give myself and my sufferings to you.

DAILY WORD: I share in your work.

EVENING REVIEW: How did I share Christ's Cross?

September 16: Sts. Cornelius (d. 253) and Cyprian (d. 258)

Though they lived across the Mediterranean Sea from one another and never met, Pope Cornelius and Bishop Cyprian of Carthage wrote to each other during one of the controversies of the early Church: whether Christians who renounced the faith under torture could be readmitted to the Church. Both agreed that God's mercy can touch those who wavered in their faith, and both gave their own lives for the faith.

St. Cyprian wrote:

> The world hates Christians, so why give your love to it instead of following Christ, who loves you and has redeemed you? The world and its allurements will pass away, but the one who has done the will of God shall live forever. Our part is to be single-minded, firm in faith, and steadfast in courage, ready for God's will, whatever it may be. Banish the fear of death and think of the eternal life that follows it. That will show people that we really live our faith. We are living here now as aliens and only for a time. When the day of our homecoming puts an end to our exile, we should welcome it. We look upon paradise as our country, and a great crowd of our loved ones awaits us there, a countless throng of parents, brothers, and children longs for us to join them. Assured though they are of their own salvation, they are still concerned about ours. What joy both for them and for us to see one another and embrace! O the delight of that heavenly kingdom where there is fear of death! O the supreme and endless bliss of everlasting life!

Jesus, I want to be with you forever. May each day draw me closer to you and my true homeland.

DAILY WORD: This is not my home.

EVENING REVIEW: What attachments to this life did I struggle with?

September 17: St. Robert Bellarmine (1542–1621)

Robert, considered the greatest theologian of his time, was a Jesuit, teacher, theological advisor to popes, archbishop, and cardinal, yet he always lived with great simplicity. A catechism he wrote has been translated more frequently than any other book except for the Bible and "The Imitation of Christ".

The following passage from *The Mind's Ascent to God* echoes the "First Principle and Foundation" meditation of St. Ignatius' "Spiritual Exercises":

> If you are wise, then, know that you have been created for the glory of God and your own eternal salvation. This is your goal; this is the center of your life; this is the treasure of your heart. If you reach this goal, you will find happiness. If you fail to reach it, you will find misery. May you consider truly good whatever leads to your goal and truly evil whatever makes you fall away from it.

With my goal in mind, I offer myself with these words of St. Robert:

Sweet Lord, you are meek and merciful. Who would not give himself wholeheartedly to your service? What command, Lord, do you give your servants? Take my yoke upon you, you say. And what is this yoke of yours like? My yoke, you say, is easy and my burden light. Who would not be glad for a burden that does not weigh heavy but refreshes? And what is this yoke of yours that does not weary, but gives rest? It is, of course, that first and greatest commandment: You shall love the Lord your God with all your heart. What is easier, sweeter, more pleasant, than to love goodness, beauty, and love, the fullness of which you are, O Lord, my God?

DAILY WORD: For God's glory and my salvation.

EVENING REVIEW: What led me toward my goal, and what made me fall away from it?

September 18

On this day in 1663, a sixty-year-old Franciscan priest, St. Joseph Cupertino, died in Italy. His family's poverty forced them to sell their house, and Joseph was born in a stable. As a youth he wandered aimlessly with his mouth open, earning him the nickname "Boccaperta" or "The Gaper". His work skills were poor, and the Conventual Franciscans rejected him when he tried to join them. The Capuchin Franciscans accepted him but dismissed him after eight months because he was forgetful and clumsy. Finally, the Conventuals, one of whom was his uncle, accepted him. When he heard the names of Jesus and Mary or saw their statues, he entered into a mystical trance from which slaps or pin pricks could not revive him but only the voice of his superior. Well-documented are the cases of levitation where he left the ground during his trances and moved through the air. This led to his being named the patron saint of pilots, aircraft crews, and air travelers.

Many people fear heights and have never flown. Others make sure they make an act of contrition before getting on a plane. But statistics show there is a greater chance someone will be killed in a car accident on the way to the airport than on a plane. Yet people generally feel no need to pray the act of contrition before driving. Why? Because in the car they feel they are in control.

Life is more like flying than driving. We are not in the driver's seat of life, and the sooner we realize this and surrender the care of our lives to God, our Pilot, the more peaceful we will be.

Loving God, I surrender to you my day and my very self because I trust your care for me.

DAILY WORD: Let go and let God.

EVENING REVIEW: How was I called to surrender?

September 19: St. Januarius (d. 305)

Januarius, a bishop in the early Church, is now the patron saint of Naples. Little is known about him, but he has become famous because his relic—a tube of dried blood—has liquefied several times a year since 1389. Scientists have thoroughly studied this phenomenon but have been unable to come up with any natural explanation for it.

What is its meaning? Perhaps this is God's way of telling us that the saints are alive in him and can be powerful intercessors for us. Christians believe that death is not the end of human existence. Joined to the Body of Christ who is risen and alive in glory, Christians live on after their deaths. They are part of the Communion of Saints. We may be separated from them physically, but they are very close to us spiritually, especially at the Eucharist.

When we gather to celebrate the Eucharist, we do so with the Communion of Saints. Stained-glass windows, statues, and icons remind us that we are not alone but are surrounded by angels and saints who worship God with us. The Letter to the Hebrews, referring to those who have died, says that "we are surrounded by so great a cloud of witnesses" (12:1). At Mass we gather together to witness a greater miracle than the liquefying of dried blood. We see Jesus make his life-giving death and Resurrection present, and we see the bread and wine become the Body and Blood of Jesus.

Jesus, I believe that I am never alone. I am part of your Body, the Communion of Saints. I offer myself to you for the building up of that part of the Body that is still on earth.

DAILY WORD: I am not alone.

EVENING REVIEW: How did the saints and I work together to build up Christ's Body, the Church?

September 20: Martyrs of Korea (19th Century)

The faith came to Korea, not through foreign missionaries, but through one layman. He was a government official who found Chinese Christian books, and, when he went on a diplomatic mission to China, he looked for a priest. He was baptized and brought the faith with him when he returned to his native land. Ten years later, when a Chinese priest arrived in Korea, he found 4,000 Christians. The spread of Christianity was not received well by the government, which began a persecution. When he canonized them in 1984 during a visit to Korea, Pope St. John Paul II said: "From the thirteen-year-old Peter Yu to the seventy-two-year-old Mark Chong, men and women, clergy and laity, rich and poor, ordinary people and nobles . . . they all gladly died for the sake of Christ."

Speaking of the martyrs during his 2014 visit to Korea, Pope Francis said:

> They were willing to make great sacrifices and let themselves be stripped of whatever kept them from Christ—possessions and land, prestige and honor—for they knew that Christ alone was their true treasure. So often we today can find our faith challenged by the world, and in countless ways we are asked to compromise our faith, to water down the radical demands of the Gospel and to conform to the spirit of this age. Yet the martyrs call out to us to put Christ first and to see all else in this world in relation to him and his eternal Kingdom. They challenge us to think about what, if anything, we ourselves would be willing to die for.

Jesus, I give myself completely to you. I want nothing to be more important to me than you.

DAILY WORD: Christ is my treasure.

EVENING REVIEW: How was I challenged to put Christ first?

September 21: St. Matthew

Matthew, apostle and Gospel-writer, was a tax-collector, one of a group of public sinners because they were generally dishonest and they collaborated with the hated Roman occupiers. Reflecting on this, Pope Benedict XVI said:

> Jesus does not exclude anyone from his friendship. Indeed, precisely while he is at table in the home of Matthew-Levi, in response to those who expressed shock at the fact that he associated with people who had so little to recommend them, he made the important statement: 'Those who are well have no need of a physician, but those who are sick; I came not to call the righteous, but sinners' (Mk 2:17). . . . Those who seem to be the farthest from holiness can even become a model of the acceptance of God's mercy and offer a glimpse of its marvelous effects in their own lives.

When Jesus called, Matthew responded immediately. Pope Benedict said:

> Matthew understood that familiarity with Jesus did not permit him to pursue activities of which God disapproved. The application to the present day is easy to see: it is not permissible today either to be attached to things that are incompatible with the following of Jesus. . . . Jesus once said, mincing no words: "If you would be perfect, go, sell what you possess and give to the poor, and you will have treasure in heaven; and come, follow me" (Mt 19:21). This is exactly what Matthew did: he rose and followed him! In this "he rose", it is legitimate to read detachment from a sinful situation and, at the same time, a conscious attachment to a new, upright life in communion with Jesus.

Jesus, I want to leave behind anything that separates me from you so that I may be with you always.

DAILY WORD: I am called.

EVENING REVIEW: Did I do anything incompatible with following Jesus?

We find a striking example of making an offering of the moments and activities of the day in the Carmelite, Brother Lawrence of the Resurrection (1614–1691). His superior wrote: "He told me that one day, while looking at a tree stripped of its leaves, and reflecting that before long its leaves would bloom, he received an insight into the providence and the power of God which was never erased from his soul."

Not only did God use the world around him to speak to Brother Lawrence, but he told God of his love by his actions. He wrote in a letter: "I flip my little omelet in the frying pan for the love of God, and when it's done, if I have nothing to do, I adore my God who gave me the grace to do it. When I can do nothing else, it is enough for me to pick up a straw from the ground for the love of God."

His superior wrote down these words of his: "That we ought not to be weary of doing little things for the love of God, who regards not the greatness of the work, but the love with which it is performed. That our sanctification did not depend upon changing our works, but in doing that for God's sake, which we commonly do for our own."

I renew my offering with this prayer of his:

My God, since you are with me, and since I must apply myself to these duties by your order, I beg you to give me the grace to remain with you and keep you company. Even better, my Lord, work with me, accept my efforts, and take possession of all my affections.

DAILY WORD: All for the love of God.

EVENING REVIEW: How did God speak to me? How did I speak to God?

September 23: St. Pius of Pietrelcina (1887–1968)

Padre Pio, whom Pope St. John Paul II visited in 1947 when he was a young priest studying in Rome and whom he called "a living image of Christ suffering and risen", was a Capuchin Franciscan who received the mystical gift of the stigmata in 1918. He spent many hours hearing confessions and founded a hospital called "Home for the Relief of Suffering".

Padre Pio gave advice about discerning the different ways in which the Holy Spirit and the evil spirit work. He said:

> The Spirit of God is a spirit of peace. Even in the most serious faults he makes us feel a sorrow that is tranquil, humble, and confident, and this is precisely because of his mercy. The spirit of the devil, instead, excites, exasperates, and makes us feel, in that very sorrow, anger against ourselves, whereas we should on the contrary be charitable with ourselves first and foremost. Therefore if any thought agitates you, this agitation never comes from God, who gives you peace, being the Spirit of Peace, but from the devil.

When we are tempted, the devil encourages us to sin and the Holy Spirit tries to dissuade us. But after we sin, the roles are reversed. The devil, known as "the accuser" (Rev 12:10), discourages us, tempting us to give up. The Holy Spirit, called the "Paraclete", from the Greek for "encouragement", encourages us to turn to God for mercy and to keep trying.

Holy Spirit of Peace, strengthen me against discouragement. Help me to humbly accept the fact that I am not perfect but that little by little, as I offer each day to the Father, I can grow and become more like Christ.

DAILY WORD: I trust in God's mercy.

EVENING REVIEW: How were the Holy Spirit and the evil spirit at work?

September 24

Today, some places are celebrating a feast of the Blessed Virgin Mary under the title "Our Lady of Ransom" or "Our Lady of Mercy". In 1218, when many Christians were imprisoned or enslaved by the Moors, who controlled much of Spain, Mary appeared in separate visions to St. Peter Nolasco, St. Raymond of Peñafort (see January 7), and King James I of Aragon. She asked them to found the Order of Our Lady of Ransom, also known as the Mercedarians, who collected money to ransom Christians and who even took a vow to give themselves as hostages should all else fail in their efforts to free them. This work went on until 1779, when the last captive was freed, but the Mercedarians continue the work of liberation, focusing now on people who are enslaved in other ways, through poverty and addictions, or who are in prisons and in hospitals.

A similar and increasingly popular devotion is to "Our Lady Undoer of Knots". This goes back to a German painting of 1700 and ultimately to St. Irenaeus (see June 28), who wrote: "the knot of Eve's disobedience was loosed by the obedience of Mary."

As I offer myself, I pray that God, through Mary, may untie the knots of my life and use me to untie others' knots:

Virgin Mary, Mother of Fair Love, Mother whose hands never cease to work for her children because they are moved by the Divine Love and Infinite Mercy that exists in your heart, turn your compassionate eyes toward us and see the snarl of knots that exist in the world. In your hands, no knot can remain undone. Our Lady Undoer of Knots, pray for us!

DAILY WORD: Obeying God's will, I undo knots.

EVENING REVIEW: What knots did I encounter?

Ninety percent of Jesus' life is called "hidden". In the Gospels we read about his conception, birth, presentation in the temple, and flight into Egypt, but then, except for an incident when he was twelve and that Luke records (2:41 – 52), we know nothing about his life until, according to tradition, he was thirty and began his ministry of teaching and healing. He did this for three years and then was crucified, died, was buried, and rose.

We might think that those three years and their culmination in his life-giving death and Resurrection were Jesus' "real" work. But the entire life of Jesus, including what is called the "hidden life", played a part in the work of salvation. Why? Because it was lived in obedience to the will of the Father, who wanted Jesus to live that hidden life— to grow up in Nazareth, play and do household chores, and work as a carpenter side-by-side with Joseph.

Pope St. John XXIII once wrote:

> Jesus, who came to this world to save humanity, spent most of his life as a workman, in ordinary manual labor. We learn a sublime lesson from this: work is a noble thing, and the better a work is done, the nobler it is. Work done for God in all humility—who could not say that this is worth doing? Indeed, it is a wonderful thing, and all work becomes supremely great when it is done in the spirit of our Lord.

Father, like your Son Jesus, I want to live in total obedience to you. In that way, all that I do will play a role in the ongoing work of salvation.

DAILY WORD: I work with Jesus.

EVENING REVIEW: What "hidden" work did I do for God?

September 26: Sts. Cosmas and Damian (d. 303)

Today's saints were twin brothers, physicians, and martyrs who lived in Syria and were called "the moneyless ones" because they did not charge their patients. Our work is the way that we support ourselves, our families, our society, our Church, and other organizations. In fact, St. Paul went so far as to write: "For even when we were with you, we gave you this command: If any one will not work, let him not eat" (2 Thess 3:10). But the goal of work is not to amass wealth or possessions. We are to use the good things of the earth not simply to satisfy our own desires but in God's service.

While we cannot be consciously thinking of God at every moment, we can make an offering of our work to God and ask God to guide it. This is especially important for those who work in health care. I renew the offering of my day with a special prayer for doctors and those who assist them: that their work today may show deep reverence for the sacredness of human life.

The following is adapted from a prayer that Pope St. John Paul II wrote:

Lord Jesus, Divine Physician, who in your earthly life showed special concern for those who suffer and entrusted to your disciples the ministry of healing, make all health-care workers ever ready to alleviate the trials of their brethren. Make them, aware of the great mission that is entrusted to them, strive always to be, in the performance of daily service, an instrument of your merciful love. Enlighten their minds, guide their hands, make their hearts diligent and compassionate. Ensure that in every patient they know how to discern the features of your divine Face.

DAILY WORD: My work serves you, Lord.

EVENING REVIEW: In what ways did I maintain a pure intention in my work?

September 27: St. Vincent de Paul (1580–1660)

The name of today's saint and the word "charity" are synonymous, though St. Vincent de Paul Societies were founded years after his death by Frédéric Ozanam (see September 7). After his ordination and several years of priestly ministry, Vincent felt called to devote his entire life to serving the poor. He founded various confraternities and congregations to meet the needs of the poor and the sick, as well as to give parish missions and provide good formation for seminarians. Toward the end of his life, he was afflicted with swollen and ulcerous legs, a suffering that he cheerfully offered up for the poor whom he so loved.

He wrote:

> Since Christ willed to be born poor, he chose for himself disciples who were poor. He made himself the servant of the poor and shared their poverty. He went so far as to say that he would consider every deed which either helps or harms the poor as done for or against himself. If a needy person requires medicine or other help during prayer time, do whatever has to be done with peace of mind. Offer the deed to God as your prayer. Do not become upset or feel guilty because you interrupted your prayer to serve the poor. God is not neglected if you leave him for such service. One of God's works is merely interrupted so that another can be carried out. So when you leave prayer to serve some poor person, remember that this very service is performed for God.

Jesus, there are so many people for whom I am praying. I offer my day as a prayer for them and especially for the poor of the world. May this prayer touch both them and you with my love.

DAILY WORD: Whatever I do, I do for Christ.

EVENING REVIEW: Where did I see Christ in others?

September 28: St. Wenceslaus (907–929) and St. Lawrence Ruiz and Companions (d. 1637)

Wenceslaus was ruler of Bohemia and so devoted to spiritual practices and works of charity that some said he belonged in a monastery and not on the throne. Hostile and jealous, his own brother Boleslaus and his cronies killed him as he entered a church.

Centuries later, we find the first Filipino saint, whom Pope St. John Paul II called the "most improbable of saints". Lawrence, the son of a Chinese father and a Tagala mother, worked as a calligrapher for the Dominicans in Manila. A husband and father of three, he was implicated in a murder. He went to the priests for help, and they, believing his innocence but fearing an unfair trial, put him on a ship. Lawrence thought the ship was going to Taiwan, where, because he was half Chinese, he thought he would find refuge until the situation was resolved. Instead, the ship went to Japan, where he and the missionaries on board were soon arrested and killed.

When he beatified Lawrence in 1981, Pope John Paul II said: "The example of Lorenzo Ruiz . . . reminds us that everyone's life and the whole of one's life must be at Christ's disposal. Christianity means daily giving, in response to the gift of Christ who came into the world so that all might have life and have it to the full" (Jn 10:10). And when he canonized him in 1987, he said that Lawrence "proved that sanctity and heroism are there for anybody, and the final victory is made to size for each one of us."

Lord Jesus, you gave your life for me. I give you my life. Give me the grace I need today to be faithful to this offering.

DAILY WORD: Sanctity and heroism, always.

EVENING REVIEW: How did unexpected events help me grow?

September 29: Archangels Michael, Gabriel, and Raphael

The *Catechism of the Catholic Church* (no. 358) says "God created everything for man." Thus, even the angels were created for man—to help, guide, and protect us. We see this in the biblical accounts of the three archangels. Michael, whose name means "Who is like God", is "the great prince who has charge of your people" (Dan 12:1), and in Revelation he leads the angels in battle against the ones who had rebelled and become devils (12:7). Gabriel ("Power of God") also appears in Daniel (8:16; 9:21) but is known primarily as the messenger of salvation who appeared to Mary at the Annunciation (Lk 1:26–38). Finally, Raphael ("God has Healed") appears in the Book of Tobit, where he guides and heals.

Pope Benedict XVI reflected on these angels:

> All three names of the archangels end with the word "El",
> which means "God". God is inscribed in their names, in
> their nature. Their true nature is existing in his sight and
> for him. In this very way the second aspect that character-
> izes Angels is also explained: they are God's messengers.
> They bring God to men, they open heaven and thus open
> earth. Precisely because they are with God, they can also
> be very close to man. Indeed, God is closer to each one of
> us than we ourselves are. The angels speak to man of what
> constitutes his true being. . . . In this sense, we human be-
> ings must also always return to being angels to one another
> —angels who turn people away from erroneous ways and
> direct them always, ever anew, to God.

Loving God, I give myself to you so that, like the angels, I may always live in your presence and guide people to you.

DAILY WORD: Christ's name is inscribed in me for I am Christian.

EVENING REVIEW: How did I bring God to others?

September 30: St. Jerome (340–420)

Jerome studied Latin and Greek literature in Rome and was baptized around the age of eighteen. He withdrew to the Syrian desert as a hermit where he experienced such strong temptations of lust that, to distract himself, he studied Hebrew. In time he left the desert, was ordained, and accompanied his bishop to a council in Rome where Pope St. Damasus I (see December 11) made him his secretary. The pope asked Jerome to translate the Bible from its original Greek and Hebrew into a new Latin edition. After the pope's death, he went to Bethlehem, where he continued the work of translation and wrote commentaries on the Scriptures. He said, "Ignorance of Scripture is ignorance of Christ."

Jerome was hot-tempered, harsh, and sarcastic. Centuries after his death, Pope Sixtus V (d. 1590), looking at a painting of Jerome beating his chest with a rock in penance, is said to have remarked, "If it were not for that rock, the Church would have never declared you a saint." In 404, when barbarians invaded Rome and many Christians found refuge in the Holy Land, Jerome took a break from his work of translation, saying, "Today we must translate the words of the Scripture into deeds; instead of speaking saintly words, we must act them."

My offering is part of a prayer that St. Jerome wrote:

Show me, O Lord, your mercy and delight my heart with it. Let me find you, whom I so lovingly seek. I am the sheep who wandered into the wilderness. Seek me and bring me home. Do with me what you will that all the days of my life I may abide with you and praise you.

DAILY WORD: I delight in your mercy.

EVENING REVIEW: What temptations did I face? How did I deal with them?

OCTOBER

October 1: St. Thérèse of Lisieux (1873–1897)

Thérèse Martin enrolled in the Apostleship of Prayer when she was twelve, entered a cloistered Carmelite convent when she was just fifteen, and died nine years later, virtually unknown to the world. But her autobiography and the way she kept her promise to spend her heaven doing good on earth led to her being called by Pope St. Pius X "the greatest saint of modern times". Calling her the "star" of his pontificate, Pope Pius XI beatified her in 1923, canonized her in 1925, and named her, along with the great Jesuit missionary St. Francis Xavier, the co-patron of the missions. In 1997, Pope St. John Paul II named her a Doctor of the Church.

She showed by her life and her writings that one can become a great saint, not by doing great things, but by doing everything—even small and hidden things—with great love for God.

Inspired by her example, I renew the offering of my day with these words of St. Thérèse:

O my God! I offer You all my actions this day for the intentions and for the glory of the Sacred Heart of Jesus. I desire to sanctify every beat of my heart, my every thought, my simplest works, by uniting them to His infinite merits; and I wish to make reparation for my sins by casting them in the furnace of His merciful love. O my God! I ask of You for myself and for those dear to me the grace to fulfill perfectly Your holy will, to accept for love of You the joys and sorrows of this passing life, so that we may one day be united together in Heaven for all eternity. Amen.

October 2: Guardian Angels

Angelic spirits appear frequently in the Scriptures. Psalm 91 says "For he will give his angels charge of you to guard you in all your ways." The Letter to the Hebrews asks: "Are they not all ministering spirits sent forth to serve?" (1:14). When Jesus challenged his disciples to respect children, he said: "See that you do not despise one of these little ones; for I tell you that in heaven their angels always behold the face of my Father who is in heaven" (Mt 18:10).

Nicolas Marasco, when he was sixteen and suffering from a brain disorder, wrote to Pope Francis: "Every night I pray to my guardian angel to watch over you and help you. You can be sure that he is good at it because he watches over me and is with me every day." Pope Francis wrote back: "Dear Nicolas, thank you so much for your letter. Thank you so much for praying for me. Keep helping me with your prayers, and also keep praying to your guardian angel, who is surely friends with my guardian angel, who also watches over me."

Nicolas' mother commented on this exchange: "What has happened to us has made us realize that the simple things are what matter, a word of encouragement, someone who listens, someone who doesn't look the other way, as we sometimes experience out on the street."

God, I thank you for my guardian angel. With my Protector's guidance and help, I want all my thoughts, words, and deeds of this day to lead me and all those I meet and pray for to our homeland in heaven, where we will be greeted by our angels.

DAILY WORD: Angel of God, my guardian dear, be with me.

EVENING REVIEW: How was I conscious of God's help coming to me through the intercession of my guardian angel?

October 3: St. Théodore Guérin (1798–1856)

Mother Théodore was born in France, joined the Sisters of Providence, and came to the U.S. with five others Sisters in 1844. They started the first Catholic women's liberal arts college—St. Mary-of-the-Woods in Terre Haute, Indiana—and other schools and orphanages throughout the Midwest. Pope Benedict XVI canonized her in 2006, calling her "a beautiful spiritual figure and a model of the Christian life".

With great trust in God's providential care, she came, in her words, "to look upon all events of life as directed by Him." She wrote: "I derive my hope above all, and most especially, from our utter incapacity, for it is always upon nothingness that God is pleased to rear His works. If at any day we accomplish some good here, the glory will certainly be His alone, since He has employed for this end instruments more capable of spoiling everything than of making it succeed." Difficulties became opportunities to exercise trust and to draw closer to God: "What strength the soul draws from prayer! In the midst of a storm, how sweet is the calm it finds in the heart of Jesus."

Father, you chose Mary to be the mother of your Son. She trusted you and your plan even when she did not understand how it could be fulfilled. She knew, as St. Paul would later write, that you are all-powerful and all-loving and so you can make everything work together for the good of those whom you love (Rom 8:28). I offer myself to you today so that your desires for me may be fulfilled. I know that separated from you I can do nothing. Keep me always close to you by drawing me into the Heart of your Son, Jesus. Amen.

DAILY WORD: I trust in Providence.

EVENING REVIEW: How did I see God's providential care?

October 4: St. Francis of Assisi (1182–1226)

The son of a wealthy textile merchant, Francis lived a wild life until he underwent a deep conversion that led him to leave home and wealth and to embark on a life designed to imitate the simplicity, poverty, and humility of Jesus. The joy he displayed in this way of life attracted many followers and soon the Friars Minor and the Poor Clares were founded. As a result of his devotion to the Passion and suffering of Jesus, he was given the mystical gift of the stigmata. St. Francis found God in all things and made his life one act of worship and praise.

I offer my day to God as an act of worship and join all creation in giving praise with part of St. Francis' Canticle of Creation:

Most high, all powerful, all good Lord! All praise is yours, all glory, all honor, and all blessing. Be praised, my Lord, through all your creatures, especially through my Brother Sun, who brings the day. You give light through him, and he is beautiful and radiant in all his splendor! Of you, Most High, he bears the likeness.

Be praised, my Lord, through Sister Moon and the stars. In the heavens you have made them bright, precious, and beautiful. Be praised, my Lord, through Brothers Wind and Air, and clouds and storms, and all the weather, through which you give your creatures sustenance.

Be praised, my Lord, through Sister Water. She is very useful, and humble, and precious, and pure. Be praised, my Lord, through Brother Fire, through whom you brighten the night. He is beautiful and cheerful, and powerful and strong. Be praised, my Lord, through our Sister Mother Earth, who feeds us and rules us, and produces various fruits with colored flowers and herbs.

DAILY WORD: All creation praises God.

EVENING REVIEW: How was I conscious of creation praising God?

October 5: St. Faustina (1905–1938)

Helena Kowalska was born in Poland and entered the Sisters of Our Lady of Mercy where she received the name "Faustina". In 1931, Jesus appeared to her and, in the course of many such appearances, told her: "Proclaim that mercy is the greatest attribute of God. All the works of my hands are crowned with mercy." He also said: "Mankind will not find peace until it turns trustfully to divine mercy."

I offer myself today as an instrument of mercy with this prayer of St. Faustina:

O Most Holy Trinity! As many times as I breathe, as many times as my heart beats, as many times as my blood throbs through my body, so many thousand times do I want to glorify Your mercy. I want to be completely transformed into Your mercy and to be Your living reflection, O Lord. Help me, O Lord, that my eyes may be merciful, so that I may never suspect or judge from appearances. Help me, that my ears may be merciful, so that I may give heed to my neighbors' needs and not be indifferent to their pains and moanings. Help me, O Lord, that my tongue may be merciful, so that I should never speak negatively of my neighbor, but have a word of comfort and forgiveness for all. Help me, O Lord, that my hands may be merciful and filled with good deeds. Help me, that my feet may be merciful, so that I may hurry to assist my neighbor. Help me, O Lord, that my heart may be merciful so that I myself may feel all the sufferings of my neighbor. O my Jesus, transform me into Yourself, for You can do all things.

DAILY WORD: Let mercy flow through me.

EVENING REVIEW: How did I experience and share mercy?

October 6: St. Bruno (1030–1101)

Today's saint was the founder of the Church's strictest religious order, about which Pope Pius XI said: "The Carthusians have so well retained the spirit of their founder that unlike other religious bodies, their Order has never needed any amendment, or, as they say, 'reform'." They live strict lives of prayer and penance and in that way make themselves channels for God's love and mercy to enter our cold and dark world.

Devotion to the Heart of Jesus became very popular among the Carthusians, one of whom, Ludolph of Saxony, wrote the following.

> The Heart of Christ was wounded for us with the wound of love, that through the opening of His side we may in return enter His Heart by means of love, and there be able to unite all our love with His divine love into one love, as the glowing iron is one with the fire. Therefore, for the sake of this wound which Christ received for us on the Cross, when the dart of unconquerable love pierced His Heart, we should bring all our will into conformity with the will of God. But to fashion ourselves into conformity with Christ's sufferings, we should consider what surpassingly noble love our Lord has shown us in the opening of His side, since through it He has given us the wide open entrance into His Heart. Therefore, let us make haste to enter the Heart of Christ: let us gather up all our love and unite it with the divine love.

Jesus, you invite me in this moment of silence to enter more deeply into your Sacred Heart and to see there the deep love you have for me and all people. I unite my love to yours by offering you this day.

DAILY WORD: Heart of Jesus, I trust in you.

EVENING REVIEW: How did the love of Jesus' Heart flow through me?

October 7: Our Lady of the Rosary

This feast was instituted in the sixteenth century by Pope St. Pius V, who had asked the Church to pray the rosary for the successful outcome of the Christian navy's effort to bring safe travel to the Mediterranean Sea. Since then, praying the rosary has opened the way for many heavenly graces to enter the lives of individuals, families, nations, and the world.

Pope St. John Paul II called the rosary an essentially contemplative prayer because the calm recitation of the vocal prayers frees the mind to meditate upon the mysteries of Christ's life. Pope Benedict XVI said:

> Christ is put at the center of our life, of our time, of our city, through the contemplation and meditation of his holy mysteries of joy, light, sorrow, and glory. May Mary help us to welcome within ourselves the grace emanating from these mysteries, so that through us we can "water" society, beginning with our daily relationships, and purifying them from so many negative forces, thus opening them to the newness of God.

Lord Jesus, because Mary was your Mother and I am now a member of your Body, Mary is my Mother as well. She was there at your conception and birth and throughout your life. She was there at your death on the Cross and saw you risen in glory, ascending to the right hand of the Father. Help me to see you through her eyes. In that way, I will come to know you better, love you more intimately, and follow you more closely. I give you this day, asking for this grace and that your will may be accomplished in me today.

DAILY WORD: Blessed is the fruit of Mary's womb, Jesus!

EVENING REVIEW: What "mysteries of joy, light, sorrow, and glory" did my day contain?

October 8

Today is the anniversary of the Great Chicago Fire, which, in 1871, destroyed 3.3 square miles of the city and killed an estimated three hundred people. An even more devastating fire hit northern Wisconsin the same day. 1,875 square miles near Peshtigo were destroyed, and over 1,200 (and by some estimates 2,500) people were killed; so many perished that, in some cases, there were no survivors to identify their bodies.

And across the part of Lake Michigan known as Green Bay, another fire raged through the countryside. As the fire approached a chapel near Champion, Wisconsin, a woman named Adele Brise refused to leave and instead organized a procession around the perimeter of the grounds where people had gathered to pray. When light dawned the next morning, they saw black and charred fields all around the haven of green where they had safely spent the night.

Twelve years earlier, the Blessed Virgin Mary had appeared there to the sixteen-year-old Adele and told her "I am the Queen of Heaven who prays for the conversion of sinners, and I wish you to do the same." Today this place is known as the Shrine of Our Lady of Champion and is the first and only approved Marian apparition in the United States.

I make my offering now with part of a prayer written by Green Bay Bishop David Ricken:

O Dear Lady of Champion, I trust that as you called Adele to holiness, you are calling me, in my station in life, to live a holy life, devoted to Jesus Christ with the help of your maternal love. I bring before you now my worries and anxieties. I abandon my attachments to them and place them at your feet.

DAILY WORD: God is my help today.

EVENING REVIEW: What worries and difficulties did I abandon?

October 9: St. Denis and Companions (3rd Century) and St. John Leonardi (1541–1609)

John Leonardi was an Italian pharmacist who became a priest in 1571 and devoted himself to the Christian education of children by means of a group he founded—the Confraternity of Christian Doctrine, or CCD. He also started a religious congregation of priests dedicated to the foreign missions that in time became the Society for the Propagation of the Faith.

St. Denis was a missionary to France and became the first bishop of Paris. Tradition has it that he was martyred with two members of his clergy. In a reading chosen to honor these martyrs, St. Ambrose wrote about different kinds of martyrdom. Not everyone may be called to die for the faith, but everyone is called to witness to it. We do so when we battle the temptations that come our way.

St. Ambrose wrote that

> there are many kinds of martyrdom. Every day you are a witness to Christ. You were tempted by the spirit of fornication, but did not want your purity of mind and body to be defiled: you are a martyr for Christ. You were tempted by the spirit of avarice to seize the property of a child and violate the rights of a defenseless widow, but remembered God's law and saw your duty to give help, not act unjustly: you are a witness to Christ. You were tempted by the spirit of pride but saw the poor and the needy and looked with loving compassion on them, and loved humility rather than arrogance: you are a witness to Christ. What is more, your witness was not in word only but also in deed.

Jesus, I want to be a witness to you today. May everything I say and do be what you would say and do.

DAILY WORD: "Christ first of all!" [St. John Leonardi]

EVENING REVIEW: What were my victories over temptation?

October 10

Yesterday was the anniversary of the day that St. John Henry Newman (1801–1890) became a Roman Catholic. Priest, theologian, and prolific author he was made a cardinal by Pope Leo XIII in 1879. When he beatified him in 2010, Pope Benedict XVI said: "Cardinal Newman's motto, *Cor ad cor loquitur*, or 'Heart speaks unto heart', gives us an insight into his understanding of the Christian life as a call to holiness, experienced as the profound desire of the human heart to enter into intimate communion with the Heart of God. He reminds us that faithfulness to prayer gradually transforms us into the divine likeness."

The following prayer from St. John Henry was a favorite of Mother Teresa, and the Missionaries of Charity continue to recite it daily:

Dear Jesus, help me to spread Your fragrance everywhere I go. Flood my soul with Your spirit and life. Penetrate and possess my whole being so utterly that my life may only be a radiance of Yours. Shine through me, and be so in me that every soul I come in contact with may feel Your presence in my soul. Let them look up and see no longer me, but only Jesus! Stay with me and then I shall begin to shine as You shine, so to shine as to be a light to others; the light, O Jesus, will be all from You; none of it will be mine; it will be You, shining on others through me. Let me thus praise You the way You love best, by shining on those around me. Let me preach You without preaching, not by words but by my example, by the catching force of the sympathetic influence of what I do, the evident fullness of the love my heart bears to You. Amen.

DAILY WORD: Shine through me.

EVENING REVIEW: How did I preach Jesus without words?

October 11: Pope St. John XXIII (1881–1963)

On this day in 1962, today's saint convoked the Second Vatican Council. I make my offering today with his "Daily Decalogue".

Just for today . . .

1. I will seek to live the livelong day positively without wishing to solve the problems of my life all at once.

2. I will take the greatest care of my appearance: I will dress modestly; I will not raise my voice; I will be courteous in my behavior; I will not criticize anyone; I will not claim to improve or to discipline anyone except myself.

3. I will be happy in the certainty that I was created to be happy, not only in the other world but also in this one.

4. I will adapt to circumstances, without requiring all circumstances to be adapted to my own wishes.

5. I will devote 10 minutes of my time to some good reading, remembering that just as food is necessary to the life of the body, so good reading is necessary to the life of the soul.

6. I will do one good deed and not tell anyone about it.

7. I will do at least one thing I do not like doing; and if my feelings are hurt, I will make sure that no one notices.

8. I will make a plan for myself: I may not follow it to the letter, but I will make it. And I will be on guard against two evils: hastiness and indecision.

9. I will firmly believe, despite appearances, that the good Providence of God cares for me as no one else who exists in this world.

10. I will have no fears. In particular, I will not be afraid to enjoy what is beautiful and to believe in goodness. Indeed, for 12 hours I can certainly do what might cause me consternation were I to believe I had to do it all my life.

DAILY WORD: Come Holy Spirit.

EVENING REVIEW: How did I do with these ten rules?

October 12

In 1966, in the middle of the Vietnam War, Pope St. Paul VI wrote a letter to the Church entitled "On Prayers for Peace during October". He was concerned not only with that conflict and the threat that it would spread, but also with the arms race, and, as he put it, "the senseless nationalism, the racism, the obsession for revolution, the separations imposed upon citizens, the nefarious plots, the slaughter of innocent people."

Things have not changed. The need to pray for peace is stronger than ever. Pope Paul went on:

> Nothing seems more appropriate and valuable to us than to have the prayers of the whole Christian family rise to the Mother of God, who is invoked as the Queen of Peace, begging her to pour forth abundant gifts of her maternal goodness in the midst of so many trials and hardships. . . . If evils increase, the devotion of the People of God should also increase. . . . And so, we want you to pray ardently to our most merciful mother Mary by saying the Rosary during the month of October.

Pope St. John Paul II, speaking of "the grave challenges confronting the world", also encouraged praying the rosary. He said it "is by its nature a prayer for peace, since it consists in the contemplation of Christ, the Prince of Peace, the one who is 'our peace' (Eph 2:14). Anyone who assimilates the mystery of Christ—and this is clearly the goal of the Rosary—learns the secret of peace and makes it his life's project. . . . In a word, by focusing our eyes on Christ, the Rosary also makes us peacemakers in the world."

I offer myself as an instrument of peace today.

DAILY WORD: Christ is our peace.

EVENING REVIEW: How did I help or hinder peace?

October 13

On this day in 1917, the last apparition of Mary at Fatima, Portugal, occurred. It was accompanied by a miracle that Bishop José Alves Correia da Silva, who gave official Church approval to the apparitions in 1930, related:

> The solar phenomenon, described in the press of the time, was most marvelous and caused the greatest impression on those who had the happiness of witnessing it. This phenomenon, which no astronomical observatory registered and which therefore was not natural, was witnessed by persons of all categories and of all social classes, believers and unbelievers, journalists of the principal Portuguese newspapers, and even by persons some miles away. Facts that annul any explanation of collective illusion.

In her last words to the three children—Lucia, Jacinta, and Francisco—that day, Mary told them to tell the people "that I am the Lady of the Rosary and that they continue to say the rosary every day."

Pope St. John Paul II, in Fatima on the anniversary of the 1981 assassination attempt, reminded people:

> If the Church has accepted the message of Fatima, it is above all because that message contains a truth and a call whose basic content is the truth and the call of the Gospel itself. 'Repent, and believe in the gospel' (Mk 1:15): these are the first words that the Messiah addressed to humanity. The message of Fatima is, in its basic nucleus, a call to conversion and repentance, as in the Gospel. The call to repentance is a motherly one, and at the same time it is strong and decisive.

Jesus, thank you for the concern you show to your human family by sending your own Mother to speak to us. I accept her call to live this day repenting and believing in the Gospel.

DAILY WORD: I believe.

EVENING REVIEW: How did I live the message of Fatima?

October 14: St. Callistus (d. 222)

Callistus was a Roman slave who mishandled the funds of his master and ended up working in Sardinian salt mines as a punishment. Eventually released, he was made the administrator of a cemetery and did so well that he was ordained by Pope St. Zephyrinus, whom he succeeded as pope in 217. Many considered him too lenient because he allowed public sinners to receive Holy Communion after showing remorse and doing penance. Tradition has it that he was killed by a mob during an uprising against Christians.

Some people, because of youthful mistakes, spend their entire lives carrying a burden or reputation. Others don't expect them to change. They don't expect them to have learned from their mistakes. But mistakes, like experience, can be the best teacher. We see this in the life of St. Callistus, who overcame past failures. He brought the experience he gained from his mistakes and the mercy that was shown to him as he served the Church.

St. Paul wrote about his mistakes and how God could use his past in making it clear to others that anyone can be saved:

> [T]hough I formerly blasphemed and persecuted and insulted him, . . . I received mercy because I had acted ignorantly in unbelief. . . . The saying is sure and worthy of full acceptance, that Christ Jesus came into the world to save sinners. And I am the foremost of sinners; but I received mercy for this reason, that in me, as the foremost, Christ

Jesus might display his perfect patience for an example to those who were to believe in him for eternal life. (1 Tim 1:13, 15–16)

Jesus, take me as I am with my weaknesses as well as my strengths.

DAILY WORD: I am not my mistakes.

EVENING REVIEW: How did my experience of past mistakes and mercy help me today?

October 15: St. Teresa of Ávila (1515–1582)

When Teresa was twenty, she entered a Carmelite convent that had become very lax. She was fine with this for eighteen years, but then felt called to a deeper prayer life and to begin a reformed branch of the Order known as the Discalced or "Shoeless" Carmelites. In 1970, Pope St. Paul VI named her a Doctor of the Church.

St. Teresa of Jesus was a great contemplative who understood well that "the reason for prayer is the birth always of good works." "Let us understand", she wrote, "that true perfection consists in love of God and neighbor." In fact, if someone received "the prayer of perfect contemplation" and did not have "a very resolute desire to pardon any injury however grave it may be," she said, "do not trust much in that soul's prayer."

One translation of a poem she wrote about the Body of Christ goes: "Christ has no body now on earth but yours, no hands but yours, no feet but yours; yours are the eyes through which he looks with compassion on the world, yours are the feet with which he is to go about doing good, and yours are the hands with which he blesses all the world."

She also wrote the following verse on a bookmark she used: "Let nothing disturb you. Let nothing make you afraid. All things are passing. God alone never changes. Patience gains all things. If you have God, you will want for nothing. God alone suffices."

O God, who are Love itself, you created me in your image to love you and your other children. I give you the hours and minutes of this day in order to fulfill your purpose for me.

DAILY WORD: "God alone suffices."

EVENING REVIEW: What were my "good works" that revealed my love for God?

October 16: St. Margaret Mary Alacoque (1647–1690)

Today's saint was the Visitation nun to whom Jesus revealed his Heart, saying, "My divine Heart is so passionately fond of the human race that it cannot keep back the pent-up flames of its burning charity any longer. They must burst out through you and reveal my Heart to the world, so as to enrich man with my precious treasures."

In response, Margaret Mary made this offering:

I give myself to the Sacred Heart of our Lord Jesus Christ and consecrate to Him my person and my life, my actions, cares, and sorrows, so that my whole being may be entirely in the service of His love, honor, and glory. It is my irrevocable decision to belong to Him completely and to do all things for the love of Him, at the same time renouncing with all my heart whatever may displease Him. I therefore take You, O Sacred Heart, as the only object of my love, the guardian of my life, my assurance of salvation, the remedy of my weakness and inconstancy, the atonement for all the faults of my life, and my sure refuge at the hour of death. O Heart full of love, I put all my trust in You, for I fear everything from my weakness but hope for all things from Your goodness. Consume in me all that may displease You or resist Your holy will; let Your pure love imprint itself so deeply on my heart that I shall nevermore be able to forget You or be separated from You. I beseech You in Your goodness and mercy, write my name in Your Heart, for I want to find my happiness and glory in living and dying as Your servant. Amen.

DAILY WORD: Sacred Heart of Jesus, I trust in you.

EVENING REVIEW: How did the love of Jesus' Heart "burst out" through me today?

October 17: St. Ignatius of Antioch (d. 110)

Before St. Peter became the bishop of Rome, he was the bishop of Antioch in Syria. Today's saint was the second successor there to Peter, and during a time of persecution, he was arrested and sent in chains to Rome, where he was martyred. Along the way he wrote seven letters to Christians in various cities.

To the Romans he wrote:

> I am writing to all the churches to let it be known that I will gladly die for God if only you do not stand in my way. Let me be food for the wild beasts, for they are my way to God. I am God's wheat and shall be ground by their teeth so that I may become Christ's pure bread. Pray to Christ for me that the animals will be the means of making me a sacrificial victim for God. No earthly pleasures, no kingdoms of this world can benefit me in any way. I prefer death in Christ Jesus to power over the farthest limits of the earth. He who died in place of us is the one object of my quest. He who rose for our sakes is my one desire. The time for my birth is close at hand. My desire is to belong to God. My love of this life has been crucified, and there is no yearning in me for any earthly thing. Rather, within me is the living water that says deep inside me: "Come to the Father."

Lord Jesus, you are my one desire. You gave yourself for me on the Cross, and you continue to offer yourself to me in the Eucharist. I offer myself to you now, praying that I may be bread broken for my brothers and sisters.

DAILY WORD: "Come to the Father."

EVENING REVIEW: How was I bread for others?

October 18: St. Luke the Evangelist

St. Luke, a Greek-speaking Gentile, was a doctor by profession (see Col 4:14) who became a co-worker of St. Paul. He wrote both a Gospel and an account of the early Church—the Acts of the Apostles.

In the conclusion of the Apostolic Exhortation "The Word of the Lord", Pope Benedict XVI wrote that a

> close relationship between God's word and joy is evident in the Mother of God. Let us recall the words of Saint Elizabeth: "Blessed is she who believed that there would be a fulfillment of what was spoken to her by the Lord" (Lk 1:45). Mary is blessed because she has faith, because she believed, and in this faith she received the Word of God into her womb in order to give him to the world. The joy born of the Word can now expand to all those who, by faith, let themselves be changed by God's word. The Gospel of Luke presents this mystery of hearing and joy in two texts. Jesus says: "My mother and my brothers are those who hear the word of God and do it" (8:21). And in reply to a woman from the crowd who blesses the womb that bore him and the breasts that nursed him, Jesus reveals the secret of true joy: "Blessed rather are those who hear the word of God and obey it!" (11:28). Jesus points out Mary's true grandeur, making it possible for each of us to attain that blessedness which is born of the word received and put into practice.

Word of God, you became flesh for love of me. You continue to speak to me through the Gospel. I give myself to you so that your word may become flesh in me today.

DAILY WORD: Word of God, transform me!

EVENING REVIEW: How did I give flesh to the Gospel?

October 19: North American Martyrs (1600s)

Today we honor the memory of six Jesuit priests and two Jesuit Brothers who came from France to bring the Gospel to the Native American tribes of Canada and New York. They were caught in the middle of tribal wars and the competition between France and England for control of North America. Some of them suffered terrible tortures as they tried to spread the faith in a hostile environment. What motivated them to leave the safety of Europe and to persevere in the midst of the difficult life here and the tortures they experienced? Their passionate love of Jesus Christ. Sharing the love that God has for every human being, their only fear was that anyone would die not knowing that love.

In 1984, Pope St. John Paul II visited their shrine in Midland, Ontario, and said:

> Saint Paul tells us how firmly he believed in the love of Christ and in its power to overcome all obstacles: "Nothing can come between us and the love of Christ" (Rom 8:35). . . . A similar confidence in God's love guided the lives of the Martyrs who are honored at this Shrine. They, like Paul, had come to consider the love of Christ as the greatest of all treasures. And they, too, believed that the love of Christ was so strong that nothing could separate them from it, not even persecution and death.

Lord Jesus, I believe that nothing can separate me from you. Only I can separate myself from you by sin. But even then, your love is there. You desire to forgive and to heal. I offer myself to you. May I not take back this offering by separating myself from you.

DAILY WORD: Nothing can separate me from God's love.

EVENING REVIEW: How did the knowledge of God's love for me give me strength and courage today?

October 20: St. Paul of the Cross (1694–1775)

As a young man in Italy, Paul lived a prayerful life and worked among the poor. In 1720, he had a vision that inspired him to start a religious congregation dedicated to the Passion of Jesus and known as the Passionists. He and his first followers were ordained in 1727 and dedicated themselves to a life of prayer, penance, and preaching about the love of God revealed on the cross.

St. Paul of the Cross wrote:

> It is very good and holy to consider the Passion of our Lord and to meditate on it, for by this sacred path we reach union with God. Love is the unifying virtue. It is a fire reaching through to the inmost soul. It transforms the lover into the one loved. Therefore, be constant in practicing every virtue, and especially in imitating the patience of our dear Jesus, for this is the summit of pure love. Live in such a way that all may know that you bear outwardly as well as inwardly the image of Christ crucified, the model of all gentleness and mercy. For if a man is united inwardly with the Son of the living God, he also bears his likeness outwardly by his continual practice of heroic goodness, and especially through a patience reinforced by courage, which does not complain either secretly or in public.

Jesus, when I look at a crucifix, I see how much you love me. You died on the Cross to free me from sin and death. You would rather suffer and die than to live without me. I want to show you some sign of my gratitude and love. I do so now by offering myself and my day to you.

DAILY WORD: By your Cross, you saved me.

EVENING REVIEW: How did I practice heroic goodness and patience?

Besides being the month of the Holy Rosary, October is also World Mission month, a time to reflect on the fact that all the baptized are called to the work of evangelization. Some do that by becoming missionaries in other countries, like St. Francis Xavier, co-patron of the missions. Others do that by their prayers and sacrifices with which they support the work of missionaries, like St. Thérèse of Lisieux, who never left her cloistered Carmelite convent and is the other co-patron. All of us are called to evangelize by witnessing to the Gospel every day through our words and deeds.

In his Message for World Mission Day 2015, Pope Francis wrote:

> Mission is a passion for Jesus and at the same time a passion for his people. When we pray before Jesus crucified, we see the depth of his love, which gives us dignity and sustains us. At the same time, we realize that the love flowing from Jesus' pierced heart expands to embrace the People of God and all mankind. We realize once more that he wants to make use of us to draw closer to his beloved people and all those who seek him with a sincere heart. In Jesus' command to "go forth", we see the scenarios and ever-present new challenges of the Church's evangelizing mission. All her members are called to proclaim the Gospel by their witness of life.

Lord Jesus, I share your passion for mankind. You passionately desire all people to know your love, receive it, and find eternal life in heaven with you. Sharing your desire, I offer myself to you. Draw close to people through me. May all I do today proclaim to others the good news of your love.

DAILY WORD: Mission is my passion.

EVENING REVIEW: How did sharing Jesus' Passion influence what I thought and did?

October 22: Pope St. John Paul II (1920–2005)

At the end of his 2005 book, *Memory and Identity*, Pope John Paul II wrote:

> The evil of the 20th century was an evil of gigantic proportions. At the same time, however, divine grace has been superabundantly revealed. There is no evil from which God cannot draw forth a greater good. Offering himself freely in his passion and death on the Cross, the Son of God took upon himself all the evil of sin. It is this suffering which burns and consumes evil with the flame of love. In the love that pours forth from the heart of Christ, we find hope for the future of the world.

When Pope Francis canonized today's saint on Divine Mercy Sunday in 2014, he called him a man of courage who had lived through the tragic events of the twentieth century yet was not overwhelmed by them. He said that for Pope John Paul II, "God was more powerful; faith was more powerful—faith in Jesus Christ the Redeemer of man and the Lord of history; the mercy of God, shown by those five wounds, was more powerful; and more powerful too was the closeness of Mary our Mother."

Pope John Paul II said that remaining united to God in the midst of the activities of the day "is a vital necessity to bear witness to His Love". I commit myself to this with his words:

Lord, may my soul be flooded with your light and know you more and more profoundly! Lord, give me so much love, love forever, serene and generous, that I will be united with you always! Lord, let me serve you and serve you well, on the pathways that you wish to open to my existence here below.

DAILY WORD: Nothing can take away my hope and joy.

EVENING REVIEW: How did I maintain hope and joy?

October 23: St. John of Capistrano (1386–1456)

Today's saint studied law in Perugia, Italy, where he became the governor in 1412. During hostilities with a neighboring city, he was imprisoned and went through a deep conversion as a result of the humiliation and suffering he endured. He became a Franciscan priest and was so famous for his preaching that the pope sent him as his personal emissary to places as diverse as Palestine, France, and Poland.

John wrote:

> Those who are called to the table of the Lord must glow with the brightness that comes from the good example of a praiseworthy and blameless life. Their upright lives must make them like the salt of the earth for the rest of mankind. The brightness of their wisdom must make them like the light of the world that brings light to others. They must learn from their eminent teacher, Jesus Christ, what He declared to His apostles and disciples when He said: You are the salt of the earth. But what if salt goes flat? How can you restore its flavor? Then it is good for nothing but to be thrown out and trampled underfoot. You are the light of the world. Now a light does not illumine itself, but instead it diffuses its rays and shines all around upon everything that comes into its view. So it must be with your glowing lives. By the brightness of your holiness, you must bring light and serenity to all who gaze upon you.

Jesus, I give myself to you. May the flame of your love, given to me in the Eucharist, burn within me so that I may "bring light and serenity to all who" will see me today.

DAILY WORD: Make me salt; make me light.

EVENING REVIEW: Whose lives were touched by my light?

October 24: St. Anthony Mary Claret (1807–1870)

Today's saint was a Spaniard who became a priest and tried to enter both the Carthusian and Jesuit Orders but was turned away because of his poor health. Providence had other plans, for in 1850, he was sent to Cuba and became its archbishop. His strong preaching led many to hate him, and he survived several assassination attempts. He had a deep love for the Immaculate Heart of Mary and founded the Claretians, also known as the Missionary Sons of the Immaculate Heart of Mary. It is estimated that he preached over 10,000 sermons and published 200 books.

He wrote:

> Driven by the fire of the Holy Spirit, apostolic missionaries have reached, are now reaching, and will continue to reach the ends of the earth. They are deservedly able to apply to themselves those words of the apostle Paul: The love of Christ drives us on. The love of Christ arouses us, urges us to run, and to fly, lifted on the wings of holy zeal. The one who truly loves God also loves his neighbor. The one who burns with the fire of divine love is a child of the Immaculate Heart of Mary, and wherever he goes, he enkindles that flame; he desires and works with all his strength to inflame all people with the fire of God's love. Nothing deters him: he rejoices in poverty; he labors strenuously; he welcomes hardships; he laughs off false accusations; he rejoices in anguish. He thinks only of how he might follow Jesus Christ and imitate him by his prayers, his labors, his sufferings, and by caring always and only for the glory of God and the salvation of souls.

O God, I offer my day for your glory and the salvation of souls.

DAILY WORD: The love of Christ urges me on.

EVENING REVIEW: How did the Holy Spirit lead me?

October 25

Yesterday was the anniversary of the death, in 1915, of St. Luigi Guanella, who was born in the Alps of northern Italy in 1842. When he was a twenty-year-old seminarian, he enrolled in the Apostleship of Prayer, which he said "is like the center of the devotion to the Sacred Heart of Jesus. The prayer of the agonizing Jesus pierces the Heart of God. The prayer of the Apostleship, thus passing through the Sacred Heart, penetrates heaven and earth. Thus the prayer of good people sustains the world today, that it may not crash under the weight of iniquity."

When he canonized him in 2013, Pope Benedict XVI said: "Thanks to the profound and continuing union with Christ, in the contemplation of his love, Don Guanella, led by Divine Providence, became a companion and teacher, comfort and support to the poorest and weakest." These included the developmentally disabled. Today the two Orders he founded, the Servants of Charity and the Daughters of St. Mary of Providence, continue his work.

He wrote: "Jesus offered Himself to God the Father. Learn to offer to the Lord the sweat of your brow. During the day, whenever hardships affect you, pray with lively faith: God is with me, and I am with him! Offer your suffering to Jesus, who has endured so much to come to meet you."

I offer myself now with this prayer of St. Luigi:

O Jesus, my father and master, the effect of your word and example remains forever in my heart. I want to be patient. I want to be humble of heart. Eternal Father: I beg you through the incarnate Heart of Jesus, grant that I may always be gentle of heart and humble in affection until the end.

DAILY WORD: God is with me.

EVENING REVIEW: How was I patient, gentle, and humble?

October 26

This is the month of the Holy Rosary, a prayer that played an amazing role in the life of Bl. Bartolo Longo (1841 – 1926). Raised in a strong Catholic family that prayed the rosary together every night, Bartolo drifted away from the Church and eventually into the occult. He was even ordained a priest in a Satanic cult.

It seems as though the Blessed Virgin, through all those rosaries of his childhood, kept a "chain" on him. He felt himself slipping into insanity, but through the help of a professor and a Dominican priest, he left the occult and returned to the Church. Yet, his struggles were not over. He felt his involvement in evil was so deep that he despaired of his salvation. Finally, praying the rosary and putting his confidence in Mary's promise that no one devoted to her would ever be lost, he found peace. He became a lay Dominican, established a shrine to Our Lady of the Rosary near Pompei, and started orphanages and trade schools for the poor.

Pope St. John Paul II called him "Our Lady's Man" and wrote:

> Just as two friends, frequently in each other's company, tend to develop similar habits, so too, by holding familiar converse with Jesus and the Blessed Virgin, by meditating on the mysteries of the Rosary and by living the same life in Holy Communion, we can become, to the extent of our lowliness, similar to them and can learn from these supreme models a life of humility, poverty, hiddenness, patience, and perfection.

O God, I offer myself to you through Mary, Mother of your Son and my Mother. With her help, keep me from all harm today and every day until the end of my life on earth.

DAILY WORD: Hope through Mary.

EVENING REVIEW: How was Mary present during my day?

October 27

In many places, the trees have changed colors and the leaves have fallen from them. Nature reminds us that change is part of life. The Jesuit poet Gerard Manley Hopkins in his poem "Spring and Fall", writes of a girl named Margaret, who, gazing upon a "Goldengrove unleaving", sheds tears. He asks "why?" and concludes that she is crying, not for the trees that are losing their leaves, but for herself: "It is the blight man was born for, / It is Margaret you mourn for." The changes of autumn show her that all things change and have an end.

Our Christian faith, however, tells us that death is not the end of our story. St. Clement, the fourth pope, in a letter to the Corinthians, wrote that even nature shows us resurrection:

> Day and night show us a resurrection; the night lies in sleep, day rises again; the day departs, night takes its place. Let us think about the harvest. The sower goes out and casts each seed onto the ground. Dry and bare, they fall into the earth and decay. Then the greatness of the Lord's providence raises them up again from decay, and out of one many are produced and yield fruit. In this hope, then, let your hearts be bound fast to him who is faithful in his promises.

Creator God, you made the sun to rise and to set, the trees to leaf out and to lose their leaves, and me, to be born and to die. I believe that death will not be the end of my story and that you have made me for eternal life. I offer myself to you, trusting in your care for me this day and every day.

DAILY WORD: Let my heart be bound fast to God.

EVENING REVIEW: How did I deal with change today?

October 28: Apostles Simon and Jude

Little is known about Jude who is called "Thaddaeus" in two of the Gospels and who, according to tradition, wrote the letter that bears his name. He is known as the patron saint of the impossible. From a human perspective, it would have certainly been impossible for the twelve apostles to live and work together. The other saint we honor today is Simon, known as "the Zealot". The Zealots were terrorists who fought to rid Israel of Roman occupation. Yet Jesus called him and also his enemy, Matthew, who collaborated with the Romans by collecting taxes.

Pope Benedict XVI commented on this:

> Simon was worlds apart from Matthew. . . . This shows that Jesus called his disciples and collaborators, without exception, from the most varied social and religious backgrounds. . . . And the best thing is that in the group of his followers, despite their differences, they all lived side by side, overcoming imaginable difficulties: indeed, what bound them together was Jesus himself, in whom they all found themselves united with one another. This is clearly a lesson for us who are often inclined to accentuate differences and even contrasts, forgetting that in Jesus Christ we are given the strength to get the better of our continual conflicts.

Jesus once said that for humans, some things are impossible, "but with God all things are possible" (Mt 19:26). The apostles had firsthand experience of this.

Jesus, you called people of diverse personalities and political views to join you in the work of spreading the Gospel. You continue to call diverse people today. I want to be close to you, to be part of your group of followers. I offer myself for your service, asking that I may work to overcome the conflicts I encounter today.

DAILY WORD: "For God all things are possible."

EVENING REVIEW: How did I deal with conflict today?

St. Teresa of Kolkata said: "Joy is a net of love by which you can catch souls." Called, as the apostles were (Lk 5:10), to fish for people, we know that success in fishing depends upon the right bait. Our bait is a joy-filled life. Even in the midst of suffering, we can have joy. Bl. Pier Giorgio Frassati once wrote to his sister: "You ask me if I am happy. How could I not be? As long as faith gives me strength, I am happy. A Catholic could not be other than happy. The goal for which we were created involves a path which has its thorns, but it is not a sad path. It is joy, even when it involves pain."

In 2012, Pope Benedict XVI encouraged young people "to be missionaries of joy". He said,

"We cannot be happy if others are not. Joy has to be shared." After saying that "joy is the sign of God's presence and action within us", he went on:

> Seek joy in the Lord: for joy is the fruit of faith. It is being aware of his presence and friendship every day. . . . Dear friends, learn to see how God is working in your lives and discover him hidden within the events of daily life. Believe that he is always faithful to the covenant which he made with you on the day of your Baptism. Know that God will never abandon you. Turn your eyes to him often. He gave his life for you on the cross because he loves you. Contemplation of this great love brings a hope and joy to our hearts that nothing can destroy. Christians can never be sad, for they have met Christ, who gave his life for them.

Jesus, I offer you my joys as well as my sufferings.

DAILY WORD: You are my joy.

EVENING REVIEW: How did the joy of being a Christian help me?

October 30

Blessed Dominic Collins was born in Ireland in 1566 at a time when Catholics experienced severe persecution. When he was twenty, he went to France to become a soldier and in a short time advanced to the rank of captain. But after a pilgrimage in 1598 to the famous Spanish shrine of St. James, Santiago de Compostela, he left to join Christ's army as a Jesuit Brother. He was sent to his native Ireland but within a year was arrested and sentenced to death.

According to an eyewitness, on October 31, 1602,

> as he was led between soldiers to the place of execution, he displayed every sign of fortitude. When he came to the gallows, he greeted it with great joy of spirit and gave a brief exhortation to those who stood around. When the enemies of the Church heard this, they could no longer restrain themselves from putting a stop to his words. Around his neck they placed the noose.
>
> He bore this with a very joyous spirit and gave such a smile of gladness that an English captain who stood nearby remarked, "I say, what kind of man is this who goes to his death as eagerly as I would go to a banquet?" To this Dominic replied, "For this cause I would most willingly suffer not just one but a thousand deaths." As he mounted the steps he began to recite the psalm, "In you, O Lord, I have hoped." When he arrived at the top he murmured, "Into your hands, O Lord, I commend my spirit," and was dropped to his death.

Dominic and sixteen other Irish martyrs were beatified in 1992.

Lord God, you have given me life. Give me also the courage to give my life to you one day at a time.

DAILY WORD: "In you I have hoped."

EVENING REVIEW: How did I maintain a joyous spirit?

October 31

Today is Halloween, a day that began as a religious celebration but has taken on dark and in many cases evil overtones. "All Hallows Eve" is the day before All Saint's Day, when we honor all holy people of every time and place, recognized as well as unknown. Nature, as it's been said, abhors a vacuum, and so when religious festivals are downplayed or forgotten, people create new ones that may be spiritually unhealthy. St. Paul, writing to the Church in Philippi, had some good advice: "Whatever is true, whatever is honorable, whatever is just, whatever is pure, whatever is lovely, whatever is gracious, if there is any excellence, if there is anything worthy of praise, think about these things" (4:8). Or, as another translation puts it: "Fill your minds with everything that is true, noble, good and pure, everything we love and honor, and everything that can be thought virtuous or worthy of praise."

As children and adults put time and attention into costumes, we can think about the best costume of all. It's not a disguise or something designed to scare people or make them laugh. It's a costume that helps us be who we are called to be. That costume is Christ.

St. Paul again gives us some helpful words about this: "For as many of you as were baptized into Christ have put on Christ" (Gal 3:27). And to the Romans he wrote: "Put on the Lord Jesus Christ, and make no provision for the flesh" (13:14). This is what the saints did, and as we prepare to honor them, we commit ourselves to following their example.

Jesus, I give myself to you so that you may clothe me in yourself today.

DAILY WORD: I put on Christ.

EVENING REVIEW: How did people see Christ through me?

NOVEMBER

November 1: All Saints Day

The Church, the Body of Christ and Communion of Saints, consists of three parts. We, the "saints-in-the-making", are the Church Militant, fighting the good fight on earth. The other two parts—the Church Triumphant and the Church Suffering—are people who have died and are separated from us through time and space but who are spiritually close to us. Today we honor all those people, known and unknown, who have arrived in heaven and share in God's glory. They triumphed over sin and continue to support us with their love and prayers.

The Letter to the Hebrews states: "Therefore, since we are surrounded by so great a cloud of witnesses, let us also lay aside every weight, and sin which clings so closely, and let us run with perseverance the race that is set before us, looking to Jesus the pioneer and perfecter of our faith" (12:1–2). We are in a marathon, and the saints in heaven are spiritually present, cheering us on. Jesus is there at the finish line waiting to greet us.

St. Cyprian spoke about this heavenly finish line: "We look upon paradise as our country, and a great crowd of our loved ones awaits us there, a countless throng of parents, brothers and sisters, and children longs for us to join them. Assured though they are of their own salvation, they are still concerned about ours. What joy both for them and for us to see one another and embrace!"

Jesus, you ran the race of earthly life and blazed a trail for me to follow. I want to stay on this path, and so I offer myself to you. Carry me, for on my own I am inclined to get off track. Bring me home to heaven.

DAILY WORD: Saints of God, give praise!

EVENING REVIEW: How did the saints help me?

November 2: All Souls Day

Today we remember all "the faithful departed", those who have died and who, like us, are in need of purification. They were not perfect at the time of death. They had "unfinished business", perhaps people with whom they had not reconciled, and they need to let go of the burden of resentments. They had residue from their sins that needs to be cleansed. Their sins had consequences in their and in others' lives, and those effects need healing. They had become accustomed to shadows and darkness and need to adjust their sight as they approach Jesus, the Light of the world, and his glory.

St. Paul speaks of the purification that occurs after death in terms of fire (1 Cor 3:10–15). It is not so much punishment but the encounter with God who appeared to Moses in a burning bush and whom the Letter to the Hebrews says "is a consuming fire" (12:29). Our earthly lives are like a building project. The "foundation" on which we build is the solid rock—Jesus Christ. But the materials with which we build are of varying degrees of value—"gold, silver, precious stones, wood, hay, straw"—and "each man's work will become manifest." Paul says that "the fire will test what sort of work each one has done. If the work which any man has built on the foundation survives, he will receive a reward. If any man's work is burned up, he will suffer loss, though he himself will be saved, but only as through fire" (1 Cor 3:12–15).

Loving God, as we remember the deceased members of the Body of your Son today and throughout this month, I offer myself to you for their ultimate healing. May my prayers and work today help their final process of purification.

DAILY WORD: "Our God is a consuming fire" (Heb 12:29).

EVENING REVIEW: What did I build with today?

November 3: St. Martin de Porres (1579–1639)

Martin, the son of a Spanish knight and a freed African slave, was born in Lima, Peru. For eight years his father would not acknowledge him, and then, when a second child was born, he abandoned the family. With God's grace, Martin weathered the rejection, the social stigma of being the child of an inter-racial union, and the poverty that resulted. When he was twelve, his mother asked a local doctor and barber to make Martin an apprentice. In time, he began helping the local community of Dominican friars, and after nine years they insisted he join them as a Brother.

When he canonized Martin in 1962, Pope St. John XXIII said:

> The example of Martin's life is ample evidence that we can strive for holiness and salvation as Christ Jesus has shown us: first, by loving God with all your heart, with all your soul, and with all your mind; and second, by loving your neighbor as yourself. When Martin had come to realize that Christ Jesus suffered for us and that he carried our sins on his body to the cross, he would meditate with remarkable ardor and affection about Christ on the cross. He had an exceptional love for the great sacrament of the Eucharist and often spent long hours in prayer before the Blessed Sacrament. He loved people because he honestly looked on them as God's children and as his own brothers and sisters. Common people responded by calling him, "Martin the charitable". He excused the faults of others. He forgave the bitterest injuries. He lovingly comforted the sick; he provided food, clothing, and medicine for the poor.

Loving God, make me a saint like Martin, faithful in loving you above all and loving my neighbor as myself.

DAILY WORD: Love God and neighbor at all times.

EVENING REVIEW: Did I see everyone today as my own brother or sister?

November 4: St. Charles Borromeo (1538–1584)

Charles was born in Italy and earned a doctorate in civil and Church law. His uncle, Pope Pius IV, called him to Rome in 1560 and named him archbishop of Milan and secretary of state. In this role he helped with the preparations for the Council of Trent and its reforms. He was a model bishop who lived a simple and austere life, imitating Jesus, who came to serve and not to be served. He established many seminaries, colleges, hospitals, orphanages, and homeless shelters. When the plague struck Milan, he cared for the sick and buried the dead with his own hands.

Speaking of his namesake on the fourth centenary of his death, Pope St. John Paul II, whose baptismal name was Karol or Charles, said:

> Charles Borromeo's entire life was a path to sanctity. And sanctity is born from the understanding of love, in order to fill one's thoughts, words, and deeds with it. "The way we came to understand love was that he laid down his life for us; we too must lay down our lives for our brothers and sisters." These words from the First Letter of St. John [3:16] are the voice of an eyewitness. Charles understood love. He understood this love which was revealed in human history through Christ and in Christ. In Jesus Christ was revealed the love which is from God himself. This was the greatest discovery of his life, the greatest "understanding". This understanding gave a direction to all his thoughts, words, and deeds. In each of them rings out a loud echo of this understanding: I too must lay down my life for my brethren.

Jesus, may the knowledge of your love for me inspire me to "lay down my life" today.

DAILY WORD: Jesus died for me.

EVENING REVIEW: How did I lay down my life for others?

November 5

The saints in glory do not need our attention or devotion, but when we read about them, we are inspired to follow their example. Reading about the saints moved St. Ignatius Loyola from worldly thoughts to thoughts of serving God as they did. It also inspired in him the desire to one day be with them in heaven.

In a similar vein, St. Bernard wrote:

> Why should our praise or even celebration mean anything to the saints? What do they care about earthly honors when their heavenly Father honors them? The saints have no need of honor from us; neither does our devotion add the slightest thing to what is theirs. Clearly, if we venerate their memory, it serves us, not them. But I tell you, when I think of them, I feel myself inflamed by a tremendous yearning. Calling the saints to mind inspires, or rather arouses in us a longing to enjoy their company. We long to share in the citizenship of heaven. We long to be united in happiness with all the saints. Come, let us spur ourselves on. We must rise again with Christ, we must seek the world which is above and set our mind on the things of heaven. Let us long for those who are longing for us, hasten to those who are waiting for us, and ask those who look for our coming to intercede for us.

God, source of my life and of all holiness, you made me for union with yourself and for communion with the saints. I embrace this desire of yours and offer myself wholeheartedly to you. Fulfill your desires in me today and every day.

DAILY WORD: "Set your minds on things that are above, not on things that are on earth" (Col 3:2).

EVENING REVIEW: What inspired my thoughts for good or bad today?

November 6

The saints, like God, can seem so distant, their lives an inspiration but not something we think we can really imitate. Yet just as God is present in the moments of daily life, so the opportunity to exercise love and all the virtues is present in the moments of my day. This is what made them saints. This is what makes me a saint.

Pope Francis said:

> The Saints are not supermen, nor were they born perfect. They are like . . . each one of us. They are people who, before reaching the glory of heaven, lived normal lives with joys and sorrows, struggles and hopes. What changed their lives? When they recognized God's love, they followed it with all their heart without reserve or hypocrisy. They spent their lives serving others, they endured suffering and adversity without hatred and responded to evil with good, spreading joy and peace. This is the life of a Saint. Saints are people who for love of God did not put conditions on him in their life; they were not hypocrites; they spent their lives at the service of others. They suffered much adversity but without hate. . . .
>
> Being holy is not a privilege for the few; in Baptism we all have an inheritance to be able to become saints. Holiness is a vocation for everyone. Thus we are all called to walk on the path of holiness, and this path has a name and a face: the face of Jesus Christ. He teaches us to become saints. In the Gospel he shows us the way, the way of the Beatitudes.

Jesus, knowing your love, I offer myself to you today with no conditions, and I place myself at your service and the service of all your brothers and sisters.

DAILY WORD: Holiness is my vocation.

EVENING REVIEW: How did I walk on the path of holiness?

November 7

St. Paul often referred to the people to whom he wrote as "saints". In Baptism they were joined to Christ and tried to be true to what sanctifying grace made them—saints.

C. S. Lewis wrote: "There are only two kinds of people in the end: those who say to God, 'Thy will be done,' and those to whom God says, in the end, 'Thy will be done.'" In other words, I either say to God, "Yes! Your will is that I be a saint in union with you and in communion with all the saints. I want this. Your will be done!" Or, God says to me, "Yes, but I am sorry. Your will is to reject my love for you and for all. I cannot force my love on you. I cannot make you do what you do not want to do, for that is not love. Love is free. Therefore, if it is your will to not be with me and the Communion of Saints forever—let it be done as you desire!"

Each day I am faced with decisions that influence what kind of person I am. When I say "Yes" to God's will for me, I am a saint. I am, in Pope Francis' words, a "hidden saint". He said: "In God's great plan, every detail is important, even yours, even my humble little witness, even the hidden witness of those who live their faith with simplicity in everyday family relationships, work relationships, friendships. There are the saints of every day, the 'hidden' saints, a sort of 'middle class of holiness' to which we can all belong."

Father, I pray, as Jesus prayed in the Garden of Gethsemane: "Thy will be done!" Help me be the saint you have made me to be.

DAILY WORD: Yes to God's will!

EVENING REVIEW: Whose will did I choose today?

November 8: St. Elizabeth of the Trinity (1880–1906)

Elizabeth's father was a French army captain, and she was born in a military camp. A lively, stubborn girl with a bad temper, she once locked herself in her room where she stomped around and kicked the door until, exhausted, she fell asleep. When she was twenty-one, she entered a cloistered Carmelite convent. She wrote: "How serious life is: each minute is given us in order to 'root' us deeper in God, as St. Paul says, so that the resemblance to our divine Model may be more striking, the union more intimate. But to realize this plan, which is that of God Himself, here is the secret: forget self, give up self, ignore self, look at the Master, look only at Him, receive as coming directly from His love both joy and suffering; this places the soul on such serene heights!"

My offering today is from part of St. Elizabeth's Prayer to the Trinity:

O my God, Trinity whom I adore; help me to forget myself entirely that I may be established in You as still and as peaceful as if my soul were already in eternity. O my beloved Christ, crucified by love, I wish to love You even unto death! But I feel my weakness, and I ask You to 'clothe me with Yourself', to substitute yourself for me that my life may be but a radiance of Your Life. O consuming Fire, Spirit of Love, create in my soul a kind of incarnation of the Word: that I may be another humanity for Him in which He can renew His whole Mystery. And You, O Father, bend lovingly over Your poor little creature; "cover her with Your shadow", seeing in her only the "Beloved in whom You are well pleased".

DAILY WORD: Word of God, take flesh in me.

EVENING REVIEW: How did I radiate Christ?

November 9: Dedication of the Basilica of St. John Lateran

Today is the feast of the "Mother and Head of all Churches, in the City and the World", the anniversary of the consecration of the pope's cathedral. Many people mistakenly think that St. Peter's Basilica is the Holy Father's home church or cathedral, but that distinction belongs to St. John Lateran. This church dates back to 324, when the Emperor Constantine converted part of the Laterini family residence into a church and gave the property to Pope St. Sylvester I. Over the centuries, it was destroyed or damaged by earthquake, fire, and invasions, but each time it was rebuilt. Within it is a precious relic from the wooden altar on which St. Peter himself celebrated the Eucharist.

Though nothing earthly lasts, and buildings come and go, including church buildings, the Church itself was made to last. Jesus promised that to St. Peter when he told him: "And I tell you, you are Peter, and on this rock I will build my Church, and the gates of Hades shall not prevail against it" (Mt 16:18). The Church continues because of Jesus' promise to Peter and his successors, the bishops of Rome.

United with St. Peter, the other apostles, and all the baptized, we are, in the words of the First Letter of Peter, "living stones" who are being "built into a spiritual house, to be a holy priesthood, to offer spiritual sacrifices acceptable to God through Jesus Christ" (2:5).

Jesus, you are the one foundation of the house of God. You called St. Peter to be one with you as a rock. I, as a living stone, offer the sacrifice of my day to the Father with you and through you.

DAILY WORD: All for God's glory!

335

EVENING REVIEW: What did my spiritual sacrifice look like today?

November 10: Pope St. Leo the Great (400–461)

Leo, one of three popes officially called "great", became the bishop of Rome when he was forty. A wise administrator and teacher, he saved the city of Rome from total destruction at the hands of barbarian invaders through his courageous and persuasive meetings with Attila the Hun and Gaiseric the Vandal.

In a Christmas homily he said:

> Rouse yourself and recognize the dignity of your nature. Remember that you were made in God's image; though corrupted in Adam, that image has been restored in Christ. Use creatures as they should be used: the earth, the sea, the sky, the air, the springs, and the rivers. Give praise and glory to their Creator for all that you find beautiful and wonderful in them. If we are indeed the temple of God and if the Spirit lives in us, then what every believer has within himself is greater than what he admires in the skies. For we are born in the present only to be reborn in the future. Our attachment, therefore, should not be to the transitory; instead, we must be intent upon the eternal. Let us think of how divine grace has transformed our earthly natures so that we may contemplate more closely our heavenly hope.

St. Leo echoed these thoughts in a homily on the Beatitudes: "Remember, Christian, the surpassing worth of the wisdom that is yours. Mercy itself wishes you to be merciful, righteousness itself wishes you to be righteous, so that the Creator may shine forth in His creature, and the image of God be reflected in the mirror of the human heart as it imitates His qualities."

God, I commit myself to using the things of this world as you want me to—for your glory and the good of your other children.

November 11: St. Martin of Tours (316–397)

Today, Veterans Day, is also known as Armistice Day because it was on this day in 1918, the 11th day of the 11th month at the 11th hour, that an armistice ending World War I went into effect. It was known as the "Great War" and the "War to End All Wars". It wasn't. A greater war and other conflicts have followed. Today we remember all who served in the military as the Church honors Martin of Tours, a soldier in the Roman Army, who left the service of an earthly king to serve the King of kings as a monk and a bishop.

The story is told that when Martin was still a catechumen preparing for Baptism, he was riding along and met a poor beggar shivering in the cold. He took his heavy woolen cloak and, with his sword, cut it in two, giving half to the beggar. That night he had a dream in which Jesus appeared to him wearing the half cloak that he had given away and saying: "Here is Martin, the Roman soldier who is not baptized; he clothed me."

Jesus said that whatever we do or do not do for the least of God's children, we do or do not do for him. Vatican II's *Gaudium et spes* says that "by His incarnation the Son of God has united Himself in some fashion with every man" (no. 22).

With his act of charity, Martin won the only war that will end all wars—the war against self-concern, self-centeredness, selfishness, sin. Ultimately it is only in following God's law—to love God above all and to love one's neighbor as oneself—that peace will come.

Lord, help me win the war today.

337

DAILY WORD: I see you in others.

EVENING REVIEW: What did I do or fail to do for Christ?

November 12: St. Josaphat (1580–1623)

Today's saint has been called an "Apostle of Union" because he gave his life to promote union between the Orthodox and Catholic Churches. He was born in Ukraine, was baptized Orthodox, and, as a result of the 1596 Union of Brest, was united with the Catholic Church. He became a Basilian monk and was made archbishop of Polotsk in what is now Belarus. Opposing his efforts to bring the Sister Churches together, a mob attacked and killed him.

Pope Pius XI wrote an encyclical on the 300th anniversary of his death in which he said:

> The Church of God, by a wondrous act of Divine Providence, was so fashioned as to become in the fullness of time an immense family that embraces all men. The Church possesses as one of her visible marks that of a worldwide unity. Christ, Our Lord, impressed upon the apostles in the strongest possible terms the supreme need of this unity (Jn 17:11, 21, 22). In His last soul-stirring prayer, he asked His Father for this unity, and His prayer was heard: 'He was heard for his reverence' (Heb 5:7). Since this communion of all the peoples of the earth in a worldwide unity is, above all things, the work of God, and therefore to be had only with the divine help and assistance, let us have recourse with all care to prayer, following in this both the teachings and example of St. Josaphat, who, in his apostolate for unity, trusted above all else in the power of prayer.

Jesus, I offer all my prayers, works, joys, and sufferings for what you desire for your Church—that we may be one as you and the Father are one.

DAILY WORD: United we stand, divided we fall.

EVENING REVIEW: How did I foster unity among Christians?

November 13: St. Frances Xavier Cabrini (1850–1917)

Frances was born in Italy and as a child dreamed of becoming a missionary. She dressed her dolls as nuns and floated boats across ponds imagining that she was sending them to China. She rejected candy and sweets because she didn't think she would have any in China. As an adult, she could not find an Order in which to fulfill her dream, and she approached Pope Leo XIII, who told her to start a new Order of missionaries. In 1880, she founded the Missionary Sisters of the Sacred Heart. Though her heart was set on going to China, the pope instead sent her to the United States to care for Italian immigrants. She founded 67 houses around the world and crossed the Atlantic 25 times. In 1909, she became a U.S. citizen, and in 1947, she became the first such citizen to be canonized.

With the following prayer of hers, I renew my offering:

Fortify me with the grace of Your Holy Spirit and give Your peace to my soul that I may be free from all needless anxiety, solicitude, and worry. Help me to desire always that which is pleasing and acceptable to You so that Your Will may be my will. Grant that I may rid myself of all unholy desires and that, for Your love, I may remain obscure and unknown in this world, to be known only to You. Do not permit me to attribute to myself the good that You perform in me and through me, but rather, referring all honor to Your Majesty, may I glory only in my infirmities, so that renouncing sincerely all vainglory that comes from the world, I may aspire to that true and lasting glory that comes from You. Amen.

DAILY WORD: May all know you, Jesus.

EVENING REVIEW: How was God's will my will today?

November 14

Faith gives me hope that my life on earth is not all there is and that, with God's grace, I will be reunited with loved ones who have died. I pray that I will not be disappointed. Pope Francis spoke of this hope:

> To see God, to be like God: this is our hope. And today, [as] we commemorate the faithful departed, we need to think a little about this hope: this hope that accompanies us in life. The first Christians depicted hope with an anchor, as though life were an anchor cast on Heaven's shores and all of us journeying to that shore, clinging to the anchor's rope. This is a beautiful image of hope: to have our hearts anchored there, where our beloved predecessors are, where the Saints are, where Jesus is, where God is. This is the hope that does not disappoint. . . .
>
> Today before evening falls each one of us can think of the twilight of life: "What will my passing away be like?" All of us will experience sundown, all of us! Do we look at it with hope? Do we look with that joy at being welcomed by the Lord? This is a Christian thought that gives us hope. . . . Let us think about the passing away of so many of our brothers and sisters who have preceded us, let us think about the evening of our life, when it will come. And let us think about our hearts and ask ourselves: "Where is my heart anchored?" If it is not firmly anchored, let us anchor it beyond, on that shore, knowing that hope does not disappoint because the Lord Jesus does not disappoint.

Jesus, in giving my day to you I anchor myself in you.

DAILY WORD: "Hope does not disappoint" (Rom 5:5).

EVENING REVIEW: Where was my heart anchored today?

November 15: St. Albert the Great (1206–1280)

Today's saint is called "The Great" because he was the greatest scholar of his time. He was a Dominican who had an encyclopedic knowledge of the physical sciences, astronomy, philosophy, and theology. One of his students, Thomas Aquinas, went on to become the greatest theologian of his time. Yet, Albert's greatness lies not so much in his intellectual gifts, but in his holiness. He made an explicit connection between the Eucharist and the Heart of Christ, writing that in the "Heart of Our Lord, in which the Divinity dwells, is preserved the grace which bestows the Holy Eucharist upon us."

Reflecting on Jesus' words at the Last Supper, "Do this in memory of me", he wrote:

> Certainly he would demand nothing more pleasant, nothing more beneficial, nothing more desirable. This sacrament is profitable because it grants remission of sins; it is useful because it bestows the fullness of grace on us in this life. Nor could he have commanded anything more lovable, for this sacrament produces love and union. It is the characteristic of the greatest love to give itself as food, as if to say: I have loved them and they have loved me so much that I desire to be within them, and they wish to receive me so that they may become my members. There is no more intimate or more natural means for them to be united to me, and I to them. Eternal life flows from this sacrament because God with all sweetness pours himself out upon the blessed.

Eucharistic Heart of Jesus, make my heart like yours. Transform my heart and all of me so that I may become more and more a pleasing offering to God our Father.

DAILY WORD: I in you and you in me.

EVENING REVIEW: How did I live my union with Christ?

November 16: St. Gertrude (1256–1302) and St. Margaret of Scotland (1046–1093)

Margaret, Queen of Scotland, brought the best out of her cruel husband, leading him to a conversion. She raised eight children, two of whom are honored as saints, and is said to have invited twelve poor people to her table every day and washed their feet.

Gertrude, when she was only five, was entrusted to the care of a group of Benedictine nuns in Germany, and in time she joined them. At twenty-five, she had a mystical experience and continued to receive profound revelations. An early proponent of devotion to the Heart of Jesus, she wrote:

> The Divine Heart is like a treasury which contains all riches, like a lyre touched by the Holy Spirit at the sounds of which the most Holy Trinity rejoices. In this Heart was conceived the Our Father, the Lord's Prayer. It supplies for all the homage we have neglected to offer to God. In It alone our works acquire that perfection, that dignity, which renders them pleasing to the Divine Majesty. Through It alone flow all the graces that can descend on earth.

Moved by the love of the Heart of Jesus, I make my offering with these words of St. Gertrude:

O Sacred Heart of Jesus, living source of eternal life, infinite treasure of the Divinity, and burning furnace of divine love. You are my refuge and my sanctuary, O my amiable Savior. Consume my heart with that burning fire with which yours is ever inflamed. Pour down on my soul those graces which flow from your love, and let my heart be so united with yours that our wills may be one and mine, in all things, may be conformed to yours. May your divine will be the standard and rule of all my desires and actions.

DAILY WORD: Heart of Jesus, be my strength.

EVENING REVIEW: How did God's gifts increase in me?

November 17: St. Elizabeth of Hungary (1207–1231)

Princess Elizabeth married Ludwig when she was only four-teen and they had, in Pope Benedict XVI's words, "a pro-foundly happy" marriage because "[Elizabeth] helped her husband to raise his human qualities to a supernatural level and he . . . stood up for his wife's generosity to the poor and for her religious practices."

The pope said:

> Elizabeth diligently practiced works of mercy: she would give food and drink to those who knocked at her door, she procured clothing, paid debts, cared for the sick and buried the dead. Coming down from her castle, she often visited the homes of the poor with her ladies-in-waiting, bringing them bread, meat, flour, and other food. She distributed the food personally and attentively checked the clothing and mattresses of the poor. This behavior was reported to her husband, who not only was not displeased but answered her accusers, "So long as she does not sell the castle, I am happy with her!"

Ludwig also told her, "It is Christ whom you have cleansed, nourished, and cared for."

Just eighteen days before the birth of their third child, Ludwig died of the plague on his way to the Crusades. Elizabeth joined the Secular Franciscans and is now their patron saint. Her charity and holiness were so universally recognized that within four years of her death, she was de-clared a saint.

Lord Jesus, you call people from all walks of life to follow you. In fol-lowing you, they not only learn to see as you see and to have hearts that are moved as your Heart is moved; they also find you in others. I give myself to you so that we may meet each other often during this day.

DAILY WORD: I meet Jesus in others.

EVENING REVIEW: How did Jesus meet me today?

November 18: St. Rose Philippine Duchesne (1769–1852)

Today the Church celebrates the anniversary of the dedication of two major basilicas that were built over the graves of two apostles—St. Peter and St. Paul. But it also honors a French woman who came to the United States as a missionary. Rose Philippine, a Visitation Sister whose community was suppressed by the French Revolution, ended up joining the Religious of the Sacred Heart and coming to St. Louis, Missouri, in 1818. At the age of seventy-two, she was sent to Kansas to start a school for Potawatomi children. Though the school succeeded, Rose did not. She couldn't learn the difficult Native language.

In one of her letters home, she wrote the following: "I carry in my heart a great fear of spoiling things wherever I shall be, and this because of the words I heard in the depths of my soul: 'You are destined to please Me, not so much by success as by bearing failure.'" From a human perspective, she, like Jesus, was a failure. But like him, she brought the love of God to all. The Native people called her "Woman Who Prays Always".

Rose shows us that God does not so much judge the results, which are often out of our control, as the love we bring to our efforts. This doesn't mean we shouldn't try our best, but in the end, we are called to surrender the results to God. We want to succeed for his glory and not our own.

Lord God, I am nothing without you. I am reminded of this so often. Do not let me give in to discouragement that shows that I am more interested in how I look than in you. Use the offering of my day for your glory.

DAILY WORD: For God's glory, not mine.

EVENING REVIEW: How did successes and failures both give glory to God?

November 19

In November we pray for those who have died. Pope Benedict XVI, in his encyclical "On Christian Hope", states emphatically that no one is an individual, isolated from others, whose actions only affect him or herself:

No man is an island, entire of itself. Our lives are involved with one another, through innumerable interactions they are linked together. No one lives alone. No one sins alone. No one is saved alone. The lives of others continually spill over into mine: in what I think, say, do and achieve. And conversely, my life spills over into that of others: for better and for worse. So my prayer for another is not something extraneous to that person, something external, not even after death.

Because death is not the end of a person's existence, our relationships continue after the physical body loses its life force—the soul. Our prayers and good works can help even those who, in dying, leave space and time and enter eternity. Writing about the purification from sin and its consequences that accompanies each person at death, Pope Benedict said: "We cannot calculate the 'duration' of this transforming burning in terms of the chronological measurements of this world. The transforming 'moment' of this encounter eludes earthly time-reckoning—it is the heart's time, it is the time of 'passage' to communion with God." Thus, "there is no need to convert earthly time into God's time: in the communion of souls simple terrestrial time is superseded. It is never too late to touch the heart of another, nor is it ever in vain."

God of life, thank you for the precious minutes of time you give me. I offer them to you for the good of both the living and the dead.

DAILY WORD: I am not saved alone.

EVENING REVIEW: How did I live today conscious of my connection with those who have died?

In *Lumen gentium*, the Second Vatican Council spoke of the "Mystical Body of Jesus Christ" and how on earth, "the pilgrim Church from the very first ages of the Christian religion has cultivated with great piety the memory of the dead."

Pope Francis said: "Remembering the dead, caring for their graves and prayers of suffrage are the testimony of confident hope, rooted in the certainty that death does not have the last word on human existence, for man is destined to a life without limits, which has its roots and its fulfillment in God."

Then Pope Francis shared a prayer of Passionist Father Antonio Rungi, part of which will be our offering prayer today:

God of infinite mercy, we entrust to your immense goodness all those who have left this world for eternity, where you wait for all humanity, redeemed by the precious blood of Christ your Son, who died as a ransom for our sins. Look not, O Lord, on our poverty, our suffering, our human weakness, when we appear before you. . . . Look upon us with mercy, born of the tenderness of your heart, and help us to walk in the ways of complete purification. Let none of your children be lost. We entrust to you, O Lord, the souls of our beloved dead, of those who have died without the comfort of the sacraments, or who have not had an opportunity to repent, even at the end of their lives. May none of them be afraid to meet You, . . . but may they always hope to be welcomed in the embrace of your infinite mercy. . . . Lord, may no earthly thing ever separate us from You, but may everyone and everything support us with a burning desire to rest peacefully and eternally in You. Amen.

DAILY WORD: I desire to rest in God.

EVENING REVIEW: What supported or hindered my desire to be with God?

November 21: Presentation of the Blessed Virgin Mary

According to an ancient tradition, when Mary was a child, her parents, Joachim and Anne, brought her to the Temple in Jerusalem and "presented" her to God so that she might be raised by the holy women who lived there. This feast reminds us that God prepared Mary in every way. She was conceived without sin. Her first years were spent in an environment that kept the fullness of grace safe and prepared her Immaculate Heart to receive the angel's message and to embrace God's will.

In 1997, Pope St. John Paul II asked that this day be set aside to thank God for the gift of cloistered and monastic life in the Church and to pray for and support those called to that vocation.

St. Alphonsus Liguori wrote:

> As the holy child Mary presented and offered herself to God in the temple with promptitude and without reserve, so let us also present ourselves this day to Mary without delay and without reserve; and let us entreat her to offer us to God, who will not reject us when He sees us presented by the hand of that blessed creature, who was the living temple of the Holy Spirit, the delight of her Lord, and the chosen Mother of the Eternal Word.

O Mary, Mother of Jesus and my Mother, as you were presented in the temple, so was I presented to God at my Baptism. May I now be completely open to God's will for me, just as you were completely open to God's will at every moment of your life. I offer myself— every thought, word, and action of this day—to God through you, Mary. Amen.

DAILY WORD: I belong to God as Mary did.

EVENING REVIEW: How did I live my "presentation"?

November 22: St. Cecilia (3rd Century)

According to tradition, Cecilia was a young Roman woman who took a vow of virginity. As she was being beheaded for refusing to renounce her vow and her faith, the executioner botched his work and fled in fear as his third attempt failed. Cecilia lingered, and as she lay dying for three days, she sang God's praises. For this reason, she is the patron saint of musicians.

In good times or in bad, we too are called to praise God. That is what St. Paul told the Ephesians would help them live a good life: "Be filled with the Spirit, addressing one another in psalms and hymns and spiritual songs, singing and making melody to the Lord with all your heart, always and for everything giving thanks in the name of our Lord Jesus Christ to God the Father" (5:18–20).

It has been said that singing is praying twice. But we must live the song we sing, as St. Augustine tells us:

> My dear brothers and sisters, fruit of the true faith and holy seed of heaven, all you who have been born again in Christ and whose life is from above, listen to me: or rather, listen to the Holy Spirit saying through me: "Sing to the Lord a new song." Look, you tell me, I am singing. Yes indeed, you are singing; you are singing clearly, I can hear you. But make sure that your life does not contradict your words. Sing with your voices, your hearts, your lips and your lives: "Sing to the Lord a new song." If you desire to praise him, then live what you express. Live good lives, and you yourselves will be his praise.

Lord, make me your song today.

DAILY WORD: "I will sing to the LORD as long as I live" (Ps 104:33).

EVENING REVIEW: How was I God's praise?

November 23: Bl. Miguel Pro (1891–1927)

Fr. Miguel Pro was born in Mexico and entered the Jesuit Order in 1911. Three years later, Mexico entered upon a time of rebellion and anti-Catholicism. Miguel was forced to flee and continued his studies in California and Belgium, where he was ordained. Though the persecution worsened, he returned home to serve his beleaguered people for eighteen months. On November 18, 1927, he was captured. Five days later, he faced the firing squad after offering them his forgiveness. Holding a crucifix in one hand and a rosary in the other, he held out his arms in the form of a cross and shouted his last words as the order to shoot was given: "Viva Cristo Rey!"

When he beatified him in 1988, Pope St. John Paul II said:

> Neither suffering nor serious illness, neither the exhausting ministerial activity, frequently carried out in difficult and dangerous circumstances, could stifle the radiating and contagious joy which he brought to his life for Christ and which nothing could take away. Indeed, the deepest root of self-sacrificing surrender for the lowly was his passionate love for Jesus Christ and his ardent desire to be conformed to Him, even unto death.

O Christ Jesus, I acknowledge You to be the King of the universe. All that has been made was created for You. Exercise over me all Your sovereign rights. I hereby renew the promises of my Baptism, renouncing Satan and all his works and empty promises, and I commit myself to leading a truly Christian life. Divine Heart of Jesus, I offer You my poor actions to obtain the acknowledgment by every heart of Your sacred kingly power. In this way, may the Kingdom of Your peace be firmly established throughout the earth. Amen.

DAILY WORD: "Viva Cristo Rey!"

EVENING REVIEW: How did I show Christ's kingship?

November 24: Martyrs of Vietnam (19th Century)

Today we honor St. Andrew Dung-Lac and 116 other martyrs (59 lay people, 50 priests, 8 bishops), Native Vietnamese and foreign missionaries, who gave their lives for the faith. Years later, their witness bore fruit in the life of Cardinal Francis Xavier Nguyen Van Thuan, who, after the fall of Saigon in 1975, spent the next thirteen years in prison. During that time he wrote:

> There are so many gifts that are freely received: the morning dew on the grass, the light of the sun, the heat of the day, sparkling water from a fountain, the freshness of the wind, the warbling of a bird. Have I ever thought of giving thanks for all of this? I enjoy all these gifts without having paid a penny. If I keep my eyes open and my spirit alert, I will live in continual thanksgiving. I am overwhelmed by the memory of so many graces: my mother's womb, my father's labor and sweat, the knowledge and formation received from teachers.

He concluded his reflection with this prayer, which will be mine today:

Thank you, Lord, for having chosen me to be your child. Thank you for having given me Mary for my Mother. Thank you for so many brothers and sisters who sustain me. Thank you for the people who place obstacles on my path and cause me trouble; they help me to become holy. I should sing your praise my whole life long for just one of these gifts. How much more praise I should give you for the innumerable graces, which I alone know, and for all the graces I am not aware of or do not remember. I will need an eternity to thank you unceasingly. How can I repay you, Lord, for filling my life with so many good things?

DAILY WORD: Thank you always.

EVENING REVIEW: For what, in my whole life, am I thankful?

November 25: St. Catherine of Alexandria (d. 307)

Today's saint was born in Alexandria, Egypt—a center of learning in the ancient world. After denouncing the emperor for persecuting the Church, she was arrested and brought before fifty philosophers who were unable to refute her arguments. In the end, to silence and to punish her, she was beheaded. She is the patron saint of philosophers.

Philosophy is the love of wisdom, which is necessary to know how best to use the knowledge that science gives us. Like the wisest man of his time, King Solomon, we need to ask God for wisdom as he did:

O God of my fathers and Lord of mercy, who have made all things by your word, and by your wisdom have formed man, to have dominion over the creatures you have made, and rule the world in holiness and righteousness, and pronounce judgment in uprightness of soul, give me the wisdom who understands what is pleasing in your sight and what is right according to your commandments. Send her forth from the holy heavens, and from the throne of your glory send her, that she may be with me and toil, that I may learn what is pleasing to you (Wis 9:1–4, 9–10).

With wisdom I acknowledge God's goodness and offer myself in gratitude:

Father of all gifts, I praise you, the source of all I have and am. Teach me to acknowledge always the good things your infinite love has given me. Help me to love you with all my heart and all my strength as my expression of thanksgiving for your many blessings. These days in particular, I remember that you fulfilled our ancestors' faith in your divine providence by making and keeping this land rich in the abundance of your creation.

DAILY WORD: Is this wise?

EVENING REVIEW: What wise or foolish decisions did I make?

November 26

After learning the words "mama" and "papa", most children learn another word that includes a life lesson. Children often grab what they want, and their parents ask them, "What do you say?" They reply, "Please", and the parent gives them what they want. But then, after receiving the desired item, the parent often asks a second question, "And now what do you say?" The response is "Thank you."

In prayer, we ask God for what we want, but, then, we shouldn't forget the second part of the lesson—to say "Thank you." Expressing thanks is not just for once a year but for every day and throughout the day. Ultimately, all is a gift. Life, health, the talents we have, and the time we have to use them in supporting ourselves and our families—all of these are gifts. But after "Please" and "Thank you", there is one more thing that parents often teach their children. If the child has brothers or sisters, the parent often coaches the child to share what he has received with others. Part of true gratitude is not holding on to our gifts and using them just for ourselves, but sharing what we have with others.

Pope Benedict once said that the custom of praying before meals "teaches people not to take their 'daily bread' for granted but to recognize it as a gift of Providence." He went on to point out that in our prayer we ask "not for 'my' but for 'our' daily bread." With this prayer we commit ourselves to showing our thanks by sharing.

Father, please give me "our daily bread"—what I need and more—so that I may show my gratitude by offering myself to you and sharing my gifts with others.

DAILY WORD: Thank you, God.

EVENING REVIEW: How did I show my gratitude to God?

On this day in 1830, the Blessed Virgin Mary appeared to a Sister of Charity in Paris named Catherine Labouré (canonized in 1947) and asked her to have a special medal made. On one side would be an image of Mary standing on a globe with rays streaming from her hands and the words "O Mary conceived without sin, pray for us who have recourse to Thee." On the other side would be the letter "M" with a cross and two hearts, representing the hearts of Jesus and Mary.

Four years later, ten million medals had to be made in France to meet the demand, and by the time Catherine died in 1876, over a billion had been distributed. So many conversions, cures, and other graces were attributed to this medal that it was called "The Miraculous Medal".

Catherine lived the rest of her life in obscurity, working in a residence for elderly men—feeding chickens, cooking, repairing clothes, and nursing the sick. Asked if she ever got bored with the grind of her daily routine, she responded: "One is never bored with doing the Will of God." She described her prayer life thus: "When I get to the chapel, I put myself before the good God and say to Him: 'Lord, here I am, give me what You wish.' If He gives me something, I am happy and thank Him. If He gives me nothing, I thank Him still, because I do not deserve anything more. Then I tell Him all that comes into my mind. I tell Him my sorrows and my joys—and I listen."

Loving God, I give myself to you. Take my day with its sorrows and joys. Give me what you wish.

DAILY WORD: "Lord, here I am."

EVENING REVIEW: What did God give me today?

November 28

Lutheran Pastor Martin Rinkart (1586–1649) served his home town of Eilenburg, Germany, during the bloody Thirty Years War (1618–1648). Since Eilenburg was a walled city, many refugees sought shelter there, but with the overcrowding a plague broke out in 1637. During this time, Pastor Rinkart celebrated forty to fifty funerals a day, including that of his own wife, who was among the eight thousand who died. In the midst of this tragic situation, Rinkart wrote the hymn "Now Thank We All Our God."

Writing a hymn of thanks in the midst of war, famine, and plague must have been a challenge. But in doing so, Rinkart was following St. Paul's instructions: "Give thanks in all circumstances, for this is the will of God in Christ Jesus for you" (1 Thess 5:18). The first stanza of the Pastor's song is based on Sirach 50:22–24.

I offer my day in gratitude to God with the words of this hymn:

Now thank we all our God, with heart and hands and voices,
Who wondrous things has done, in Whom this world rejoices;
Who from our mothers' arms has blessed us on our way
With countless gifts of love, and still is ours today.

O may this bounteous God through all our life be near us,
With ever joyful hearts and blessed peace to cheer us;
And keep us in His grace, and guide us when perplexed;
And free us from all ills, in this world and the next!

All praise and thanks to God the Father now be given;
The Son and Him Who reigns with Them in highest Heaven;
The one eternal God, whom earth and Heaven adore;
For thus it was, is now, and shall be evermore.

DAILY WORD: "In all circumstances give thanks."

EVENING REVIEW: For what do I give thanks?

November 29: Bl. Bernardo Francisco de Hoyos (1711–1735)

Today is the anniversary of the death of a young Jesuit priest who has been called "the first apostle of the Sacred Heart in Spain". He was a month shy of his fifteenth birthday when he entered the Jesuits and was given a dispensation to be ordained when he was twenty-three. Pope Benedict XVI beatified him in 2010.

Bernardo wrote:

> Try to have a divine and heavenly peace in your heart. I do not speak of peace with others, called by another name, charity. I speak of peace within one's own heart, which often is the greater struggle for us, arousing in the soul a thousand disturbances, anguishes, and disquiet with which the demon succeeds in his aim of thwarting us in the way of perfection. The distinguishing characteristic of the friends of God consists in this interior peace, which Christ so often recommended to his disciples, repeating: "Peace be with you" (Lk 10:5; 24:36). Disturbance, on the contrary, is characteristic of reprobates: "There is no peace for the wicked" (Is 48:22). Jesus cannot abide where there is no peace. The soul is a mirror; it is a crystal-clear stream which reflects all the beauties placed before it; in which the image of our God is reflected: into the same image we are being transformed (2 Cor 3:18), so long as the waters of this stream are not disturbed or agitated, so long as the clarity of this mirror is not dimmed or obscured.

Jesus, as I give myself to you, give me peace—the peace of a clear conscience, the peace of knowing that in all that I will do today I am doing the will of our Father.

DAILY WORD: Heart of Jesus, be my peace.

EVENING REVIEW: When was my heart agitated or at peace?

November 30: St. Andrew

According to the first chapter of the Gospel of John, Andrew was Simon Peter's brother and a disciple of John the Baptist who one day pointed to Jesus and declared "Behold, the Lamb of God." Andrew and another, unnamed disciple heard this and followed Jesus, who asked them, "What are you looking for?" They replied, "Rabbi, where are you staying?" They were so thrilled to see "the Lamb of God" or "Messiah" that they wanted to know where he lived so that they might get to know him better. Jesus answered, "Come, and you will see." They stayed with Jesus the entire day.

Spending that quality time with him convinced Andrew that this was indeed the promised Messiah or Savior of Israel. He could not keep this good news to himself but immediately went to find his brother to tell him "We have found the Messiah." Then he took Peter to see Jesus, who, with one look at Peter, saw his potential and changed his name from "Simon" to "Cephas" (Rock) or "Peter".

Regarding this scene, Pope Benedict XVI said: "The Apostle Andrew, therefore, teaches us to follow Jesus with promptness, . . . to speak enthusiastically about him to those we meet, and especially, to cultivate a relationship of true familiarity with him, acutely aware that in him alone can we find the ultimate meaning of our life and death."

Jesus, I want to give you quality time today so that I may get to know you better. But I am so busy. Come to me then through the people and events of my day. I give you not only my time of prayer but my entire day so that you may encounter me in it.

DAILY WORD: Jesus, I look for you.

EVENING REVIEW: How did I spend time with Jesus and share him with others?

DECEMBER

December 1: St. Charles de Foucauld (1858–1916)

St. Charles de Foucauld was killed on this day in 1916. Orphaned at the age of six in 1864, he rejected God, sought pleasure above all else, and joined the army. While serving in Algeria, he encountered Muslims. He wrote: "Islam really shook me to the core. The sight of such faith, of these people living in the continual presence of God, made me glimpse something greater, truer than worldly concerns." He returned to the faith, saying, "As soon as I believed that God existed, I understood that I could do nothing else but live for him alone."

In time he went to the Holy Land, where he spent seven years as a Trappist monk and four years as a hermit, writing: "Anyone who loves tries to imitate. I have lost my heart to this Jesus of Nazareth, and I spend my life trying to imitate him as much as my weakness allows." He returned to Algeria, where he determined "To continue with the hidden life of Jesus in the Sahara, not to preach, but to live in solitude and poverty doing the humble work of Jesus."

I make his Prayer of Abandonment my own:

Father, I abandon myself into Your hands; do with me what You will. Whatever You do I thank You. I am ready for all, I accept all. Let only Your will be done in me, as in all Your creatures. I ask no more than this, my Lord. Into Your hands I commend my soul; I offer it to You, O Lord, with all the love of my heart, for I love You, my God, and so need to give myself—to surrender myself into Your hands, without reserve and with total confidence, for You are my Father.

DAILY WORD: I live for you alone, God.

EVENING REVIEW: How was or was not God's will done in me?

December 2

The word "Advent" means "Coming", and during this season we remember the "comings" of Jesus. We are preparing for the celebration of the Nativity of Our Lord, Christmas, the first coming of Jesus when he was born in Bethlehem so many years ago. This preparation reminds us of his Second Coming at the end of time. Jesus told us that this world will end and that he will come to establish a new heaven and a new earth where death will be no more.

But there are other "comings" as well. Because "the Word became flesh" (Jn 1:14) in Mary's womb, the Son of God was able to give his flesh on the Cross for the life of the world. He makes that offering present in every Eucharistic celebration where he comes and gives us his Body and Blood.

And then there is his "coming", as St. Teresa of Kolkata put it, "in the distressing disguise of the poor". In a parable about the judgment that will accompany his Second Coming (Mt 25:31–46), Jesus identifies with those in need and says that if we ignore them, we ignore him, and if we help them, we help him.

Lastly, we may not survive until his Second Coming at the end of the world, but we can speak of his coming at the end of our lives. All of these "comings" are related, as are our preparations—for a holy celebration of Christmas, for Holy Communion, for meeting Jesus in others, for meeting him when we pass from this life to the next, and at the end of time.

Lord Jesus, I believe that you came, that you come to me every day, and that you will come in the end. I give myself to you. Help me prepare today to meet you.

DAILY WORD: Come, Lord Jesus!

EVENING REVIEW: How did my preparations go?

December 3: St. Francis Xavier (1506–1552)

One of the founding fathers of the Jesuits, Francis, set sail for India in 1541 and began the work that led to his being named patron saint of the missions. He became the first missionary to enter Japan, but when people there expressed dismay that the wisest people in the world—the Chinese—had not heard of Christianity, he decided that he had to go to China. He died on an island off the coast of China on this day in 1552.

On his feast in 1844, a group of French Jesuit students, who were anxious to follow in his footsteps as missionaries, heard a talk from their spiritual director, Fr. Francis Xavier Gautrelet. He told them they did not have to wait to be apostles; they could be apostles of prayer by making an offering of their entire day—their prayers, studies, work in the community, frustrations, and sufferings—as a powerful spiritual sacrifice for the spread of the Gospel. This idea, embodied in the Daily Offering, caught on and led to the creation of the Apostleship of Prayer, now known as the Pope's Worldwide Prayer Network, from which we get this Trinitarian offering prayer:

God, our Father, I offer you my day. I offer you my prayers, thoughts, words, actions, joys, and sufferings in union with the Heart of Jesus, who continues to offer Himself in the Eucharist for the salvation of the world. May the Holy Spirit, who guided Jesus, be my guide and my strength today so that I may witness to your love. With Mary, the Mother of our Lord and the Church, I pray for all Apostles of Prayer and for the prayer intention proposed by the Holy Father this month. Amen.

DAILY WORD: My life is an offering.

EVENING REVIEW: What did I consciously offer with Jesus for the salvation of the world?

December 4: St. John Damascene (645–749)

John was the chief treasury official of the Muslim caliph of Damascus, Syria, but he left to become a monk at St. Sabbas Monastery near Jerusalem. He became a great theologian whose writings summarized the faith and defended the use of holy pictures and statues. He wrote: "It is not the material that we honor but what it represents; the honor paid to images goes to the one who is represented by the image."

St. John wrote this prayer of gratitude and offering:

O Lord, you formed me in my mother's womb. By the blessing of the Holy Spirit, you prepared my creation and my existence. You sent me forth into the light by adopting me, and you enrolled me among the children of your holy Church. You kept me alive with the solid food of the body of Jesus Christ, your only-begotten Son and our God, and you let me drink from the chalice of his life-giving blood, poured out to save the whole world. In this way, you have humbled yourself, Christ my God, so that you might carry me, your stray sheep, on your shoulders. You let me graze in green pastures, refreshing me with the waters of orthodox teaching at the hands of your shepherds. Like a shining lamp, lead me along the straight path. When I open my mouth, tell me what I should say. By the fiery tongue of your Spirit, make my own tongue ready. Stay with me always and keep me in your sight. Do not let my heart lean either to the right or to the left, but let your good Spirit guide me along the straight path. Whatever I do, let it be in accordance with your will, now until the end. Amen.

DAILY WORD: I am your living image.

EVENING REVIEW: How did the Spirit guide me and my words?

December 5

Jesus spoke of his Second Coming in frightening terms (Mt 24). He said it would be preceded by various calamities and that "all the tribes of the earth will mourn, and they will see the Son of man coming on the clouds of heaven with power and great glory" (v. 30). Jesus challenges us to be alert and compares himself to a "thief" (v. 43).

This image is repeated in the Book of Revelation, where he is quoted as saying "Behold, I am coming like a thief" (16:15). St. Paul also used this image: "For you yourselves know well that the day of the Lord will come like a thief in the night" (1 Thess 5:2).

It seems odd that Jesus would speak of himself as a thief, yet that is how many people see him. A thief takes something that does not belong to him. Many people think of their lives as their own, and so, when Jesus comes for them at the end of their lives, they see him as taking something that is not his. But the reality is we do not belong to ourselves. St. Paul writes: "Do you not know that your body is a temple of the Holy Spirit within you, which you have from God? You are not your own; you were bought with a price. So glorify God in your body" (1 Cor 6:19–20). Our daily offering helps us remember that.

God, you made me. I belong to you. You redeemed me, and the price that was paid was the Blood of your Son. I give you this day that in its many minutes I may glorify you in my body.

DAILY WORD: I belong to God.

EVENING REVIEW: Did I take back my offering in any way today? How?

December 6: St. Nicholas (270–350)

Today's saint, bishop of Myra in Turkey, was present at the first ecumenical council of the Church, the Council of Nicaea, which affirmed the divinity of Christ and gave us the creed we proclaim every Sunday. About this, Pope Benedict XVI wrote:

> Was Jesus of Nazareth only a great religious man, or had God himself actually become, in him, one of us? Is God so mighty that he can make himself small; is he so mighty that he can love us and really enter our lives? For if God is too far away from us to love us effectively, then human love too is only an empty promise. If God cannot love, how can we be expected to do so? In professing faith in God's Incarnation, therefore, it was ultimately a case of affirming also our capacity to live and die in a human manner. The figure of St. Nicholas, Santa Claus, illustrates and symbolizes this connection.

Moreover, St. Nicholas is associated with gift-giving because, according to tradition, he heard about a poor man whose wife had died and whose three daughters were unable to marry because he could not provide their dowries. On three successive nights, when the streets were deserted and everyone was asleep, Nicholas passed their house and tossed a bag of gold through an open window. Commenting on this, Pope Benedict said: "This is the message of all the St. Nicholas and Santa Claus figures: from the light of Christ we are to light the flame of a new humanity, caring for the persecuted, the poor, the little ones—this is the core of the legend of St. Nicholas."

Jesus, you gave all to save us. I continue your work by giving all today.

DAILY WORD: There is more joy in giving than in getting.

EVENING REVIEW: How did I imitate St. Nicholas?

December 7: St. Ambrose (340–397)

Ambrose was the governor of northern Italy who addressed the crowd that assembled to elect a new bishop for their city of Milan. The crowd was deeply divided, and Ambrose encouraged them to proceed in a spirit of charity and peace. His speech made such an impression that even before he finished, a voice from the crowd called out: "Ambrose! Bishop!" The crowd took up the cry and insisted that their governor become their bishop. The problem was that Ambrose was a catechumen, not yet baptized. This and his ordination were soon arranged, and on this day in the year 374, Ambrose was consecrated bishop. His eloquent preaching touched the hearts of many, including a man named Augustine, whose mother, Monica, had been praying fervently for his conversion.

Ambrose's teaching on prayer reminds us that we do not pray alone but as parts of the Body of Christ:

> The apostle [Paul] teaches us to pray anywhere, while the Savior says "Go into your room"—but you must understand that this "room" is not the room with four walls that confines your body when you are in it, but the secret space within you. That is your prayer-room, always with you wherever you are, always secret wherever you are, with your only witness being God. Above all, you must pray for the whole people: that is, for the whole body, for every part of your mother the Church, whose distinguishing feature is mutual love. If you ask for something for yourself, then you will be praying for yourself only. If each person prays for all people, then all people are effectively praying for each.

Lord Jesus, I offer myself today for the good of your entire Body.

DAILY WORD: One Body, of which I am a part.

EVENING REVIEW: How did my offering encompass all?

December 8: Solemnity of the Immaculate Conception

About the mystery we celebrate today, Pope Francis said:

> The Gospel of Luke presents us with Mary, a girl from Nazareth, a small town in Galilee. Yet the Lord's gaze rested on her, on the one he had chosen to be the mother of his Son. In view of this motherhood, Mary was preserved from original sin, from that fracture in communion with God, with others, and with creation, which deeply wounds every human being. But this fracture was healed in advance in the Mother of the One who came to free us from the slavery of sin.

As a result of this gift of grace that kept Mary sinless from the moment of her conception, she had a pure heart. In it there was no obstacle to receiving God's Word. Her pure heart was purely devoted to doing God's will.

God's "gaze rested" on Mary, and, Pope Francis continued, "God rests his loving gaze on every man and every woman! The Apostle Paul states that God 'chose us in him before the foundation of the world, that we should be holy and blameless before him.' We too, from all time, were chosen by God to live a holy life, free of sin."

I renew my offering with part of a prayer that the bishops of the United States used in 2006 to renew the consecration that the twenty-three bishops in the U.S. made in 1846:

Mary, Immaculate Virgin, our Mother, Patroness of our land, we praise you and honor you and give our country and ourselves to your sorrowful and immaculate heart. Protect us from all harm. Pray for us, that acting always according to your will and the will of your Divine Son, we may live and die pleasing to God.

DAILY WORD: Let your will be done in me.

EVENING REVIEW: How was I inspired to "be holy and blameless"?

December 9: St. Juan Diego (1474–1548)

St. Paul, writing his First Letter to the Corinthians, said: "God chose what is foolish in the world to shame the wise, God chose what is weak in the world to shame the strong, God chose what is low and despised in the world, even things that are not, to bring to nothing things that are, so that no flesh might boast in the presence of God" (1:27–29). God chose a humble Aztec Indian to receive an apparition of the Blessed Virgin Mary that would lead to the conversion of millions.

On this day in 1531, Mary appeared to Juan Diego and sent him to the bishop of Mexico to tell him that she wanted a church built in her honor. Seeing his fear, she said:

> Know for certain, smallest of my children, that I am the perfect and perpetual Virgin Mary, Mother of the True God through whom everything lives, the Lord of all things near and far, the Master of heaven and earth. I am your merciful Mother, the merciful Mother of all of you who live united in this land, and of all mankind, of all those who love me. Hear and let it penetrate your heart, my dear little one. Let nothing discourage you, nothing depress you. Let nothing alter your heart, or your face. Am I not here who am your mother? Are you not under my shadow and protection? Am I not your fountain of life? Are you not in the folds of my mantle? In the crossing of my arms? Is there anything else that you need? Do not fear any illness or vexation, anxiety or pain.

Blessed Mother, give me your errands today as you gave one to Juan Diego.

DAILY WORD: I am weak but God is strong.

EVENING REVIEW: How did my weakness lead me to depend more on God?

December 10

On this day in 1941, Thomas Merton (1915–1968) visited the Trappist Abbey of Gethsemane in Kentucky and began interviews that led to his becoming a monk. Exactly twenty-seven years later, he was accidentally electrocuted in Bangkok while attending an interfaith monastic conference.

The loss of his mother when he was six and his father when he was fifteen led to his declaring, "I believe in nothing." But at the age of twenty-three, after encountering the beauty of the faith in churches and the liturgy, he asked to become Catholic.

Speaking to the U.S. Congress, Pope Francis said of him: "Merton was above all a man of prayer, a thinker who challenged the certitudes of his time and opened new horizons for souls and for the Church. He was also a man of dialogue, a promoter of peace between peoples and religions."

The following is Merton's Prayer of Abandonment:

My Lord God, I have no idea where I am going. I do not see the road ahead of me. I cannot know for certain where it will end. Nor do I really know myself, and the fact that I think I am following Your will does not mean that I am actually doing so. But I believe that the desire to please You does in fact please You, and I hope that I will never do anything apart from that desire. And I know that if I do this, You will lead me by the right road although I may know nothing about it. Therefore will I trust You always, though I may seem to be lost and in the shadow of death, I will not fear, for You are ever with me, and You will never leave me to face my perils alone.

DAILY WORD: I trust you. I will not fear.

EVENING REVIEW: How did I fulfill my desire to please God?

December 11: Pope St. Damasus I (305–384)

Damasus, who was pope from 366 to 384, introduced the chanting of psalms with the two sides of the church alternating verses, a custom that monasteries continue to this day. Another tradition that Pope Damasus started was chanting an Alleluia before the proclamation of the Gospel at Mass. He had a deep devotion to the early martyrs and fostered the veneration of their relics.

The inscription that Damasus composed for his tomb is a clear statement of his belief in the resurrection of the body:

Who calmed the wild waves of the sea,
Whose power gives life to the seed dormant in the earth,
Who for Lazarus could loosen the bonds of death,
And restore a brother on the third day to his sister
    Martha—
Christ will, so I firmly believe, awaken me, Damasus,
    from death!

Created in God's image and likeness, I am destined for eternal life. The Second Person of the Blessed Trinity shared my human life so that I could share his eternal life. According to the *Catechism of the Catholic Church*, no. 366, "The Church teaches that every spiritual soul is created immediately by God—it is not 'produced' by the parents—and also that it is immortal: it does not perish when it separates from the body at death, and it will be reunited with the body at the final Resurrection."

Lord Jesus, in Advent I prepare to celebrate how you, the Son of God, were conceived and born; how you lived our life and suffered our death. All for love of me! I believe you will come again at the end of the world and at the end of my life. I give myself to you so that you may raise me up body and soul to share your risen life.

DAILY WORD: Choose life, here and hereafter.

EVENING REVIEW: How did I choose life today?

December 12: Our Lady of Guadalupe

A few days after first appearing to Juan Diego (see December 9), the Blessed Virgin Mary gave him a sign to take to the bishop of Mexico to convince him that she had indeed appeared and that he should build a church in her honor. She pointed to roses that were growing out of season and told him to pick them. She arranged them in his tilma, or poncho, and told him to take the roses to the bishop. He did, and when he let them fall to the ground, the shocked bishop knelt down, for there, on his tilma, was imprinted the image of Our Lady of Guadalupe. This miracle led to the largest conversion in history as millions of Juan Diego's people renounced human sacrifice and embraced Christianity.

The image was not painted by human means, and the material of the tilma should have disintegrated centuries ago. A bomb placed next to it in 1921 destroyed the altar and twisted the heavy metal candlesticks but did not damage the picture. It remains visible to this day. It remains just as the loving intercession of Mary always remains with us.

When he visited Mexico in 1979, Pope St. John Paul II made this prayer:

Mother of Mercy, Teacher of hidden and silent sacrifice, to you, who come to meet us sinners, we dedicate on this day all our being and all our love. We also dedicate to you our life, our work, our joys, our infirmities and our sorrows. We wish to be entirely yours and to walk with you along the way of complete faithfulness to Jesus Christ in His Church; hold us always with your loving hand.

DAILY WORD: Our Lady of Guadalupe, pray for us.

EVENING REVIEW: How was Mary with me?

December 13: St. Lucy (d. 304)

During the darkest days of the year in the northern hemisphere, we celebrate a feast in honor of a woman whose name means "Light". St. Lucy had taken a vow of virginity that angered her fiancé whose marriage to her had been arranged by her mother. He denounced her as a Christian. She was tortured by having her eyes torn out and then stabbed. She is the patron saint of all those who suffer from afflictions or diseases of the eye.

In the first verses of his Gospel, John wrote: "In the beginning was the Word. . . . In him was life, and the life was the light of men. The light shines in the darkness, and the darkness has not overcome it. There was a man sent from God, whose name was John [the Baptist]. . . . He was not the light, but came to bear witness to the light. The true light that enlightens every man was coming into the world." That light is Jesus, who said, "I am the light of the world; he who follows me will not walk in darkness, but will have the light of life" (Jn 8:12).

But in his Sermon on the Mount, Jesus said to his followers: "You are the light of the world" (Mt 5:14). As members of his Body, I share in his light. I reflect his light through the daily witness of my life, just as Lucy did.

Jesus, united to you I am light so that others may find their way to you. I offer myself to you so that you may shine through me. May nothing in me dim your light today.

DAILY WORD: My "light [must] shine before men." (Mt 5:16).

EVENING REVIEW: In how much darkness or light did I walk today?

December 14: St. John of the Cross (1541-1591)

John entered the Carmelite Order in Spain and after his ordination felt drawn to a stricter, more contemplative life as a Carthusian. St. Teresa of Ávila, the great reformer of the Carmelite women, convinced him to remain a Carmelite and to undertake a reform. He agreed and suffered much as a result. At one point, his Brother Carmelites held him captive in a six-by-ten-foot cell and even scourged him. After six months, they gave him a pen and paper, and he composed some of his most beautiful and mystical poems about union with God. In time he escaped and carried on the work of reform.

In times of suffering and distress, it's natural to pray: "O God, where are you!? Why have you abandoned me?" John found God even as he suffered because he knew that as a temple of the Holy Spirit, God is within. He wrote: "What more do you want, O soul! What else do you search for outside, when within yourself you possess your riches, delights, satisfactions, and kingdom—the Beloved whom you desire and seek."

He knew that his sufferings, joined to the Cross of Jesus, opened up new channels for grace to enter the world. He wrote: "Everything I do, I do with love, and everything I suffer, I suffer with the delight of love. So the soul, in this union that God has ordained, joins in the work of the Trinity, not yet fully as in the life to come, but nonetheless even now in a real and perceptible way. O my soul, created to enjoy such exquisite gifts, what are you doing, where is your life going?"

Holy Spirit, as close as my breath, I give myself to you.

DAILY WORD: "Everything I do, I do with love."

EVENING REVIEW: What crosses did I join to Jesus' Cross?

If I were God, how would I choose to save the world? Would I come in power and glory with an army of angels to rid the world of sin and force people to be good? Would I come on a winter night as a tiny baby, born in a shelter for animals? God's ways are not our ways, according to Isaiah 55:8. Yet God calls me to follow his way, for it is the only one that leads to eternal and heavenly life.

Accepting God's way for me, I offer myself with this prayer of St. John Henry Newman:

God has created me to do Him some definite service. He has committed some work to me which He has not committed to another. I have my mission. I may never know it in this life, but I shall be told it in the next. . . . I am a link in a chain, a bond of connection between persons. He has not created me for naught. I shall do good, I shall do His work; I shall be an angel of peace, a preacher of truth in my own place, while not intending it, if I do but keep His commandments. . . . Therefore, I will trust Him, whatever, wherever I am, I can never be thrown away. If I am in sickness, my sickness may serve Him, in perplexity, my perplexity may serve Him; if I am in sorrow, my sorrow may serve Him. . . . He does nothing in vain. . . . He knows what He is about. He may take away my friends, He may throw me among strangers, He may make me feel desolate, make my spirits sink, hide the future from me—still He knows what He is about. . . .

DAILY WORD: Your way, not mine.

EVENING REVIEW: How was God's plan for me being fulfilled?

After Jesus was born, Mary laid him in a manger, a trough for feeding animals. What are the mangers that will receive Christ this Christmas? Catherine de Hueck Doherty wrote, "Christ desires to be born in the manger of our hearts." Naturally I want my heart to be a warm cradle to receive Christ this Christmas, but perhaps it is more like a cold, hard manger. What can I do to prepare my heart to receive him?

First, I can celebrate the Sacrament of Reconciliation, which changes my sin-hardened heart into one softened by God's love. Also, I can make some room in my heart for Christ by stopping for a few minutes every day and doing nothing but emptying my heart of all the distractions that make it easy to forget what the coming celebration is all about.

Doherty went on to say that our manger-hearts must be, as Jesus said, childlike. "A child is trusting. A child is totally open." The following Advent Wreath Prayer was written by Grace Mazza Urbanski:

> *Dear Baby Jesus,*
> *When you were born, you had no crib,*
> *No cozy sheets to sleep in.*
> *The animals helped to keep you warm,*
> *And Joseph and Mary's swaddling.*
> *I was not there to see you smile,*
> *Or to touch your tiny feet;*
> *So now I seek your loving Heart*
> *In everyone I meet.*
> *This Advent candle shines your light,*
> *Your brightness everywhere.*
> *I am a child, just like you were—*
> *Please hear my Advent prayer:*

I would like to be your crib;
Rest in me, Lord, I pray.
Make me your manger to cradle you,
and hold you every day.

DAILY WORD: Make my heart childlike.

EVENING REVIEW: How did I prepare my heart to receive the
Christ Child?

December 17

During the final preparation for Christmas, the Church gives
us a series of ancient poetic texts. They come from the Hebrew Scriptures and present various names for the Messiah.
Each asks him to come. These texts eventually became the
verses of the popular Advent hymn "O Come, O Come
Emmanuel." Today's verse goes:

> O come, O Wisdom from on high,
> Who orders all things mightily;
> To us the path of knowledge show,
> And teach us in her ways to go.

This antiphon comes from Sirach 24:3 where Wisdom
is personified and speaks, saying, "I came forth from the
mouth of the Most High . . . and I covered the earth like
a mist." We also find elements of the antiphon in Wisdom
8:1: Wisdom "reaches mightily from one end of the earth to
the other, and she orders all things well." While our world
has grown in scientific and technological knowledge, it has
not grown in the wisdom that helps us know how to use all
that knowledge for good and not for evil.

Where do we find wisdom? Jesus is wisdom in the flesh
because he is the fullest revelation of who God is and who
mankind is. Fully human, he shows us how mankind was
created to live—loving God and one another. All other

373

knowledge will end up harming people unless it is guided by this wisdom, by Jesus.

Come, Jesus, bring order to what is disordered in my life so that I may be guided by you, by wisdom. I offer myself to you so that you may guide me in the ways that will lead me and those I meet to the goal of our lives—life on high with you.

DAILY WORD: Teach me wisdom, Lord.

EVENING REVIEW: How were my actions guided by wisdom?

December 18

> O come, O come, our Lord of might,
>   Who to your tribes on Sinai's height;
> In ancient times did give the law,
>   In cloud and majesty and awe.

Today's "O Antiphon" speaks of God giving the Ten Commandments to Moses and the Israelites: "Mount Sinai was wrapped in smoke, because the LORD descended upon it in fire; and the smoke of it went up like the smoke of a kiln, and the whole mountain quaked greatly. And as the sound of the trumpet grew louder and louder, Moses spoke, and God answered him in thunder" (Ex 19:18–19). It was a terrifying experience that caused great fear in the people. They were not even to come near: "Whoever touches the mountain shall be put to death" (19:12).

Centuries later, God came again, but in a very different way. The Letter to the Hebrews says: "You have not come to what may be touched, a blazing fire, and darkness, and gloom, and a tempest, and the sound of a trumpet, and a voice whose words made the hearers entreat that no further messages be spoken to them. . . . But you have come . . . to Jesus, the mediator of a new covenant" (12:18–24).

As Pope Benedict put it: "Now—this God who has become a child says to us—you can no longer fear me, you can only love me." Pope Francis said: "The Ten Commandments are a gift from God. They come from a God who has created us for love, from a God who has forged a close alliance with humanity, a God who only wills the good for humanity. Let us trust God!"

Lord God, I trust that you want only what is good for me and that you gave the commandments for my good. I commit myself to them today.

DAILY WORD: I trust you, God.

EVENING REVIEW: How did I follow the Ten Commandments?

December 19

> O come, O Branch of Jesse's stem;
>   From ev'ry foe deliver them.
> That trust your mighty pow'r to save,
>   And give them vict'ry o'er the grave.

King David was the greatest king of Israel, and Jesse was his father. David defeated Israel's enemies and prepared the way for his son Solomon to dwell in prosperity and peace and to build the temple. In the Gospels, Jesus is often called the "Son of David". This is why Joseph and Mary had to travel to Bethlehem, David's home, to be registered in the Roman census. The original Latin in this verse, however, refers, not to the "Branch" of Jesse, but to the "Radix" or "Root". How could Jesus, who came after Jesse and David, be their "Root"? Because he is God, the origin of all people. This word is an act of faith in the divinity of Jesus, who used the divine name to refer to himself: "Truly, truly, I say to you, before Abraham was, I am" (Jn 8:58).

Jesus is both "branch" or "shoot"—a descendent of Jesse—and the "root" of Jesse because he is fully human and fully divine. The prophet Isaiah used both expressions: "There shall come forth a shoot from the stump of Jesse, and a branch shall grow out of his roots. . . . In that day the root of Jesse shall stand as an ensign to the peoples; him shall the nations seek, and his dwellings shall be glorious" (11:1, 10). Thus, Jesus alone can save us from the deadly foes of sin and death.

Jesus, Son of David, I offer myself to you. Hold me close, and deliver me from sin so that I, like you, may overcome death.

DAILY WORD: Save me from my foes.

EVENING REVIEW: What spiritual foes did I battle and with Jesus' help overcome?

December 20

> O Come, O Key of David, come,
>   And open wide our heav'nly home;
> Make safe the way that sets us free,
>   And close the path to misery.

The prophet Isaiah wrote: "I will place on his shoulder the key of the house of David; he shall open, and none shall shut; and he shall shut, and none shall open" (22:22). Centuries later, the Book of Revelation applied these words to Jesus, calling him "The holy one, the true one, who has the key of David, who opens and no one shall shut, who shuts and no one opens [says this:] 'I know your works. Behold, I have set before you an open door, which no one is able to shut'" (3:7–8).

376

Jesus is the key to heaven. Through his birth, life, death, and Resurrection, he opened the door of heaven. I have a choice to enter or to turn away. But when I turn away and sin, Jesus has also opened the way to forgiveness. He shared the power of the keys with Peter, telling him: "I will give you the keys of the kingdom of heaven, and whatever you bind on earth shall be bound in heaven, and whatever you loose on earth shall be loosed in heaven" (Mt 16:19). This power was given to all the apostles and their successors when Jesus appeared after the Resurrection and said: "Receive the Holy Spirit. If you forgive the sins of any, they are forgiven; if you retain the sins of any, they are retained" (Jn 20:22–3).

Jesus, at times I have turned from your way and have chosen the path that leads to misery here and hereafter. I give myself to you completely so that you may guide me this day and every day through the heavenly door that you opened.

DAILY WORD: Jesus is the key to life.

EVENING REVIEW: On which path did I spend most of my day?

December 21: St. Peter Canisius (1521–1597)

> O come, O Dayspring from on high,
>   And cheer us by your drawing nigh;
> Disperse the gloomy clouds of night,
>   And death's dark shadow put to flight.

Isaiah prophesied: "The people who walked in darkness have seen a great light; those who dwelt in a land of deep darkness, on them has light shined" (9:2). The "great light" is Jesus. He is the Sun that brings the dawn of a new day. We live in a world of darkness, of error and sin, of violence and hatred. God did not create the world this way, but mankind, rejecting God's ways, has allowed darkness to cover the earth.

Only Christ can transform it, and he does so, beginning with me. John the Baptist's father, Zechariah, said that he would be a "prophet" who would "go before the Lord to prepare his ways, to give his people knowledge of salvation through the forgiveness of their sins." Through Baptism, I, too, am a prophet showing others "the tender mercy of our God when the day shall dawn upon us from on high to give light to those who sit in darkness and in the shadow of death" (Lk 1:76-79).

Peter Canisius was a Jesuit whom Pope Leo XIII called "the second apostle of Germany". I renew my baptismal promise to be a prophet of light with part of St. Peter's offering prayer:

O merciful God, I give and surrender myself wholly to You, and offer You all I possess, with the prayer that You bestow Your grace on me, so that I may be able to devote and employ all the thinking power of my mind and the strength of my body in your Holy service. Amen.

DAILY WORD: Light from on high, shine on me.

EVENING REVIEW: What darkness did I help push back?

December 22

> O Come, Desire of nations, bind
>   In one the hearts of humankind;
> Make all our sad divisions cease,
>   And be for us the King of peace.

St. James wrote: "What causes wars, and what causes fightings among you? Is it not your passions?" (4:1). Jesus is the Desire that fulfills the longing of every human heart. When that longing is fulfilled in him, there will be peace.

St. Paul, writing about the unity of Jews and Gentiles in the Church, said: "For he is our peace, who has made us both one, and has broken down the dividing wall of hostility, by abolishing in his flesh the law . . . , that he might create in himself one new man in place of the two, so making peace. . . . He came and preached peace to you who were far off and peace to those who were near, for through him we both have access in one Spirit to the Father" (Eph 2:14 – 18).

The peace Jesus gives is, as he said, "not as the world gives" (Jn 14:27). Jesus' peace is the peace that comes from justice, from truth and order, from reconciliation with God and others.

Isaiah prophesied: "Of the increase of his government and of peace there will be no end, upon the throne of David, and over his kingdom, to establish it, and to uphold it with justice and with righteousness from this time forth and for evermore" (9:7).

King of Peace, I offer myself as your loyal subject today. I want to reject anything that will hinder the advance of the Kingdom. I want to choose everything that will serve to bring about greater reconciliation in my relationships with all people and with our Father.

DAILY WORD: Give me your peace.

EVENING REVIEW: Did I live as a loyal subject of the King of peace? How?

December 23: St. John of Kanty (d. 1473)

> O come, O come Emmanuel,
> And ransom captive Israel,
> That mourns in lonely exile here
> Until the Son of God appear.

Our final O Antiphon, which is the first verse of the Advent hymn, speaks of "Emmanuel", a name that according to the Gospel of Matthew, means "God is with us" (1:23). Matthew quotes Isaiah: "a virgin shall conceive and bear a son, and shall call his name Immanuel" (7:14). Jesus, fully divine and fully human, is God with mankind. God so desired to dwell among his human children, so desired to save and unite himself to mankind, that he joined in the one Person of his Son the human and divine natures.

God walked among us when Jesus lived on earth, and he remains "Emmanuel", or "God with us", in the Eucharist. Christmas is a Eucharistic feast. Moreover, in the Eucharist, Jesus unites his Body and Blood with ours, thus transforming us into his Body. Now we also meet him in one another.

The Polish philosophy professor John Kanty understood this. His college had a tradition: every day when food was prepared for students and faculty, a special meal was made for the poor. As dinner was served, one of the administrators called out, "A poor man is coming!" The president of the college then responded, "Jesus Christ is coming!" The meal was then served to a poor person in the vicinity.

Jesus, I believe that you are fully human and fully divine. When you were born, you did not leave your divinity behind in heaven. When you ascended to heaven, you did not abandon us. You remain on earth, body and blood, soul and divinity. In gratitude, I give myself to you.

DAILY WORD: You are near.

EVENING REVIEW: How was God "Emmanuel" for me today?

The Letter to the Hebrews begins: "In many and various ways God spoke of old to our fathers by the prophets; but in these last days, he has spoken to us by a Son. . . ." This son is the Son of God who took flesh in Mary's womb and was born. Hebrews continues, having the Son use Psalm 40 to refer to himself: "Then he added, 'Behold, I have come to do your will.' . . . By that will we have been sanctified through the offering of the body of Jesus Christ once for all" (10:9–10).

What our ancestral parents grasped at—"equality with God"—Jesus "emptied himself" of, "taking the form of a servant, being born in the likeness of men. . . . He humbled himself and became obedient unto death, even death on a cross" (Phil 2:6–8).

The time has come to celebrate the emptying of the Son of God, who shared our life with its joys and sorrows, its suffering and death. Speaking about this, Pope Francis said:

> Think well on this: God is with us and God still trusts us. God willed to share in our human condition to the point of becoming one with us. He chose to live in our history as it is, with all the weight of its limitations and of its tragedies. The Birth of Jesus reveals that God "sided" with humanity once and for all, to save us, to raise us from the dust of our misery, from our difficulty, from our sins. The Birth of Jesus brings us the good news that we are loved immensely and uniquely by God.

Jesus, you loved us so much that you became one with us. I love you and give myself to you so that I may always be one with you.

DAILY WORD: God is with me and trusts me.

EVENING REVIEW: How did God trust me today?

The time of waiting is over. Mankind waited thousands of years for its Savior. The Israelites waited thousands of years for their Messiah. We have waited during Advent, amidst many preparations and distractions, to celebrate the birthday of the Son of God. Some families even bake a cake, adorn it with lit candles, and sing "Happy Birthday" to Jesus.

Sometimes Christmas gift-giving can feel like a business transaction. People compare the value of the gifts given and received and assign value to their relationships. What about my relationship with God? God gave me his own Son to save me from sin and death. There is no greater gift that God could give. God must value me very much. What could I possibly give God that comes close to the value of his gift to me?

All God asks is to return his love by giving myself. But giving myself and all the minutes of my day—that means giving God everything! Like the child who has received many things and can't let go of any and so is unable to receive more, I am tempted to hold on to my life. Yet only the hands that have given all and are empty can receive even more. So I resolve to give all to God today with the following children's morning offering (sung to the tune of "Amazing Grace") from the Pope's Worldwide Prayer Network (Apostleship of Prayer).

> *For love of me you came to earth;*
> *You gave your life for me.*
> *So every day you give me now*
> *I give back happily.*
> *Take all my laughter, all my tears,*
> *Each thought, each word, each deed,*
> *And let them be my all-day prayer*
> *To help all those in need.*

DAILY WORD: I am my gift to you.

EVENING REVIEW: What gift of time did I give to God and others?

December 26: St. Stephen (1st Century)

St. Stephen was one of the first deacons and is considered the first martyr to witness to Jesus with his death (see Acts of the Apostles 6 and 7). It may seem odd that right after the celebration of the birth of the Prince of Peace, we read about a violent martyrdom. Pope Benedict XVI spoke about this:

> In the joyful atmosphere of Christmas, this commemoration may seem out of place. Why disturb the charm with the memory of such atrocious violence? In reality, from the perspective of faith, the Feast of St. Stephen is in full harmony with the deeper meaning of Christmas. The remembrance of the first martyr immediately dispels a false image of Christmas: the fairytale, sugarcoated image, which is not the Gospel! The liturgy brings us back to the authentic meaning of the Incarnation, by linking Bethlehem to Calvary and by reminding us that the divine salvation involved the battle against sin, it passes through the narrow door of the Cross.

St. Fulgentius of Ruspe wrote about the love that Jesus and Stephen shared:

> The love that brought Christ from heaven to earth raised Stephen from earth to heaven; shown first in the king, it later shone forth in his soldier. His love of God kept him from yielding to the ferocious mob; his love for his neighbor made him pray for those who were stoning him. Christ made love the stairway that would enable all Christians to climb to heaven. Hold fast to it, therefore, in all sincerity, give one another practical proof of it, and by your progress in it, make your ascent together.

Jesus, you came to earth to raise me to heaven. Like a child, I place myself in your arms. Lift me up.

DAILY WORD: Love is my stairway.

EVENING REVIEW: What practical proofs of love did I show?

December 27: Apostle John

John has traditionally been identified with "the disciple Jesus loved" who appears in the Gospel of John. He and his brother James along with Peter were invited to be close to Jesus at two critical moments in his life—at his Transfiguration and during his agony in the Garden of Gethsemane. Though his motive was to find out who the betrayer of Jesus was, John lay his head on Jesus' chest at the Last Supper. Writing about this, St. Paulinus of Nola said: "John, who rested blissfully on the breast of our Lord, was inebriated with the Holy Spirit, who searches even the deep things of God; from the Heart of all-creating Wisdom, he quaffed an understanding that transcends that of any creature." Perhaps it was this intimate contact with the Heart of Jesus that gave him courage the next day to be the only apostle to stand under the Cross as Jesus was crucified. There, Jesus gave his Mother, Mary, to John to be his Mother and ours.

I, too, am called to draw near to the Heart of Jesus. Pope Benedict XVI said: "The Lord wishes to make each one of us a disciple who lives in personal friendship with him. This is only possible in the context of a relationship of deep familiarity, imbued with the warmth of total trust. This is what happens between friends."

Jesus, at the Last Supper, you told John and the other apostles "I have called you friends, for all that I have heard from my Father I have made known to you" (Jn 15:15). I do not want a casual friendship with you. I give myself to you so that we may be friends for life and forever.

December 28: Holy Innocents

The Jewish historian Flavius Josephus, who lived shortly after the time of Jesus, called King Herod a "man of great barbarity". He was the puppet king of Israel when Jesus was born. Afraid of losing his power when he heard from the Magi that a new king had been born, he "sent and killed all the male children in Bethlehem and in all that region who were two years old or under" (Mt 2:16). Jesus escaped when his parents fled with him to Egypt. Thus, the Son of God began his earthly life under the threat of murder and as a refugee. Since the fourth century, the victims of King Herod's fear and jealousy have been venerated as martyrs.

How can these babies be considered martyrs? The word "martyr" means "witness", and the fifth-century bishop St. Quodvultdeus explained why they were martyrs: "The children die for Christ, though they do not know it. The Christ child makes of those as yet unable to speak fit witnesses to himself. They cannot speak, yet they bear witness to Christ. They cannot use their limbs to engage in battle, yet already they bear off the palm of victory." In other words, they died in place of Christ, who, in time, will die on the Cross in place of sinful mankind. Their martyrdom, unknown to them at the time, reflects the death of Jesus.

Loving God, I offer myself to you so that whether I am aware or not, no matter what I think, say, and do today will give witness to you. May I never think, say, or do anything that is not worthy of you.

DAILY WORD: All for the love of God.

EVENING REVIEW: As I look back on my day, were there times that I was giving witness even though I was unaware of it?

December 29: St. Thomas Becket (1118–1170)

In 1155, the deacon Thomas Becket, who was a personal friend of King Henry II of England, was named his chancellor. When the archbishop of Canterbury died in 1162, the king pushed for Thomas to replace him. After ordination as a priest and a bishop, Thomas took over the leadership of the Church in England. His commitment to his new responsibilities brought him into conflict with the king, who wanted to use him as a puppet to pursue his own goals. The conflict led Thomas to excommunicate the king and to flee to France. In time, King Henry reconciled with the archbishop, who returned to England, but soon more conflicts developed. At one point the king, in a fit of anger, shouted, "Who will rid me of this turbulent priest?" Four of his knights took these words literally and killed Thomas in his cathedral. As he died, Thomas declared: "For the name of Jesus and in defense of the Church, I am willing to die."

St. Paul wrote: "work out your own salvation with fear and trembling" (Phil 2:12). Thomas echoed these words in a letter:

> Remember then how our fathers worked out their salvation; remember the sufferings through which the Church has grown, and the storms the ship of Peter has weathered because it has Christ on board. Remember how the crown was attained by those whose sufferings gave new radiance to their faith. The whole company of saints bears witness to the unfailing truth that without real effort no one wins the crown.

Jesus, you died to save me, but you cannot force me to accept that salvation. Now I must, in the midst of temptations and conflicts, embrace my salvation as my deepest desire.

DAILY WORD: Salvation is most important.

EVENING REVIEW: What effort did I put into attaining my ultimate goal?

The Christmas season is a time for family gatherings and celebrations. But many families find Christmas to be difficult because they experience sharply the pain of brokenness or loss—families that are struggling to stay together and the memory of loved ones who have died. The Holy Family of Joseph, Mary, and Jesus did not have it easy either. They lived in poverty. Death threatened them. Yet they were able to stay strong because of their love and because Jesus was at the center of their life together.

Pope Benedict XVI said:

> In the poor grotto of Bethlehem shines a very bright light, a reflection of the profound mystery which envelopes that Child, which Mary and Joseph cherish in their hearts and which can be seen in their expression, in their actions, and especially in their silence. The Holy Family of Nazareth went through many trials. Yet, trusting in divine Providence, they found their stability and guaranteed Jesus a serene childhood and a sound upbringing.

He then concluded his remarks:

> Dear friends, the Holy Family is of course unique and unrepeatable, but at the same time it is a "model of life" for every family because Jesus, true man, chose to be born into a human family and thereby blessed and consecrated it. Let us therefore entrust all families to Our Lady and to St Joseph, so that they do not lose heart in the face of trials and difficulties but always cultivate conjugal love and devote themselves with trust to the service of life and education.

Loving God, recent popes have called the family the "basic cell of society". Healthy cells mean a healthy body. Cancerous cells that follow their own will kill the body. Make me a healthy cell.

DAILY WORD: Holy Family, pray for me.

EVENING REVIEW: How did I promote healthy family life?

December 31: St. Sylvester I (d. 335)

Pope Sylvester I led the Church during a time of peace after centuries of persecution. He is the first non-martyr to be venerated as a saint.

Where did the year go? Reflecting on this, I am reminded once again of how precious time is.

As Pope Francis said:

> All this induces us to think of the end of the journey of life, the end of our journey. There was a beginning and there will be an end, "a time to be born, and a time to die" (Eccles 3:2). With this truth, so simple and fundamental and so neglected and forgotten, Holy Mother Church teaches us to end the year and also our day with an examination of conscience, through which we review what has happened; we thank the Lord for every good we have received and have been able to do and, at the same time, we think again of our failings and our sins—to give thanks and to ask for forgiveness.

Pope Francis also said that "time is God's messenger." It is where I meet God and where God meets me one day at a time. Time is the medium in which God is preparing me for eternal life, when time will end and there will be an eternal "now".

Loving God, thank you for the gift of time in which you show your love for me and with which I love you. Thank you for all the blessings of the past year. In gratitude, I offer this day to you. I am sorry for all that I offered you in the past year that was not worthy of you, that was not in accordance with your loving plan.

DAILY WORD: "Time is God's messenger."

EVENING REVIEW: How did or did not this day prepare me to live better next year?

THE DAILY OFFERING

O JESUS, through the Immaculate Heart of Mary, I offer You my prayers, works, joys, and sufferings of this day in union with the Holy Sacrifice of the Mass throughout the world. I offer them for all the intentions of Your Sacred Heart: the salvation of souls, reparation for sin, and the reunion of all Christians. I offer them for the intentions of our bishops and of all Apostles of Prayer, and in particular for those recommended by our Holy Father this month.

Amen.